English Progress

Pupil Book 3

Levels 5-7

Series editor: Geoff Barton
Series consultant: Michael Jones

Authors: Claire Austin-Macrae
Bernadette Carroll
Clare Constant
Emma Lee
Liz Lockwood

PEARSON
Longman

195413 428 AUS Functional Skills

Contents

Speaking and Listening

Reading

Writing

Language

The Language strand is all about exploring and analysing the English Language. A stand-alone Language unit allows you to explore this strand in depth, but developing your skills in the Language objectives will also help you to improve your speaking and listening, reading and writing skills, so the Language objectives are also covered in a range of speaking and listening, reading and writing units shown in the tables below.

Progress in ... Exploring and analysing language		
10.1	Exploring language variation and development according to time, place, culture, society and technology	236
10.2	Commenting on language use	

Language in Speaking and listening units		
10.1	Exploring language variation and development according to time, place, culture, society and technology	AF6
10.2	Commenting on language use	

Language in Reading units		
10.1	Exploring language variation and development according to time, place, culture, society and technology	AF7

Language in Writing units		
10.2	Commenting on language use	AF5
10.2	Commenting on language use	AF6

Progress in ...
Speaking and Listening

Speaking and Listening AF1
Progress in ... Structuring talk to persuade and involve listeners

LEARNING OBJECTIVES

- Select the best way of organising your talk to present information appropriately and persuasively for your listeners in a range of contexts.
- Develop and adapt your speaking skills to suit familiar and unfamiliar situations.
- Make effective use of verbal and non-verbal techniques to actively involve listeners.

Activate your learning

Imagine you are trapped in a seaside cave with three other people. The tide water is rising fast and will fill the cave within five minutes. Inside the cave are the four items shown below – you have to get everyone out of the cave using only these items.

1 a) Working in a group of four, take it in turns present your proposal for getting everyone to safety. Organise your ideas and choose your words carefully to help the rest of the group understand your suggestion.

Hint: Think about how each item can help people escape and what is the best order in which to use them.

b) As a group, discuss which ideas would work best and agree on a plan. Working together, present your solution to the rest of the class.

2 a) What helped you to understand what other groups were suggesting? What did not help?

b) Discuss with a partner how you could improve the way you planned and presented your proposal.

Assess to Progress

How confident are you already at planning and presenting a talk in formal and informal situations? Are you good at making sure your audience is engaged with what you are saying? Rate yourself for each of the following skills by deciding where you would place yourself on the scale below.

1	2	3	4	5	6	7
I find this difficult.			I'm getting there.			I'm good at this.

- I can plan and structure my talk to present information effectively

  Self-check: In the task above, did you plan and structure the important points you wanted to make before you started talking?

- I can speak persuasively and know how to adapt the way I talk to suit familiar and unfamiliar situations.

  Self-check: Did your presentation convince the group to choose your plan? Did your language alter when you spoke to the whole class?

- I choose effectively from a range of verbal and non-verbal techniques to make sure listeners are actively involved in my talk.

  Self-check: How well did you use eye contact, gestures and tone of voice to draw the audience in?

Build your skills

The government is considering banning under-16s from using social networking sites such as MySpace and Facebook. You have been asked to plan and present a talk to a committee of MPs about whether social networking sites do more harm than good. Your talk needs to persuade your audience that your point of view is right. Follow the skill steps to help you plan your talk.

Step 1 Research your talk

1 Working with a partner, answer the questions below.

a) What is the purpose of your talk? e.g. To persuade listeners that ...

b) Decide: Who is your audience? How much do they know already? How formal should your talk be? e.g. Very formal for officials, less formal for people I know, so ...

c) What might your audience want to find out about the topic? e.g.

- Benefits of social networking – meeting people
- Drawbacks – cyber-bullying
- Health problems – lack of regular exercise travelling to see friends
- Social problems – lack of real social interaction.

d) Which details will convince your audience of your point of view? How can you present your information in a way that stimulates your listeners' interest? e.g. I can include facts, real-life stories ...

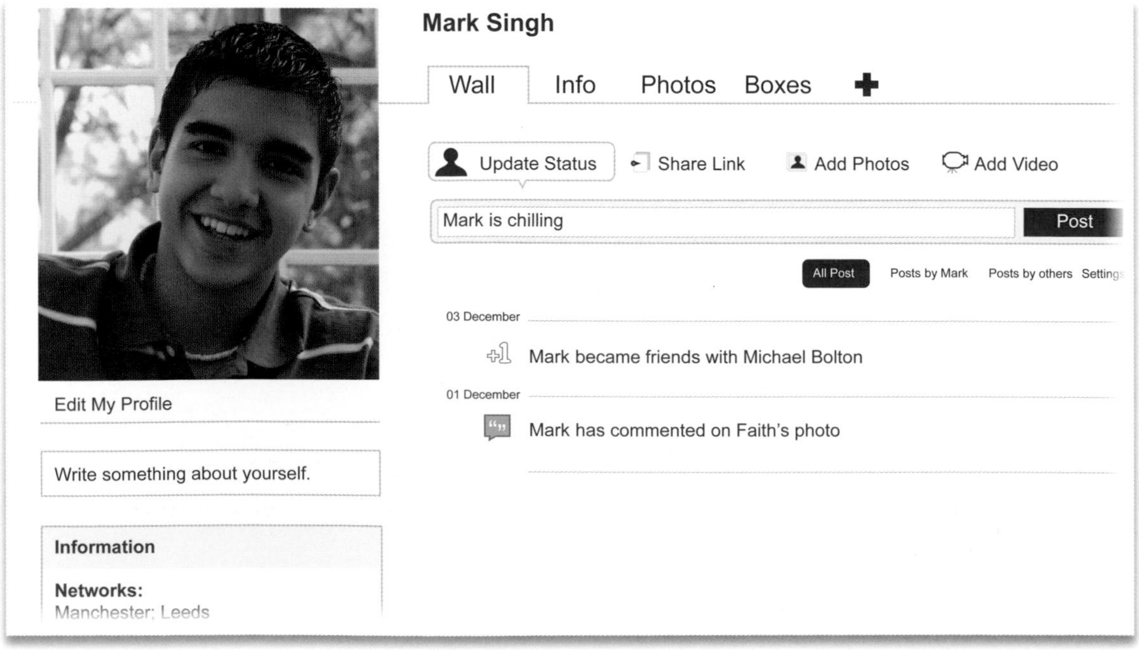

Step 2 Organise your talk

Think carefully about how to organise information to win over the audience. People will be persuaded by a clear, strongly argued talk that interests and entertains. Other speakers may contradict your view, so make sure you can prove that your points are the strongest.

1 Working with a partner, look at the planning advice below. Use this to help you organise your information.

Introduction

- Let listeners know what you are going to speak about and explain the aims for your talk,
  e.g. 'Right Honourable Members, I am here today to tell you about the negative impact that social networking can have on ...'
- Make your opening memorable. Think about how you can stimulate listeners' interest from the start,
  e.g. Use a question, an astonishing fact, or an anecdote to catch their attention ...

Main section

- Express your points clearly, remembering to include evidence and explanations.
- Think about the best way of sequencing your points to support your point of view,
  e.g. Start with a point you disagree with, then link to a point you agree with that proves the first point wrong.

Conclusion

- Summarise your key points to emphasise why your point of view is right.
- Think about the message you want your audience to take away. Try to create a memorable sentence that sticks in the mind,
  e.g. 'Don't let teenagers get tangled up in social networking sites!'

2 a) Write brief notes for your talk on separate prompt cards and number the cards in the right order, e.g. 3 health problems – Facebook addiction, Lack of exercise

b) Discuss your notes with a partner. Have you included the most important points? Does the running order help to signal where your talk is going?

Language

Reinforce your skills

The following extract is from a speech about the future of the BBC given by the TV presenter Stephen Fry. In this speech, he uses an anecdote (a story from his own life) to show how his view of the importance of the BBC was formed at a very early age.

I may have grown up just as the Golden Age of Radio had passed, but the Golden Age of Television … that grew with me.

When I was seven my parents moved house.

The week before we moved, the BBC started a new drama, starring William Hartnell. An old man, whose name appeared to be Grandfather or the Doctor, had a police phone box of the kind we saw in the street quite commonly in those days. It turned out to be a magical and unimaginably wonderful time machine.

My brother and I watched this drama in complete amazement: the first ever episode of *Doctor Who*. I had never been so excited in all my life. A whole week to wait to watch the next instalment. Never have seven days crawled so slowly by – for all that they involved a complicated house move from Buckinghamshire to Norfolk. A week later, in that new house, my brother and I turned on the good old television set in its new sitting room, ready to watch Episode 2. The TV had been damaged in transit and was never to work again.

We missed that episode and nothing that has transpired in my life since has ever, or could ever, make up for that terrible, terrible disappointment. There is an empty space inside me that can never be filled. It is amazing, amazing neither of us was turned into a psychopathic serial killers from that moment.

1 a) Working with a partner, pick out the ways in which Stephen Fry:

- creates a formal tone
  Hint: Look at the vocabulary and the types of sentence used.
- shows how enthusiastic and positive he is about the BBC
- uses humour and exaggerated language to emphasise his point.

b) Which part of Stephen's speech do you think this section is taken from? Why do you think this?

Develop and practise your own talk to MPs about social networking sites by following the skill steps opposite.

Language

Step 1 Choose the right language for your audience

1 Think about your audience and how formal the context is. Decide:

- what kind of tone you want to create, e.g. formal, polite, serious ...
- how you can make your talk persuasive, e.g. by including evidence to support your points, choosing positive language to describe the benefits of your point of view
- how you can involve your listeners in your talk, e.g. by using anecdote, asking rhetorical questions, including humour
- how you can guide your audience through your talk, e.g. by using link words to signpost the structure of your argument – 'However', 'In addition'.

2 Working in pairs, take turns to practise your draft talk. Your partner should say 'Stop!' whenever they feel they are losing interest in what you are saying. Work out what you could have said instead to keep their interest. Then carry on with your talk using the new phrase.

Step 2 Practise your delivery

Presenting your talk to one person sitting across a desk from you is very different from standing up and delivering your talk to a larger group. When you speak to an audience it is important to:

- speak loudly and clearly, but not too quickly – give time for the information you are presenting to sink in
- speak in a lively and engaged way by varying your tone of voice – if you sound interested, there is more chance your listeners will be interested too
- act confidently even if you are not feeling it – look at your listeners, make eye contact and smile while talking.

1 Working with a new partner, take turns to practise delivering your talk. As you listen to your partner's talk, check whether they hit all the bullet points above. Give feedback and discuss the ways they could improve their delivery.

2 Now join with another pair and practise delivering your talk to this new audience. Remember to think about the feedback you have been given.

Support

When you deliver your talk smile and make eye contact with different members of the audience as you speak, you should be talking to, rather than at, your audience. **Remember:** if you make a mistake, keep going – no one else knows what you meant to say!

Extend your skills

You can make your talk more interesting by using visual aids to illustrate your points or to help your audience remember information, e.g.

- Posters – to illustrate key points visually
- *PowerPoint* presentations – incorporating graphics, video and other media
- Handouts – to summarise key information
- Quiz sheets – to involve the audience
- Whiteboards – to write up key phrases or bullet points
- Objects – to create interest and emphasise points.

1 Which of these visual aids have you seen speakers use when giving a talk? How effective were they? Discuss your ideas with your partner.

Visual aids can also be distracting if the audience focuses on them more than on what you are saying. A speaker can also lose track of what they are saying because they are dealing with the visual aid.

2 What are the possible drawbacks of using each of the visual aids above? How could you avoid these dangers?

3 Which visual aids would make your talk more effective? When would you use them? Prepare the visual aids you want to use.

Stretch

Think about how you could use visual aids to present complex information in a way that the audience can understand *e.g. presenting statistics as a graph on a PowerPoint slide.*

4 In your group, take turns to present your talk, using appropriate persuasive language and visual aids. The rest of the group will act in role as MPs and give feeback.

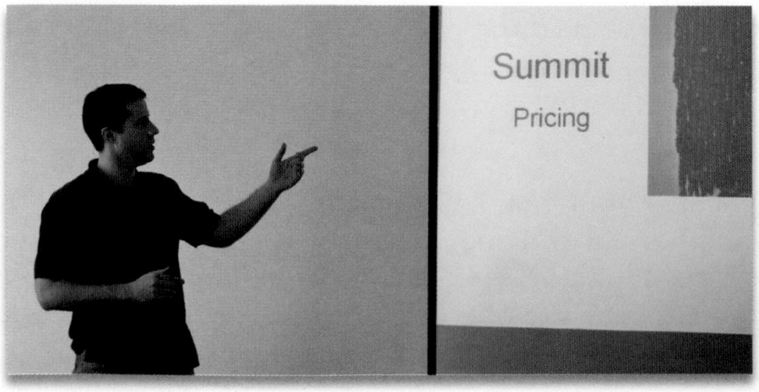

Apply your learning

Task Choose a group of people in your community who would benefit from a social networking site, e.g. people with insomnia, teenage mums, disabled people. Plan and deliver a talk which will persuade the trustees of the charity IT4You to set up this site.

1 Plan your talk. Think about:
   - what problems the group you have chosen might face
   - what dangers these users might worry about
   - how the new social networking site could help them.

2 Organise your talk. Think about how you can present information in a clear, logical way that signals the direction of your talk. Use language persuasively and prepare any prompt cards or visual aids that you will need.

3 In groups take it in turns to deliver your talk (with group members acting in role as trustees). Remember to think about the way you speak and use gestures and body language to direct the audience's attention.

Assess to Progress

How confident are you now at planning and presenting a talk in formal and informal situations? Are you good at making sure your audience is engaged with what you are saying? Look back at the ratings you gave yourself on page 3. Now rate yourself again for each of the skills. Pick out examples that show your skill level from the task you have just completed.

SKILLS FOR LIFE

You have been asked to give a talk to the regional chief constable and other senior police officers explaining how they could make your local town or city a safer place for teenagers to visit at weekends.

Work in groups of four. Use the speaking skills you have developed during this unit to plan, prepare and present your talks in turn. Think about:

- the problems teenagers face when they visit the local town centre
- how these problems could be overcome
- what the police need to do and how you can persuade them to act
- how teenagers could be persuaded to help improve the situation.

Progress in ... Listening and responding

LEARNING OBJECTIVES

- Listen to what a speaker says and respond constructively, analysing and extending a speaker's ideas.
- Identify the implications of what speakers say, using questions that probe and clarify meaning.

Activate your learning

How good are you at listening and responding? Work in a group of five, to complete the following activity.

1 One of you should begin to tell a story – this could be a true or invented story. When the teacher clicks their fingers, the speaker should stop and the next person in the group should continue the story. Remember to listen carefully to pick up details so that you can continue the story.

2 How easy or difficult did you find this activity? Did the way you listened alter when you knew you might have to continue the story?

Assess to Progress

How good are you already at listening and responding to what someone says? Rate yourself for each skill by deciding which number on the scale below best shows your skill level.

1	2	3	4	5	6	7
I find this difficult.			I'm getting there.			I'm good at this.

- I can listen and respond constructively to what a speaker says.

  Self-check: Can you recognise the key points a speaker makes and the techniques they use to communicate these, responding in a way that develops and extends these ideas?

- I can analyse the implications of what speakers say through careful questioning.

  Self-check: Can you understand how speakers feel by analysing what they say and by asking probing questions?

Build your skills

You are going to look at a presentation from the TV programme *Dragons' Den*, in which people with new business ideas give a presentation to possible investors, hoping to secure some money for their product. Here, Andy Harmer is sharing his idea for a business called *Double Dates*.

'I'm here looking for £100,000 invested into my company for 25% of the investment. My company name is Double Dates. Basically … erm … my idea is a celebrity entertainment concept which allows the everyday person to be a celebrity for the day. For the past nine years I have been a David Beckham professional lookalike and … wha … er … what my concept is … er … totally … I can't talk. (Deep breath) OK. My idea is, comes from being a celebrity for the day. The … erm … I … what I've done is I've … you … created … I can't talk. (Deep breath) The for … the Double Dates has 30 top celebrity lookalikes in the industry. I've actually brought a couple of my guys along with me today … Mr Will Smith. Mr Johnny Depp. The Double Dates has already set the foundations for this company to work in London. We've got exclusivity contracts with … casinos, night clubs, recording studios, photo studios and limousine companies and obviously with all of my celebrity doubles there's a massive industry for this. Do you have any questions?'

Step 1 Listen and respond to what the speaker says

1 Working with a talk-partner, answer the following questions to work out the key details from Andy's presentation:

a) What exactly is Andy offering the Dragons a stake in?

b) What sort of businesses are they hoping to work with?

c) What information did you expect Andy to provide that he didn't?

2 What speaking skills and techniques does Andy use to try to persuade the Dragons to invest in his idea? How do you think the Dragons will respond? Why?

3 List three reasons why the Dragons should invest in Andy's business. List another three reasons why they shouldn't. Compare your reasons with a partner's.

Support

Decide whether Andy has used any of the following techniques and the impact they have on his presentation.

- Examples to support his ideas
- Lists of three
- Repetition
- Presenting key information last

Reinforce your skills

Step 2 Use questions to probe and clarify meaning

Look at the transcript below to see how one of the Dragons, Deborah Meaden, responded to Andy by **asking questions** to get a fuller picture of Andy's business and how he would spend the £100,000 investment.

Deborah:	*So if I understand this, you've got some celebrity lookalikes …,*	
Andy:	*Yeah.*	
Deborah:	*And you're offering for people to hire them for the day to do celebrity type stuff … That's it in a nutshell?*	Question to summarise and clarify meaning.
Andy:	*That's correct.*	
Deborah:	*You should have had me over there doing your pitch for you!*	
Andy:	*Yeah.*	
Deborah:	*So what have you got in place in terms of those celebrity events?*	Question to seek clarification.
Andy:	*Well, I've signed exclusivity contracts for the celebrity experience with Grosvenor casinos, erm … er … recording studios, photo studios …*	
Deborah:	*So you're allowed to attend the casino and then put your own event on?*	Question to encourage development of ideas.
Andy:	*Yes.*	

1 Working in pairs, rework Andy's pitch using the techniques you have explored and the information above. Join with another pair and take it in turns to present your pitch, with the interviewing pair acting in role as the Dragons and asking questions.

2 Working in pairs, role-play a conversation in which a teenager is trying to persuade their parents to allow them to go to a late-night music concert. The parent should ask questions to clarify information.

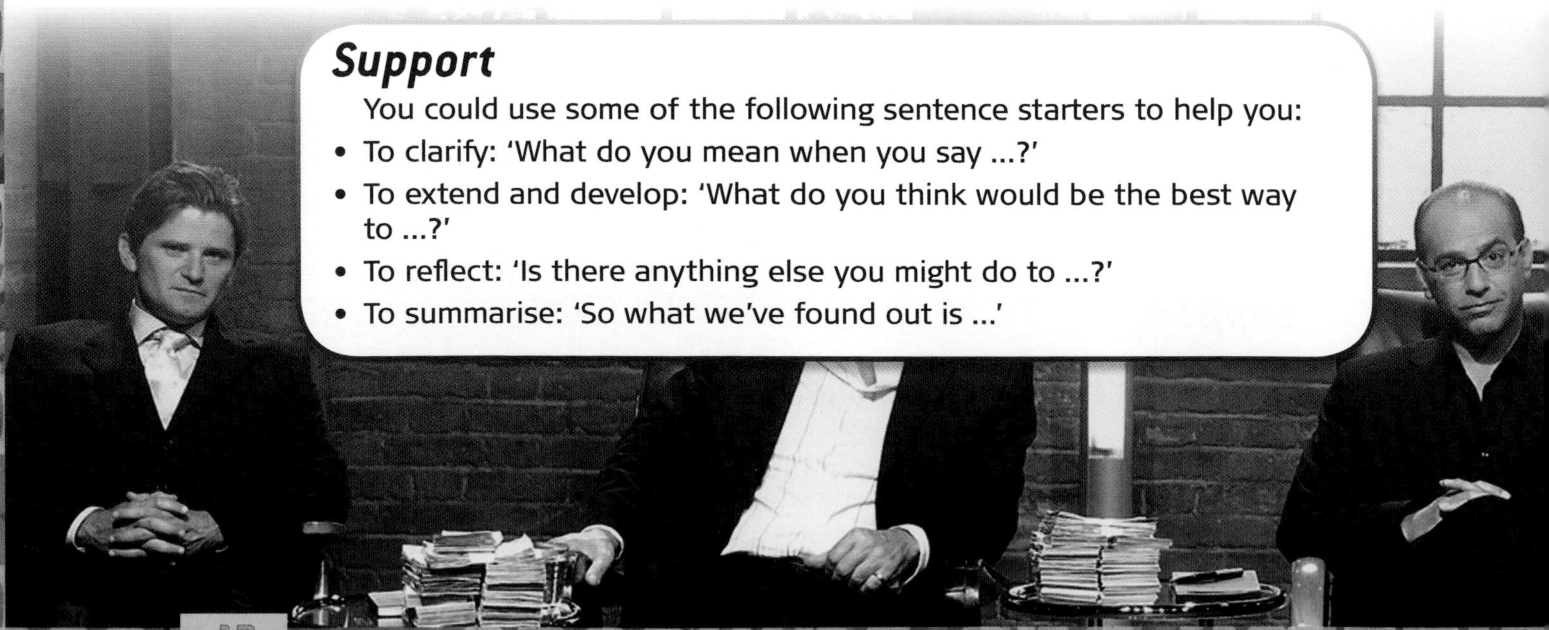

Support

You could use some of the following sentence starters to help you:

- To clarify: 'What do you mean when you say …?'
- To extend and develop: 'What do you think would be the best way to …?'
- To reflect: 'Is there anything else you might do to …?'
- To summarise: 'So what we've found out is …'

Extend your skills

Step 3 Identify the implications of what speakers say

As well as understanding what a speaker says **explicitly**, it is important to be able to recognise the **implications** of what has or has not been said by listening 'between the lines', e.g. is the speaker missing out important information that might hinder his pitch? Working this out allows you to recognise any underlying issues.

1 In pairs, work in role as Andy and the Dragon Theo Paphitis to read aloud the exchange below where Theo is trying to find out how Andy is planning to spend the money. Then discuss the following questions with your partner:

a) What techniques does Theo use to try to find out the information he wants?

b) How does the way he responds to Andy's answers show how he feels about the business idea?

c) What underlying issue has Theo identified?

Theo: *Andy … assuming that somebody decided that they were going to give you £100,000, what're you going to do with it?*

Andy: *What I'm going to do, is I'm going to … I've got £10,000 which I want to put on a launch party, which is … er …*

Theo: *Well, we've started with a really good one – the first £10,000 of my children's inheritance, you're going to blow on a party!*

Andy: *Yeah, well, I … I … I've been in negotiations with a … er … a couple …*

Theo: *Now I've got £90,000 of my children's money still. What ya gonna do with it?*

Andy: *Er … I'm gonna put £30,000 into advertising.*

Theo: *Now you've got £60,000 left of my children's money. What ya gonna do with it?*

Andy: *Well, you know we need some … we're gonna need to find somewhere, you know, there's gonna be spaces where, you know, where maybe we need to put a bit more into admin.*

Stretch

To develop a detailed awareness of a speaker's overall design, look for speakers using the following techniques:

- irony – when there is a difference between what is meant and what is said
- euphemism – when a word or phrase that could be offensive or upsetting is replaced by something more agreeable
- undertone – an underlying meaning.

1 Which of these techniques is Theo Paphitis using when he says, 'Well, we've started with a really good one'? What does he mean?

2 Swap roles and rerun the role play between a teenager and a parent from page 12. The person playing the teenager should make statements that **imply** why they should be allowed to attend the concert. The parent should ask questions to identify implications and uncover underlying issues.

Apply your learning

Task A music festival is being planned which will be held near to where you live. Listen to what the promoter has to say on a local radio phone-in show about the proposal.

I'm here today to tell you about a wonderful opportunity that will benefit all of you who live in this area: the Amazing Music Festival, planned to take place in two months' time. This will not be just another music festival, it will be a lot more than a music festival: it is a three day, three night event which takes place on a beautiful stretch of land. It's the perfect way for students to end their exams and to begin their summer! We're the only Festival in England that we know of that offers such amazing facilities. We've got camping on site and we're licensed for three days and three nights. We also pride ourselves on being very environmentally and socially responsible, particularly when it comes to the local area.

In a group of five, choose one of the following roles:

- a student who would like to go to the festival
- a parent or guardian who is worried about it
- a local resident
- a local shopkeeper
- the promoter.

1 Now regroup into specialist groups, e.g. all the shopkeepers working together and so on, except for the promoters. In your specialist group, work in role to discuss your thoughts and views about the festival and agree on questions you would like to ask the promoter.

2 The promoters should take turns to observe the different specialist groups' discussions. Think about the concerns that different people have and how you could respond to these.

3 Re-form into your original group. Role-play a meeting with the promoter to discuss the full range of views about the festival proposal. Remember to:

- listen to what different speakers say
- make perceptive responses to build and extend meaning
- use questions to probe and clarify meaning.

4 When you have finished the role play, work in your group to discuss your role play and give constructive feedback to each member on their contributions.

Assess to Progress

How good are you now at listening and responding to what somebody says? Look back at the ratings you gave yourself on page 10. Pick out examples that show your skill level from the task you have just completed. Now rate yourself again for each of the skills.

Skills for Life

Role-play a conversation between a careers adviser and a pupil discussing possible careers they are interested in and the subjects they are thinking of studying to help them. Working in a group of three, take the following parts in the role play:

- a talker, who will explain and comment (careers adviser)
- a questioner, who will prompt and seek clarification (Year 9 pupil)
- a note-taker, who will take notes and report about appropriate use of language and questions to probe and clarify meaning.

Keep swapping roles so every member of the group has a chance to play each part.

Progress in ... Developing speaking skills in formal and informal situations

LEARNING OBJECTIVES

- Understand how spoken English varies to suit different situations and purposes and apply this in different speaking contexts.
- Choose the right level of formality to suit your audience and purpose and sustain the use of spoken standard English throughout your talk.
- Consider the needs of your listeners and the features of different types of talk to help you to organise and adapt what you say.

Activate your learning

The transcripts below are taken from different speaking situations. Read each transcript carefully, thinking about the language choices made by each speaker. Working with a partner, answer the questions opposite.

Matt is talking to his friend about a film he watched at the weekend. His friend has not yet seen the film but wants to.

Of course, the cinematography was wonderful and quite anarchic: I thought the director really made excellent use of the slow-motion fight scene. It was almost surreal, almost a ballet rather than a fight. Hugely graceful. The acting was monumental. I thought there was a towering performance from the lead actor. You got a real sense of the charisma of the character, and although I didn't really empathise with him, his hubris at the end was well-acted. Didn't really think the director would kill him off – but I guess that's the shocker, really.

Dr Philippa Coxon is an MP. She is giving a speech in Parliament about nuclear power.

Well, [coughs] *hello! Hello everyone. Hello Brian [waves to the back] nice to see you all … OK. Where am I? Where am I? Gosh, I am in a muddle today! [shuffles her papers] OK. Nuclear fuel. For or against. As you all know, I've been looking into this topic for a while now. Should we? Shouldn't we? I know a lot of you will say we should be investing in the wind turbines and stuff like that – you know … what's it called? … renewable energy. Yes, renewable energy … But really, unless we want to cover the hills in turbines, nuclear power is quite clean really, what with the low emissions and whatnot.*

Language

1 What does Matt do that is not appropriate for the situation and the needs of his listener? Pick out five things he does that you would not expect in this kind of situation.

2 What does Dr Coxon do that is not appropriate for the situation and needs of her listeners? Pick out five things she does that you would not expect in this kind of situation.

3 Take turns to re-enact these speeches, choosing the right level of formality for the listeners and situation.

Assess to Progress

How well do you adapt what you say to suit your purpose for speaking and the situation you are in? Are you able to choose the right level of formality and use standard English when you speak? Rate yourself for each of the following skills by deciding where you would place yourself on the scale.

1 3 4 5 6 7

I find this difficult. I'm getting there. I'm good at this.

- I understand how spoken English varies to suit different situations and purposes and can apply this when I speak in different contexts.

  Self-check: Do you understand how language used by a BBC News presenter differs from that of a presenter on an MTV music show? Can vary your language according to the situation you are speaking in?

- I choose the right level of formality to suit my audience and purpose and sustain my use of spoken standard English.

  Self-check: Can you make a formal presentation about your school to Year 6 pupils and their parents using standard English throughout?

- I think about the needs of my listeners and the features of different types of talk to help me to organise and adapt what I say.

  Self-check: Did you understand what changes needed to be made to suit the different speaking situations on page 16 to make sure the language used was appropriate for the audience and purpose?

Language

Build your skills

Whenever you speak, it is important to think about who you are talking to, and why you are talking. This helps you to think about the type of talk you need to use and to organise and adapt what you say appropriately.

Step 1 Organise and adapt your talk appropriately for the audience and purpose

Mark Kermode is a radio and television presenter who reviews films. When he talks, he needs to think about what information people expect to hear and how best to present this.

1 Working with a partner, make a list of the information you would expect to hear in a film review. Compare your ideas with another pair and agree on a list of the five most important things.

Now look at what Mark Kermode says about the film *Casino Royale*.

He introduces what he is talking about.

A new Bond movie, and a new Bond, Daniel Craig, who of course, when he first got the role, there was a lot of press furore and people kept saying 'No! His hair's the wrong colour … he's too small … he's not handsome enough …' which is all nonsense. He's a great actor and that's all that matters. It takes you right back to the roots of the Bond story … the 007 thing … he's only just getting his licence to kill and in fact at the beginning of the film, we see him committing his first, and indeed, second, kills. It's a much tougher movie than the Bonds that we've got used to. It's got action sequences in which you feel that people genuinely get hurt, including Bond himself, and a rip-roaring crane-top opening sequence.

He then talks a little about what people thought before the movie was filmed.

He then reassures the listener that Daniel Craig is a great James Bond.

Then he gives some simple information about the plot.

He summarises three things we might enjoy about the film.

Language

With your partner, discuss and answer the following questions:

2 Look back at the list you created. Which information from your list did Mark Kermode include in his review? Was there any information you expected to hear but didn't?

3 a) Why do you think Mark Kermode mentions what people were saying before the movie came out? What will this make the audience think?

b) Why do you think he then says 'He's a great actor and that's all that matters'? What will his listeners think now?

4 Do you think this will develop into a positive or negative review of the film? How does the way Mark Kermode has organised the opening of his review show listeners his opinion?

Step 2 Choose the right level of formality and use spoken standard English

As well as giving his listeners the information they need about the film, Mark Kermode chooses the right level of formality to communicate this information effectively. In his review, he creates an informal tone but still speaks in standard English as he needs to make sure he is understood by a wide range of listeners.

1 Working with a partner, identify the ways Mark Kermode creates an appropriate level of formality without using non-standard English. Pick out examples where he:

- uses the first person and present tense to explain his ideas about the film
- expresses his ideas in complete sentences or units of speech
- uses vocabulary to make his ideas clear and easy to understand
- adds details to what he says
- involves the audience.

Language

Reinforce your skills

When you speak to explain or inform, the way in which you should express your ideas depends on the formality of the context. The transcript below is taken from the introduction to a BBC documentary about fantasy.

Imagine yourself on a journey into a wondrous and magical place. We're heading for the land of fantasy. Today, fantasy has become a worldwide phenomenon. In the twenty-first century, more and more people are turning to books, movies and video games to transport them into the worlds of the imagination. But is this explosion in fantasy simply an entertainment? A way of hiding away from the realities of our modern world? Or is it something more?

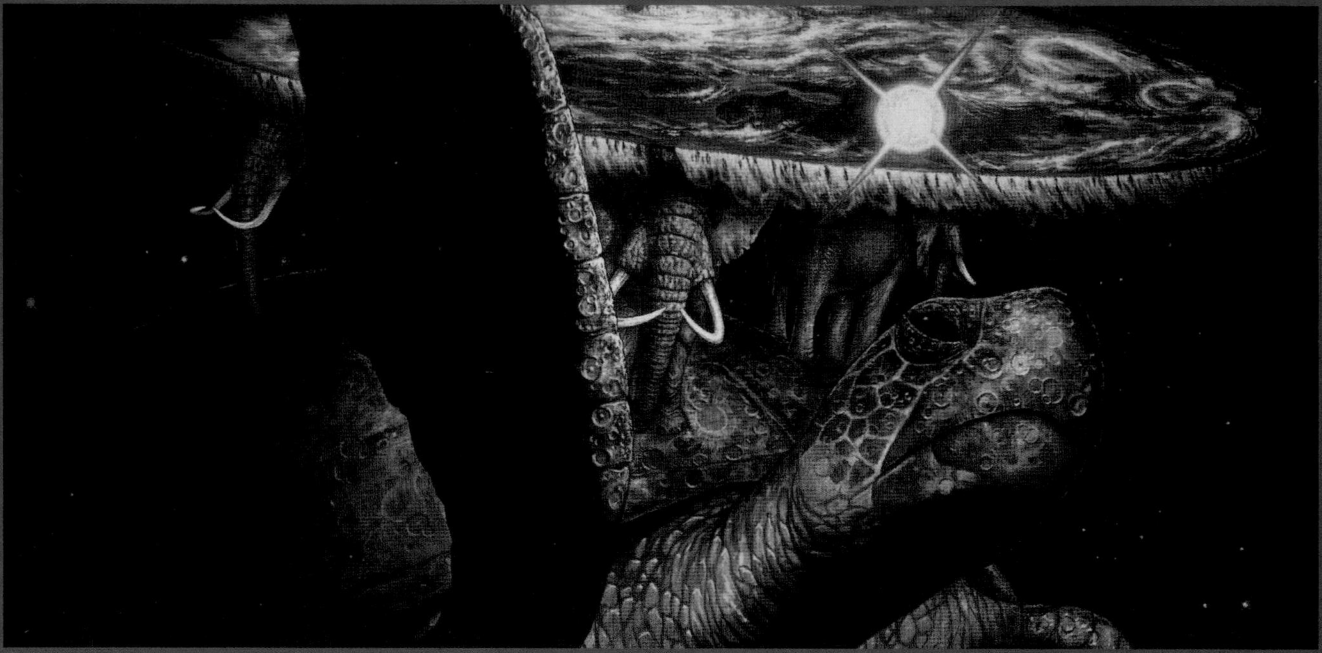

1 How does the speaker signal that this is the opening of their explanation? What features can you find that show this is designed to hook the listener?

2 What examples can you find that engage and interest the listener? Why do you think they are effective?

3 What examples can you find of the speaker crafting their language, using rhetorical devices for effect?

Support

Can you find examples of rhetorical questions, emotive language (words used for emotional impact), repetition, rule of three, contrasts, hyperbole (exaggeration), sound patterns, parallel structures (same pattern of words linked by a conjunction) or imagery?

In the transcript below, the author Terry Pratchett talks about how he became interested in fantasy fiction.

I don't recall learning to read for pleasure at school. The first book I ever read for pleasure was The Wind in the Willows. I read it all the way through and read it again ... and ... you know ... joined the local library within a couple of days and was looking for other books. I just wanted to get that magic and I quickly got through all the fantasy that they had – which wasn't so much in those days – and I read the folklore because ... you know ... that seemed pretty much like fantasy ... and then the mythology because that clearly was fantasy ... and then ancient history, which in many ways resembled the fantasy ... and one book led to another book.

4 a) Working with a partner, take turns to read the transcript aloud then discuss the ways in which Terry Pratchett's explanation sounds less formal than the documentary and more like natural speech.

b) Copy and complete the table below, picking out examples to show the level of formality in each transcript and how the speaker creates this.

Documentary	**Terry Pratchett**
More formal – speaks in complete sentences	Less formal – uses fillers such as 'you know' to give thinking time

5 a) Working with a partner, take it in turns to interview each other about which genre of books or films you enjoy most. Explain how you became interested in this genre and what its appeal is.

b) Now create an introduction for a radio documentary about this genre. Think about:

- the features you need to include – what will your listeners expect to hear?
- how to use standard English and create the right level of formality for a wide audience.

Language

Extend your skills

Sometimes you might want to speak for more than one purpose, e.g. not just explaining but persuading or justifying your ideas to your listeners.

Look at the introduction Stuart has prepared for a radio documentary about manga. The documentary will be broadcast on a station with an older audience.

Manga – for those of you who don't know – is kind of like cartoons and graphic novels, but with a twist. It's mostly Japanese or Korean, but there's some American stuff as well. But ... it's not cartoons or geeky. In Japan, there's manga for everybody. There's manga for kids, manga for lads, manga for girls, manga for women, manga for guys. And it's not just about not wanting to read a lot of words – it's visual – kind of like a movie and a book combined – so you get the best of both worlds. They don't have to tell you the character's angry or thinking, you can just see it. It's also really artistic – some of the artwork is incredible. It's like we get past seven and it's not OK to like picture books any more, but I used to love all my old picture books. Who is it that says growing up means you don't have to like pictures?

1 How does Stuart adapt his talk to persuade as well as inform?

2 What features show that Stuart is trying to justify his ideas as well as explain what manga is?

3 Discuss with a partner the changes Stuart could make to sustain his use of standard English and create a formal tone.

4 Now discuss ways in which you could adapt the introduction you wrote on page 21 to persuade your listeners and justify your ideas.

5 Take turns to present your introductions and feedback on how well you each created the right level of formality and sustained the use of standard English.

Stretch

Create a list of formal speaking situations which require the use of standard English. Choose one to practice the skills you have developed.

Support

Remember to avoid the use of dialect or colloquial language. If you have to use vocabulary that your listeners may not understand, make sure you explain what you mean. Think about how you can structure your talk in a clear and logical way.

Apply your learning

Task You are appearing as a guest film reviewer on Radio 5 Live's new late-afternoon programme aimed at people driving home from work.

1 Working in pairs, you are going to present a short film review. You need to show that you can choose the correct register and style for your talk, making decisions about the audience for the broadcast.

Think about the features of this type of talk and how you can organise and adapt these. You might want to include the following information:

- the film's plot, without giving too much away
- who you think would enjoy the film, and why
- what you thought about the film, giving your reasons.

Remember to use the right level of formality and standard English. Make sure you structure what you say to suit the needs of the audience. Take turns to work in role as the guest reviewer and the show's presenter.

2 Now adapt your film review for a two-minute slot on *FILM:UK*, a new TV programme aimed at teenagers. Present your review, changing the level of formality to suit your new audience.

Assess to Progress

How well do you adapt what you say to suit different situations and purposes now? Can you sustain your use of standard English when you speak? Look back at the ratings you gave yourself on page 17. Now rate yourself again for each of the skills. Pick out examples that best show your skill level from the task you have just completed.

Skills for Life

You have volunteered to act as host to a range of teenagers and business people visiting from your twinned town. They have come to see life in England and are looking at schools, businesses and sport and leisure facilities.

Prepare and present a talk to be given on the visitor's arrival, welcoming them to your town and persuading them that they have come to the best place. Remember to use standard English and choose the right level of formality for your audience and purpose.

Progress in ... Group discussion and interaction

LEARNING OBJECTIVES

- Take a wide variety of roles in discussion, collaborating effectively and handling challenges or disagreements.
- Move a discussion forward, building on what others say and bringing together other ideas and points of view.
- Give constructive feedback, identifying strengths and areas for development in your contributions and those of others when working in a group.

Activate your learning

Work in a group of six. Three of you will discuss whether you agree or disagree with the following statements. The other three will observe the discussion, making notes on how you work as a group.

1 The first group of three should look at these statements. Discuss whether you agree with them or not, giving examples and evidence to support what you say. You have four minutes to discuss the four statements.

> Rap music should be banned. It is responsible for the 'gangsta' culture in Britain and has created a nation of adults who think it is acceptable to carry guns and knives, or that 'bling' is the most important goal in life.

> Music is often the only way people's views and voices get heard. For many people in life, shows like *The X-Factor* and *Pop Idol* offer them a way out of a hard life.

> *Music with explicit, violent or aggressive lyrics should be banned. There's no place in this world for all that hatred.*

> All music and lyrics should be allowed; it is up to the individual to decide whether or not it is appropriate or inappropriate. If you don't like it, don't listen!

2 The observers should focus on one person each within the discussion group. Make notes about:

- how well they cooperate with each other
- how they handle interruptions
- how they support or challenge others' views.

3 a) At the end of the discussion, each speaker should pair up with an observer. The observer should feed back on how well the speaker worked in the group discussion.

b) Re-form in your group of six. Discuss the feedback, sharing what you agree you did well and what you need to work on in future group work.

Assess to Progress

How confident are you at working in groups? How good are you at moving discussion forward? Rate yourself for each of the following skills by deciding where you would place yourself on the scale below. Justify your decisions using examples from the activity you have just completed.

1 2 3 4 5 6 7

I find this difficult. I'm getting there. I'm good at this.

- I can identify strengths and areas for development in the contributions I make and those of others when working in a group.

  Self-check: When working in a group, do you recognise what you do well and also consider how well others contribute to the discussion?

- I can take a wide variety of roles in discussion and know how to collaborate effectively, handling challenges or disagreements.

  Self-check: Do you feel confident taking a range of roles in group discussion and know how to use the skills these require to organise and sustain the discussion?

- I can move a discussion forward, building on what others say and bringing together other ideas and points of view.

  Self-check: Do you know how to develop what other people have said and can bring together different ideas and viewpoints to build agreement in the group?

Build your skills

In Geography, Ben has watched a TV programme about how some fashion suppliers use children in factories in developing countries to produce their clothes cheaply. It showed how bad the conditions in the factories were, and how children as young as seven were working seventeen-hour days. He now has to discuss this in a group, exploring their responses to this issue and considering what can be done about it.

Step 1 Plan for discussion

When you want to discuss an issue you have heard about or a topic you are exploring in school, it is a good idea to plan for your discussion. This can help you to generate ideas, consider your feelings about the topic and think about what you want to say.

1 a) Create a diagram of your own thoughts and ideas on this topic, using whatever planning method you think would be most suitable.

b) Order your ideas, making notes of where you could add examples or explain what you mean. Make sure you begin with the key ideas you plan to discuss.

Step 2 Share your ideas and feelings in discussion

It is important to make sure you get your point across in discussion, but you also need to listen to others' views so that you can develop your own thinking. Look at this transcript of the discussion in Ben's group and think about how each person shares their ideas and feelings.

Ben: *I think the main issue for me is that these are children who are working. Most of them are younger than me. I can't imagine having to go out to work and not being able to survive unless I did. It made me think how lucky we were and how we shouldn't take advantage of other people.*

Kieran: *Yes, I know what you mean, but would it be any different if they were adults? I think it's all disgusting, not just that they use children to do it. Nobody should have to live like this in our day and age. But it's not going to solve the problem that we all want the most fashionable clothes and we don't want to pay a lot for them. There's nothing we can do to make people want to buy fewer clothes or to look at the label and see where it was made.*

Bilal: *You're all forgetting that this used to happen in Britain though, and not even that long ago. Being able to do this helped make us the country we are. I don't see how we can go around telling other countries they can't use child labour when it used to happen in Britain!*

1 Working with a partner, identify the point Ben makes in the discussion. How does he help the rest of the group understand this idea?

2 What other ideas do Kieran and Bilal give? How do they express these?

3 Join with another pair to form a group of four. Three of you should now discuss the topic and the fourth person should make notes of the main points and ideas people contribute.

Step 3 Develop ideas and draw together what others say

Ben responds to the points the others make in order to move the discussion forward. Look at how he does this by drawing ideas together and using them to develop his own point of view.

> *You've got a good point, Bilal. But we don't do it any more ... Maybe we can learn from history how we managed to put an end to it and how we improved conditions for adults.*

Here Ben refers to Bilal's comment that children used to work in factories in Britain and he uses this to speculate on how we might help other countries stop child labour. He also mentions improving conditions for adults, which links to Kieran's point.

1 Working in your group of four, think back to your discussion. The person who observed the discussion should share the notes they made. Discuss:

- What were the main points made by the speakers?
- What points did you make that were similar?
- What are the main ideas that could lead to further discussion?

2 Continue your discussion of this issue. Think about how you can draw together people's contributions and develop ideas to move the discussion forward.

Stretch

Listen carefully to what other people in your group say. Think about the ways you can respond to other people's comments, rather than just adding your own idea. Remember to:

- ask relevant questions
- put their ideas into your own words to show you understand
- speculate to explore the implications of what has been said
- draw on their point to develop your own idea.

Reinforce your skills

When working in a group, it is important to challenge others' views in ways that are polite and non-confrontational, yet make your point. Being assertive, rather than aggressive, is a key feature of challenging others' views.

Jeremy Paxman, is well known for his confrontational style. In the interview below, he wants an answer from Michael Howard, a politician, about whether or not he threatened to overrule a decision made by Derek Lewis to move rather than suspend Mr Marriott. Read the transcript and answer the questions.

1 What does Jeremy Paxman do that might be considered aggressive?

2 What effect does it have on Michael Howard? How does he respond?

3 Discuss with a partner whether this aggressive style is effective.

Michael Howard: Mr Marriott was not suspended. I was entitled to express my views. I was entitled to be consulted …

Jeremy Paxman: Did you threaten to overrule him?

Michael Howard: I … I was not entitled to instruct Derek Lewis and I did not instruct him and the truth of …

Jeremy Paxman: [interrupts] Did you threaten to overrule him?

Michael Howard: The truth of the matter is that Mr Marriott was not suspended. I did not …

Jeremy Paxman: [interrupts] Did you threaten to overrule him?

Michael Howard: I did not overrule Derek Lewis.

Jeremy Paxman: [interrupts] Did you threaten to overrule him?

Michael Howard: I took advice on what I could or could not do …

Jeremy Paxman: [interrupts] Did you threaten to overrule him, Mr Howard?

Michael Howard: and I acted scrupulously in accordance with that advice. I did not overrule Derek Lewis.

Jeremy Paxman: [interrupts] Did you threaten to overrule him?

Michael Howard: Mr Marriott was not suspended.

Jeremy Paxman: [interrupts] Did you threaten to overrule him?

Michael Howard: I have accounted for my decision to dismiss Derek Lewis …

Jeremy Paxman: [interrupts] Did you threaten to overrule him?

Michael Howard: in great detail before the House of Commons.

Jeremy Paxman: I note you're not answering the question whether you threatened to overrule him.

Michael Howard starts by making his point very clearly, using simple words.

Jeremy Paxman interrupts ignoring signs that he hadn't finished speaking.

Michael Howard repeats some of his words and ideas but doesn't answer the question directly.

Jeremy Paxman keeps using a polite term of address, saying 'Mr Howard' even though he's interrupting.

Michael Howard continues talking, ignoring the interruption.

Jeremy Paxman repeats the question, changing the stress when it isn't answered exactly.

To be assertive, rather than aggressive, you should:

- let the other person finish speaking before challenging them
- focus on what someone has said rather than on the speaker – don't make personal criticisms
- ask open questions to move the discussion forward, e.g. What evidence do you have for that? What do other people think?
- if your question is ignored, rephrase it and ask it in a different way
- watch your body language – make sure your gestures and your facial expressions don't become aggressive.

4 Work as a pair to role-play an interview using more assertive techniques. You could role-play the interview you just have read or create a new interview situation.

Extend your skills

Look at this grid, which shows four different types of feedback.

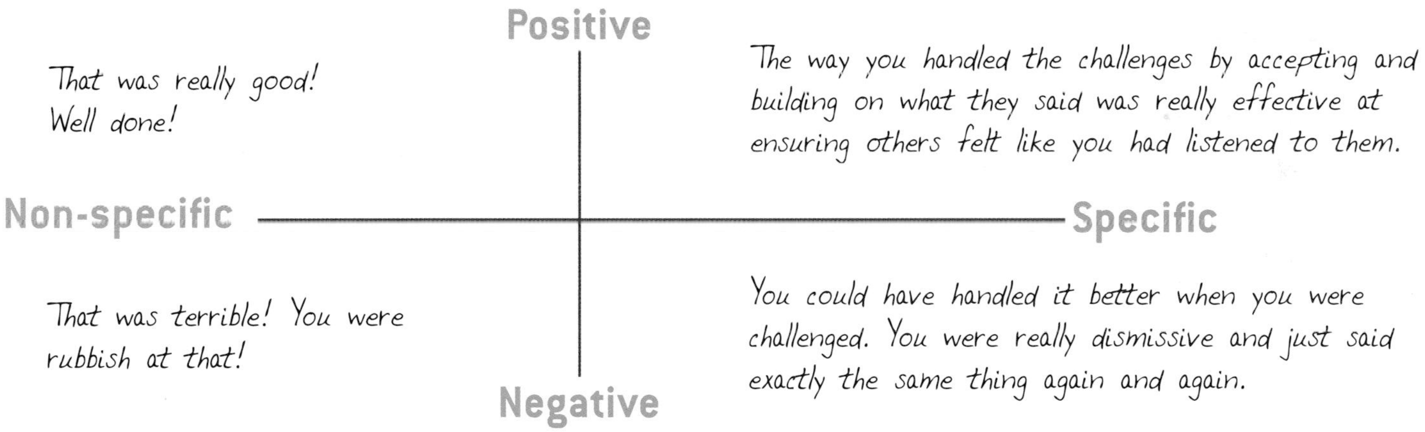

Positive specific feedback is useful because it helps you identify what you did well in order that you can do it again in future.

Negative specific feedback is useful because it helps you identify what you are doing that is less effective. It is also helpful to give some kind of prompt as to how to improve next time.

Positive non-specific feedback is not very useful. It doesn't help you identify the best bits so that you can use them again.

Negative non-specific feedback can be upsetting and doesn't identify any positives at all. Remember to avoid generalised negative comments.

1 Think about how you reflect on your own performance in group discussion and how you give feedback to others.

a) Look back to your notes from the Activate your learning activity on page 24. What kind of feedback did you give?

b) What do you do well when you give feedback to others? How might you improve your feedback to other people?

c) Now think about your performance in the activity on page 28. What strengths do you notice in your own work? What did you do well?

d) What improvements do you think you could make in your next group discussion? Discuss your ideas with the rest of the group. Think about the type of feedback you give.

Support

What different roles have you taken in discussion? Make a list of what you think are the main responsibilities of:

- a good chairperson
- a good supporting speaker
- a good listener who responds well to others.

Use this list to help you identify your own strengths and areas for improvement. Which role do you think you need to develop most?

Apply your learning

Task Work as a group of four to discuss the following issue. Two of you should argue in support of cosmetic surgery and two should argue against it.

Cosmetic surgery is pointless and vain. Some of our best surgeons have opted for cosmetic surgery when they could be performing life-saving operations. People who have cosmetic surgery have something wrong with them psychologically. They'd be better having therapy than surgery. This world is obsessed with its image and has forgotten about the more important things.

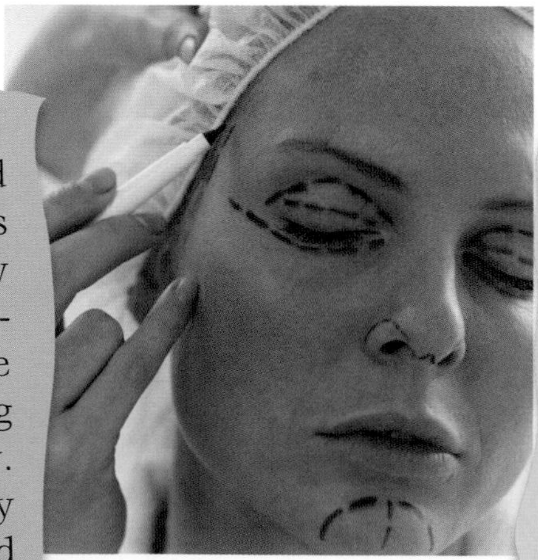

Cosmetic surgery may not save lives in the same way as a heart or brain operation might, but it is fundamental to some people's quality of life. Whether they have been bullied because of their appearance or whether they have no confidence because of how they look, cosmetic surgery helps people live the lives they want to. Appearance is just as important as what's going on underneath.

Before you start the discussion, work with your partner to generate and organise your ideas.

In your group discussion, you will need to show that you can:

- take a wide variety of roles in discussion, handling challenges
- work together with your partner to convey your argument effectively
- build on what your partner or opponents say and develop their contributions.

At the end of your discussion, give feedback to your partner about how you think they did, focusing on their strengths and any areas you think they could develop further.

Assess to Progress

How confident are you now at working in groups and developing your own and others' ideas to move a discussion forward? Look back at the ratings you gave yourself on page 25. Now rate yourself again for each of the skills. Pick out examples which best show your skill level from the task you have just completed.

SKILLS FOR LIFE

Your local council is planning to build several new schools in your area. You have been invited to the council chamber to contribute your ideas to a discussion about their plans. The council wants to know how you think the schools should look and what features they might have.

Work as a group of four to discuss the following points:

- What facilities should the schools offer? How can they be part of the community?
- What facilities will the schools need for the future?
- Are there any things that schools have now that you don't think they will need in the future?

At the end of your discussion, make a list of your recommendations to the council.

Then take the roles of councillors and compile a list of concerns and responses to the list of recommended actions.

Progress in ... Drama, role play and performance

LEARNING OBJECTIVES

- Use a variety of dramatic approaches and conventions to explore complex and challenging ideas, themes and issues.
- Use drama to develop and sustain roles and performances by selecting and adapting appropriate techniques.
- Analyse your use of different dramatic conventions and techniques and explain the impact and effects these have.

Activate your learning

1 Working in a group of four, make a list of your favourite characters from film or TV. Next to each name write a typical dramatic situation they could find themselves in,
e.g. James Bond trapped as a bomb is detonated.

2 Discuss which of the dramatic techniques below you have used before. Decide which would help you to explore a character and situation from your list.

tableau | hot-seating | thought-tracking | improvisation | conscience alley | role on the wall

3 Choose one situation and character. Working in role, use some of these dramatic techniques to develop a short scene. Think about how you can make your character believable and the situation tense or dramatic.

4 Working with your group, discuss how the techniques you used helped you create an effective performance.

Assess to Progress

How good are you at using a variety of dramatic approaches and techniques to explore ideas and texts or develop a performance in role? Rate yourself for each of the following skills by deciding where you would place yourself on the scale below. Justify your decisions using examples from the activity you have just completed.

1	4	5	6	7
I find this difficult.	I'm getting there.			I'm good at this.

- I can use a variety of dramatic techniques to explore complex and challenging ideas, texts, issues and themes.

  Self-check: Can you use techniques such as hot-seating to explore a character's situations and make thoughtful contributions analysing their responses?

- I can develop and sustain a performance in role by selecting appropriate dramatic techniques.

  Self-check: Can you use voice, gesture and movement skilfully to convey your understanding of a character to an audience?

- I can evaluate the effectiveness of the dramatic techniques I use and analyse their impact on an audience.

  Self-check: When you use a technique such as thought-tracking can you judge the audience's response and explain the effect the technique has?

Build your skills

Sometimes an event can change your life for ever. The event might be something positive, (e.g. the birth of a baby brother or sister) or it could be unexpected and unpleasant, (e.g.an accident). A life-changing event can affect the way you view your life and even alter the way you behave.

When you portray challenging issues through drama, you can use different **dramatic techniques** to explore their effects. In the extract on the next page from the play *Face* by Benjamin Zephaniah and Richard Conlon, Martin, a London teenager, remembers a night out that ended with him seriously injured and another boy dead. One actor plays 'Narrative Martin' looking back; another actor plays 'Past Martin' acting out the scene.

NARRATIVE MARTIN Look at me. I had no idea. ***(calls to his past self)*** It's all over, Martin. All over! Listen to me, you fool. You stupid fool! ***(he softens, looks to the audience)*** Oh bless … all I wanted to do was dance. That night, for the first time, I suddenly knew I could do it. If I could free myself from worrying about people watching, I could do it.

ALL STREET VOICES Just forget that people are watching.

NARRATIVE MARTIN And I did. Nervous at first, but then – one two, left right, one two, right left. Things were going OK and then – ***I put my hands in the air.***

New image
No, no hands in the air, I look like a raver and I don't want to look like a raver in this bad ass rap club. One two, left right, one two, right left. No, going wrong, thinking too much, look like Cliff Richard, I'm dancing like an uncle at a wedding. And everyone's looking at me, and woh! … There go my hands again, what can I do with my hands?

New image
Not going well. Nat and Mark and Matthew, looking embarrassed. Oh no! New guy in the ring.

New image, Past Martin is joined by another dancer.
He came out of nowhere – and he was good, smooth, supple, confident, cocky and he took over, just plain took over.

New image
And then – and then – I thought, 'I can do that'. I'm a gymnast – I can do that and better. I've done moves like that, harder than that, for years. OK, here we go, one, two, three and bounce and splits and yeah man, one, two, three and splits and bounce and yeah, I got it going on, one, two, three. Crowd clapping. Nat looking proud, yeah dead proud, and me just moving like on the gym mat. In the zone. All eyes on me and me in some other place somehow – distant. Transported. Transformed.

Step 1 Select techniques to help you create your character

1 Working with a partner, reread the extract and discuss what you can tell about the character of Martin. Think about:
- what Past Martin says and how he feels about the situation
- what Narrative Martin says that show his feelings looking back on the situation.

2 Now decide which of the following approaches would help you create the characters of Past Martin and Narrative Martin. Use these to develop your ideas about the characters.
- Hot-seating – interviewing Martin about how he was feeling on the night and now.
- Role on the wall – adding words to describe worries and feelings to the outlines of Past Martin and Narrative Martin.

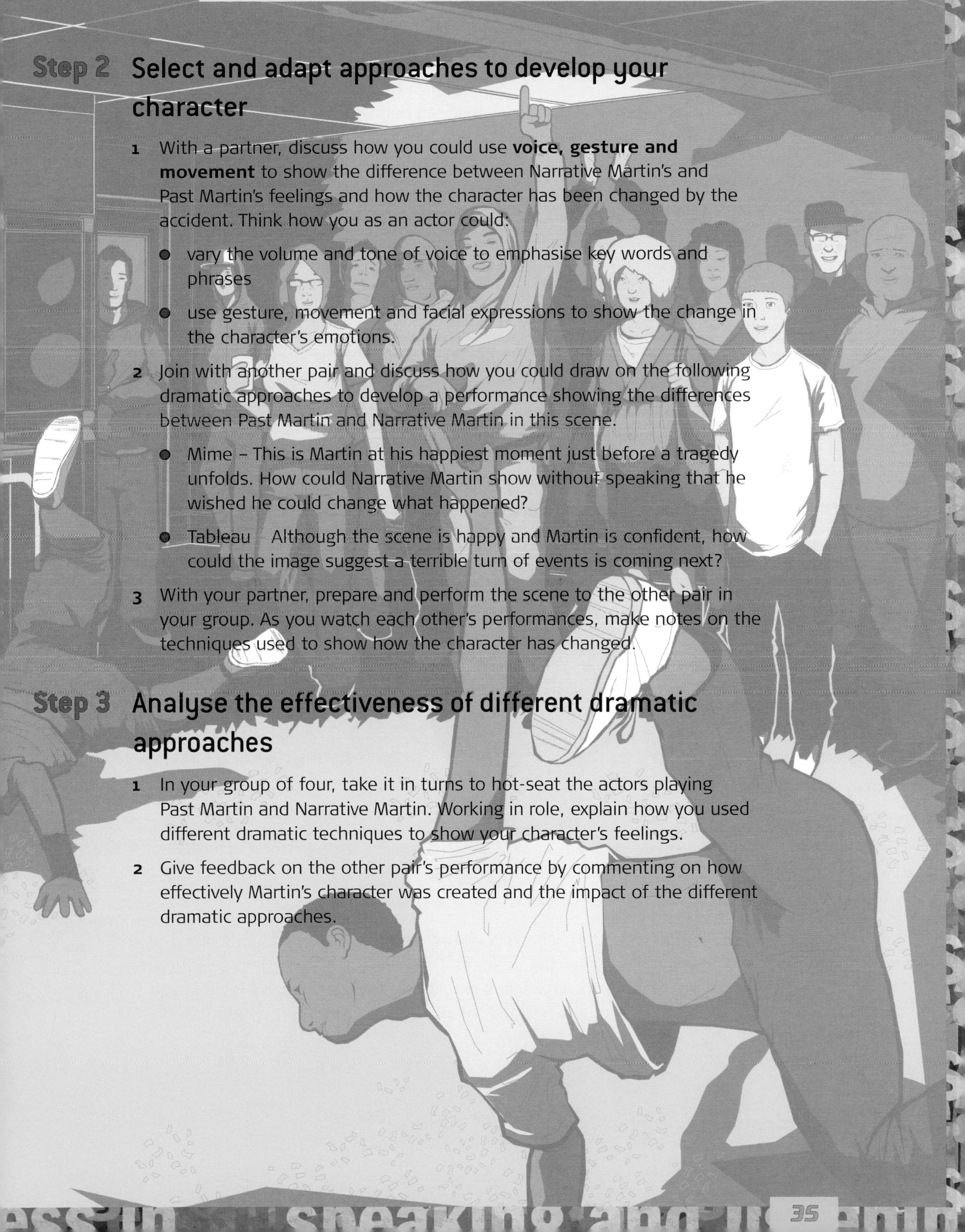

Step 2 Select and adapt approaches to develop your character

1 With a partner, discuss how you could use **voice, gesture and movement** to show the difference between Narrative Martin's and Past Martin's feelings and how the character has been changed by the accident. Think how you as an actor could:

- vary the volume and tone of voice to emphasise key words and phrases
- use gesture, movement and facial expressions to show the change in the character's emotions.

2 Join with another pair and discuss how you could draw on the following dramatic approaches to develop a performance showing the differences between Past Martin and Narrative Martin in this scene.

- Mime – This is Martin at his happiest moment just before a tragedy unfolds. How could Narrative Martin show without speaking that he wished he could change what happened?
- Tableau – Although the scene is happy and Martin is confident, how could the image suggest a terrible turn of events is coming next?

3 With your partner, prepare and perform the scene to the other pair in your group. As you watch each other's performances, make notes on the techniques used to show how the character has changed.

Step 3 Analyse the effectiveness of different dramatic approaches

1 In your group of four, take it in turns to hot-seat the actors playing Past Martin and Narrative Martin. Working in role, explain how you used different dramatic techniques to show your character's feelings.

2 Give feedback on the other pair's performance by commenting on how effectively Martin's character was created and the impact of the different dramatic approaches.

Reinforce your skills

Thought-tracking is a technique that can help you to explore a character's feelings in role. By pausing a scene at a key moment and tapping a character on the shoulder, you can get them to voice their thoughts before carrying on with the scene. This can reveal to the audience deeper feelings that the character might be hiding.

After the night at the club, Martin accepts a lift home from two joyriders in a stolen car. The car crashes, killing the driver and his friend and leaving Martin with severe burns on his face and body. Martin has plastic surgery, but has to deal with the fact that he will never look the same again.

1 Working in a group of four, discuss how you would react to such a life-changing event. Think about:

- how you would feel and how you would act
- how you think your friends and family would treat you
- how people you didn't know would react to you.

Now look at the following quotations and think about how Martin has been changed by his accident.

PAST MARTIN

'I've got nothing new to learn, my head's full.'

'I'm pretty fly for a white guy.'

'Nice face. Good-looking guy.'

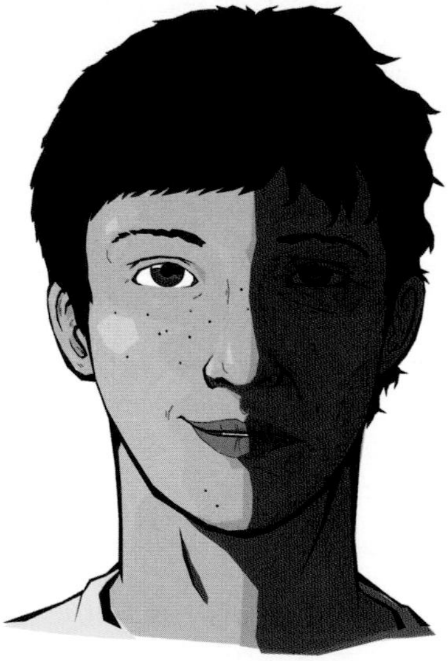

NARRATIVE MARTIN

'My skin looked so rough.'

'Rough, and ruptured and jagged and sharp and solid. Not like skin, not like a face, not like me.'

'I was so tempted to hide in my room and get on with things in secret.'

2 a) Improvise a short scene showing Martin meeting his friends again for the first time after the accident. Before you start your improvisation, discuss what the characters would be doing, saying and feeling. You could use thought-tracking to help prepare this improvisation.

b) As you prepare and act out the scene, remember to select and adapt dramatic approaches to help you create and develop the characters. Think about how you could use:

- **voice**: How would Martin sound? Would he be angry about what had happened to him? How would his friends sound - upset or trying to act like everything was normal?
- **body language and facial expressions**: Would Martin want to hide his face? How might his friends show their reactions to seeing his face for the first time?
- **mime** and **tableaux** to emphasise key moments in the scene.

Stretch

How do you think Martin's girlfriend Natalie would deal with the changes in her boyfriend's appearance? She once told Martin not to 'judge a person by what they look like' but do you think she would be able to take her own advice? Use a range of dramatic techniques to explore her thoughts and feelings. Then improvise her conversation with Martin, discussing how she feels now.

3 Evaluate your group's performance. Which techniques did you think worked well? What would you change if you did the improvisation again?

Support

When you are evaluating performances, explain the impact of the dramatic techniques using details to support your points:

- The use of hot-seating was effective because ...
- You could also use thought-tracking in order to ...

Extend your skills

In the following extract from the play, Martin is speaking to his form tutor about going back to school after the accident.

PRESENT MARTIN	***(opens the door wide)*** Term starts on Monday, yes?
FORM TUTOR	***(surprised)*** Yes, that's right.
PRESENT MARTIN	Then I'd best be there, I guess.
FORM TUTOR	Martin, do you think that's - ?
PRESENT MARTIN	***(sharply, indignantly)*** Yes, I do. I'm not going to hide. And I'm not going to wait until you've had a chance to do a nice assembly on me and what's happened. I'm not ashamed. I didn't do anything wrong. I just made a mistake, and I'm paying for it enough as it is, thank you very much. My brain still works – it's just the face that's changed and the sooner people get used to that, the better.

Conscience alley is a dramatic technique you can use to explore a character's inner feelings, particularly when there is a choice or a dilemma. In a conscience alley, a group of actors splits into two lines facing each other. Each line can represent a different way of seeing a situation. Working in role, actors take turns to walk between the lines as the rest of the group say aloud what is in the character's conscience. At the end of the line, the actor in role makes their decision about what they should do

1 Working in a group, use the conscience alley technique to explore how Martin is feeling about going back to school. One line could represent Martin's desire to carry on as normal. The other line could represent his inner fears about what might happen when he goes back to school.

2 In your group, discuss the issues that were explored in the conscience alley, e.g. What challenges does Martin think he will face? How does he think he will get over these?

Apply your learning

Task Working on your own, use the techniques and approaches you have developed in this unit to prepare and perform the scene opposite in which Martin overcomes his challenges to perform a spectacular gymnastic display at a competition.

1 Working with a partner, explore how Martin might be feeling before the competition starts. Think about the challenges Martin has faced and how he tackling these is now. Use different dramatic techniques to help you do this.

2 Adapt different dramatic techniques to help you develop and sustain a powerful performance. Think about how you could adapt the approaches you used to perform the scene on page 34.

3 Working with a partner, perform the scene, taking turns to play Narrative Martin. Try to show your understanding of Martin's experiences in the way you present him to the audience.

4 Write a short commentary reflecting on the nature of your performance and its impact.

Narrative Martin	The first event was the trampolines, nice to watch, nice not to be first up ... but then I was on. When I walked out I became so conscious of my face. I knew that every person in the hall was looking at me. I was tempted to look around to see how they were looking, I mean were they looking at a gymnast or a face? I tried not to show my nervousness, I just looked straight ahead of me, trying hard not to lose my concentration.
Announcer	And now on the floor, representing Eastmorelands, Martin Turner.
Narrative Martin	From the first move I forgot about my face, the judges, Nat, the whole room.
Street Voices	***(whispering off)*** Like no one is watching.
Narrative Martin	It was just me, the mat and gravity.
	Still images, like at the Bassment
	Two steps, turning jump, smooth landing, two hand-springs and front tucked somersault. Nice. Cartwheel, cartwheel, three Arab springs, four flick-flacks. All spot on. You know when it's right.
	Get to the far corner, change direction, fast as a cat, smooth as water, I could hear that the crowd, not one of them breathing, not yet. Two head-springs, a forward roll, another two Arab springs and four more flick-flacks ending with a back somersault. Perfect landing. Solid, stable, smooth. And the audience breathed.

Assess to Progress

How well have you used a variety of dramatic approaches and techniques to explore the issues that Martin faced and to develop effective performances in role? Look back at the ratings you gave yourself on page 33. Now rate yourself again for each of the skills. Pick out examples which best show your skill level from the task you have just completed.

Skills for Life

During a work experience placement at a removals company, you have to deal with a difficult customer on the phone. The customer is complaining about the firm breaking some valuable belongings. Working in role with a partner, improvise the phone conversation as you try to deal with the angry customer. Explore a range of dramatic approaches and compare their effectiveness. Use your findings to develop and sustain your improvisation.

Progress in ... Exploring language variation

LEARNING OBJECTIVES

- Analyse the ways in which spoken English varies depending on context and purpose as well as in a range of regions and cultural contexts.
- Consider the influences that add to and change language, exploring how and why language changes.
- Adapt how you speak to make your talk more effective when communicating with a range of listeners.

Activate your learning

When you turn on the radio, you can usually quickly tell which station you are listening to because of the way the presenter speaks. Similarly, if you overhear a conversation between two people you can often tell the type of work they do or the interests they have because of the vocabulary they use.

1 Read the following speeches aloud with a partner and discuss:

- who you think is talking and to whom
- what you think they are talking about.

Bromine is a much more efficient chemical at destroying the ozone layer and if the world had gone down that pathway, we would probably have destroyed the ozone layer. It would already have gone.

I think you have to treat him as a right-hander and if the ball pitches outside his original off stump or his original leg stump use that as the lbw because that was the way he was batting when the bowler started his run-up and got to the crease to deliver.

Course, Shonen Jump is way better than than the Tankobon versions ... manga is meant to be serialised ... Like Death Note ... you just don't get the same pleasure if you can read it all in one go. You're supposed to wonder whether L and Light know he's Kira.

Ere, mate, will you do us a favour? Will you go to the shop for us and get us some scran? Swear down I'll pay you back, like. That's boss mate. Cheers mate. You can get me owt, I don't mind, like.

Language

2 a) Which speech did you find the easiest to understand? Why?

b) Which speech was the most difficult to understand? Why?

3 a) How do you know the speakers are talking to listeners who are familiar with the topic they are discussing?

b) What do these speakers do, or what could they do, to help the listener make sense of what they are saying?

Assess to Progress

How good are you at understanding how language varies in different situations? Rate yourself for each of the following skills by deciding where to place yourself on the scale below. Justify your decisions using examples from the activity you have just completed.

1 2 3 4 5 6 7

I find this difficult. I'm getting there. I'm good at this.

- I can analyse the ways in which the language people use can vary according to the context they are speaking in.

  Self-check: Could you explain how the language used in the speeches on page 40 varied depending on who they were speaking to or why they were speaking?

- I understand the influences that add to and change language.

  Self-check: Do you understand how the words we use have changed over time and the way that new words are added to our language?

- I can adapt how I speak to make my talk more effective when communicating with a range of listeners.

  Self-check: Can you vary your speech to make it easier for a range of people to understand you if you are talking about things with a lot of jargon?

Language

Build your skills

Speaking gets a little tougher when you are speaking to someone you are less familiar with or in an unfamiliar situation.

There are four rules that you can use when you are talking to unfamiliar listeners and you think you may need to change the language you use.

- Be polite and non-confrontational.
- Be clear and specific.
- Avoid using jargon (language related to a particular profession or group).
- Make your language and vocabulary as accessible as possible without being patronising.

Look at the following transcript between two speakers who are not very familiar with each other. Abigail is trying to explain to Daisy why she doesn't like supermarket shopping. Then look at the notes Katie has made below the transcripts.

Daisy: So why don't you like supermarkets, then? What on earth is wrong with supermarkets?

Abigail: When I was younger, we didn't really have supermarkets. We had little village shops, like the butcher's and the greengrocer's. It was much more of a community, and I'd go into the shops with my mum and there was a real feeling that everyone knew each other.

Daisy has a confrontational style when she says 'What on earth?' which is quite unexpected as it is the kind of language you might use with someone you know better.

Now look at the next part of the transcript where Abigail explains why she doesn't like supermarkets. Think about how she makes her ideas clear to Daisy, who is unfamiliar with her topic. Then, working with a partner, answer the questions that follow.

Abigail: The supermarkets seem to have shot up over the last twenty years and are just getting bigger and bigger, sucking up all the land around the edge of our towns.
Daisy: So it's the fact they're so big you object to?
Abigail: Yes, but it's not just that. You see people go through the doors and get their souls sucked out. They suddenly lose any sense of anyone else, like everyone else has just evaporated and all they care about is themselves, and how many 2 for 1s they can get.
Daisy: It's like all that sense of community and knowing each other has disappeared.

Abigail explains what it was like using standard English, so that Daisy understands what she is saying. She is clear and specific about what she liked about the shops in the past.

Language

1 How does Abigail make what she is talking about clear for an unfamiliar audience?

2 How does Daisy support Abigail's point of view and show she agrees with her?

3 Imagine you have been asked to talk about something you don't like with an unfamiliar listener. Think about how you can follow the language rules to make your ideas clear to a wide audience.

Reinforce your skills

When you speak in unfamiliar situations, you need to avoid using grammar or vocabulary that excludes others, e.g. jargon, colloquial language.

However, if your listeners share your world, you can choose to use colloquial language or dialect that an outsider might not understand. Look at this conversation between Rachel and her mum.

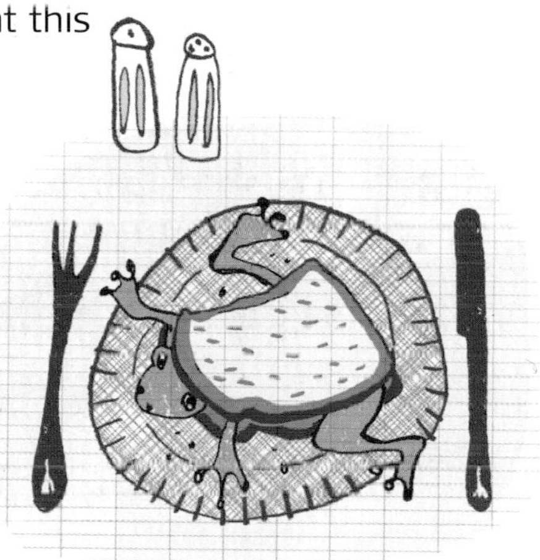

Rachel: *I'm clempt! I could eat a buttered frog! Me belly thinks me throat's been cut.*

Mum: *Not to worry! I've got tea on.*

1 Which of Rachel's words show that she expects her mother to understand her? How do you know that her mother understands what these words mean?

You may also use jargon or topic-specific language if you are familiar with your listener, or you know that they share your understanding. Look at the following conversation.

Chris: *Did you watch the test this weekend?*

Pete: *Yeah … that wicket from Jimbolina … genius. And four wickets from Monty … Genius … couldn't believe he got him lbw – you wouldn't think he'd go for a duck. Freddie's going to be hard-pushed to get selected though.*

2 Which words are difficult for an outsider to understand?

3 How might the first speaker have to adapt what they say if they were speaking to someone who wasn't familiar with the topic?

4 Working with a partner, discuss how you use dialect or jargon when speaking in certain situations. Make a list of phrases you use that could confuse other listeners.

5 Join with another pair and take turns in pairs to role-play a situation where you would use dialect or jargon. Make notes of any words that you didn't understand.

Language

Stretch

Think about the role plays and the earlier transcripts.

- How are they similar? What things do not change when we speak?
- What are the differences between them? Which do you think are most important?

Write a paragraph explaining how and why spoken English varies in these different contexts and comment on the impact of jargon, dialect and other features.

Extend your skills

'Urban' or 'modern' dictionaries document new words and phrases, explaining where they came from and how they became part of our language. In 2000, the word 'Google' was not widely known. Now it has become a common verb meaning 'search for something on the internet' – 'Google it!'

The following definition of the term 'Bling' is taken from an urban dictionary.

Bling: Bling is said to be taken from Jamaican slang for diamonds. It is taken from the sound of two diamonds colliding and can be traced through rap in America into popular culture. It could also be said to be the sound made by light reflected from diamonds. It refers to showy, ostentatious, expensive items such as jewellery or phones. It can be used as a noun, 'my bling', an adjective, 'it's very bling-bling' or 'blinging!', or a verb, 'blinged up'.

1 Work with a partner to define five examples of urban jargon that you use. Give clear definitions of what each means and examples of how you would use it. You could research the word's origins and find out when it became popular.

2 Look at the two pictures above. Decide where it would be most appropriate for the speaker to use urban jargon, explaining why.

Support

Think about using a dictionary to research each word. Has its meaning changed over time? Interview people to collect examples of slang or jargon and how they are used.

Apply your learning

Task

1 Work with a partner to create conversations for the situations below.

- A two-minute chat between friends about something they are both interested in, e.g. a hobby, or a TV programme. Use the right language, vocabulary and grammar to show that this is a conversation between friends who have a clear 'shared world'.
- A two-minute TV interview where one of you will act as an interviewer who has little knowledge of the subject matter (a topic of your choice) and the other will act as an 'expert' in this area. Your aim is to give a brief interview that explains hobby or interest. Swap roles so that you each get a turn to play the interviewer and the expert.

Remember to:

- use slang, dialect or jargon appropriately to show a 'shared world'
- keep slang, dialect, urban language or jargon to a minimum when you are speaking to someone who may not share your knowledge.

2 Write a brief commentary explaining how and why you varied your language, explaining the techniques you used to do this.

Assess to Progress

How confident are you now at exploring how language varies? Look back at the ratings you gave yourself on page 41. Now rate yourself again for each of the skills you have been practising.

SKILLS FOR LIFE

Work with a partner to role-play an interview for your dream job. Before you begin, discuss the jargon that could be included what level of formality you need to create and how you would use spoken standard English. Take turns to play the interviewer and interviewee, thinking about how you should vary your use of language in each role.

Assessing your Progress

TARGETS FOR PROGRESS

- Analyse the implications of what speakers say by using questions that probe and clarify.
- Take on different roles to move a discussion forward such as handling challenges or disagreements, collaborating and drawing together ideas effectively.
- Choose verbal and non-verbal techniques to actively involve listeners.
- Select ways of organising talk to present information appropriately and persuasively for listeners.
- Use a range of dramatic techniques to analyse complex issues.
- Use and adapt the conventions of spoken texts for different purposes.

Working through this unit will give you the opportunity to show the progress you have made in your speaking and listening skills. You will complete three tasks where you will have the chance to show your skills in talking to others, with others, and in drama.

Activate your learning

In this unit, you will explore different projects to provide laptops for schools in developing countries. Here is some information about one of these countries, Nigeria.

There are 30 million children in Nigeria's schools taught in classes of up to 80 pupils	Not all classrooms have desks or chairs, let alone text books and certainly not computers
There is no internet and often no electricity	Most teachers, parents and pupils have never seen a computer
The climate is hot and dusty	Schools are often in remote, rural communities

1 With a partner, choose one of these facts and talk about the problems it raises and the solutions that might be needed. Share your ideas with another pair and answer any questions they have about your ideas.

2 At the end of your discussion, look at the objectives for this unit and talk with your partner about where they used any of those skills during your discussion. Identify one skill that you will focus on improving.

Progress task 1: Talking with others

Two companies are producing cheap laptops for developing countries. You are a government adviser and you have been invited to an expert group discussion to decide which laptop should be chosen for your schools. This is an important decision: a lot of money is involved and the education department is desperate for pupils to be able to learn better.

In a small group, discuss the products and give your recommendation.

Assess to Progress

In this task you will be assessed on the way you:

- Use questions to clarify what other speakers mean
- Pull together different points and build on what other speakers say
- Draw speakers into the discussion, challenging and resolving disagreements.

On the next page there are some details about each of the laptops you are going to discuss.

1 Use the information about each laptop on the next page to make your own notes on the points that you think are the most relevant to the needs of schools in a developing country. Your government is going to spend a lot of money on this project and you need to make sure you advise them to do the right thing.

2 Before the meeting, you have a chance to ask each company three questions about their product. Working in pairs, decide what questions you want to ask. Then join with another pair and take it in turns to hotseat the developers.

You now have the information you need to discuss the laptops for schools project. Now think about the skills you need to use to hold a good discussion:

- Use questions to clarify what other speakers mean
- Pull together different points and build on what other speakers say
- Draw speakers into the discussion, challenge and resolve disagreements.

Features	One laptop one child (XO)	Classmate PC (Intel)
Price	$100	$300-$500
Specification	Windows and Linux	Windows XP
Features	Standard range of open-source/ shareware programs for drawing, writing, music, animation. Firebox internet browser Camera – still and moving image Educational content includes a calculator, encyclopaedia and text books Storage chip and memory slots instead of a hard drive	Standard Microsoft programs. Internet Explorer Webcam Educational content includes Maths Toolkit Games like minesweeper and pinball. Flash memory instead of CD or hard drive USB fan
Power	Mains, solar and wind-up Battery will last for up to 13 hours.	Mains Battery will last for up to 4 hours
Connectivity	Wireless VSAT satellite internet link – 128kbps connection speed (costs $2,500 to install, and $350 per month for the connection) Computers have wi-fi antennas known as 'rabbit ears'. Mesh network links each machine	Wireless Wimax – 256kbps (costs $1500 to install and $900 a month connection costs) Mesh network links each machine
Design	Waterproof screen and keyboard Rubber feet No open slots on the outside.	Water-resistant keyboard
Comments	A new version is being developed that is more like an e-book reader, with two screens instead of a screen and keyboard. This will be cheaper and could store up to 500 e-books.	The machines come as part of a computer lab with computers for teachers and an interactive whiteboard. The next generation Classmate has an optional hard drive.

3 Look at the following extract from a discussion about which laptop the government should choose. What skills can you see the speakers using? What advice would you give the speakers to improve their discussion? Discuss your ideas with a partner.

James: I think the XO laptops would be really good for our students. The materials it is made from mean it would cope with being knocked a bit, and it folds up really neatly. I particularly think the 'rabbit ears' that become a flap to protect the memory slots are a really good idea.

Harry: I prefer the Classmate laptops.

Sarah: They should just buy some more books.

Karl: OK, James, so you like the design of the XO because it seems to be suitable for the environment and the students who are going to be using it, but Harry, you prefer the other laptop. Why do you think that one would be better for the students?

Harry: Well, the Classmate has got more software that we use, like Microsoft.

Karl: Why would that be an advantage?

Harry Well, I suppose it is the sort of software they will use when they get jobs and it would let them do lots of things that they want to do.

Karl: Like what? How is that software better than the software on the other laptop? I think there could be advantages to the XO open-source software like cost, simplicity for children not used to using computers, stability of the software. We won't have a team of technicians to put things right if the machine crashes and we need to think about what they really need to use for their learning…

4 Working in a small group, discuss the products and agree your recommendation. Remember to use the skills you have explored.

Progress task 2: Talking to others

A set of one of the laptops was introduced into all of the schools in your area six months ago and the first results of the scheme are available. You are a reporter for the local television station and have been given the job of covering the story.

Work with a partner to create a report to be shown on the local evening news.

Assess to Progress

In this task you will be assessed on the way you:

- Choose verbal and non-verbal techniques to actively involve listeners in what you are saying.
- Select ways of organising talk to present information appropriately and persuasively for listeners.
- Vary the formality and informality of language to suit your listeners.

When the laptops were first launched, news reporters were keen to tell viewers about the project.

1 Look at the following points included in one of the TV reports. How should the reporter organise the points to make a logical and interesting report for viewers? Discuss with a partner what you think the best order would be.

- Quotations from pupils
- Comments from inventors
- Comments from the founder of the project
- Reporter's viewpoint
- Information about software
- Charging the laptop
- Features of the machine
- Charity Aid Agency point of view
- How the web browser works
- Where the ideas came from

2 The extracts below are from the finished TV news report. How does the reporter use verbal techniques to keep viewers interested? Make notes on:

- how new points are introduced and developed
- where reasons are given
- where evidence is used
- how formal the language is
- how the report ends.

These Brazilian school children are among the first to test a laptop its developers hope will revolutionise developing world education.

'It's cool. I took photos and did my email'.

'I used the computer to find everything my teacher asked us to find about a sport, the rules and the court size'.

The laptop is just brimming with energy-saving devices. For instance, the display goes from full colour to black and white. And out here in brilliant sunshine, you can still see it, meaning it needs no backlight.

There's also been a radical rethink of data storage systems. 'One of the things in laptops that takes up a huge amount of power is actually the hard drive, spinning around as a motor. Er, it just uses a lot of power so one of the things we've done here is make sure that er there are no moving parts that require motors.'

What about the software then? Well, the operating system XO is custom built adapted from Linux. One of the main aims is to slash the amount of power the chip sucks up so you'll find applications that don't put as much strain on the processor as a conventional computer.

'It may all seem idealistic and established aid agencies have criticised the entire concept of giving computers to some of the most impoverished nations. 'The big priority for these countries is to get all children into school, into a manageable class size. That means employing more teachers and having some fundamentally basic materials in schools and I'm afraid having laptops into school is not the first priority for these countries...'

Nevertheless, the one laptop one child project is facing some serious competition from several quarters. 'The first front is from the Intel Classmate PC. It is significantly more expensive, estimated at $400 and also Microsoft has announced that they are working hard to sell reduced packages of Windows and Office for $3 in certain countries, so in terms of the project not actually having to worry about money, I do think that is a very naive point of view. Bill Gates has said it's not really a decent computer and others have complained they're not really laptops, they're find of glorified toys.

Nevertheless, Intel's initial opposition to the project has recently subsided. In fact, it now sits on One Laptop's board alongside its once arch-rival AMD, which currently makes the processor at the computer's core.

Politics aside, the one laptop project has announced it's ready to take the laptops into main production. The first wave will see millions handed out, probably in Africa and South America. A world with truly one laptop per child will still be a long way off but at least it's a start.

3 a) Working with a partner, discuss what different non-verbal techniques the reporter could use to keep the viewers interested? Think about:

- How could the presenter use visual aids
- How the presenter should move, use his hands and facial expressions.
- How the presenter should use his voice to control the pace and give emphasis to particular points

b) Take in in turns to present the above sections of the report using these non-verbal techniques. Give feedback on the effectiveness of these.

4 Now make your own notes for your news report updating viewers about the laptops the school has been using. Think about whether the project has been a success or whether there have been some problems. You need a story that viewers will want to hear. You should:

- Decide how to organise your ideas.
- Think of reasons and evidence to give viewers enough information to understand the issues.
- Think about your choice of language. Remember to use standard English.

5 a) Working with a partner, practise delivering your report. Remember to use your voice to keep the viewer interested. Emphasise particular words to show they are important and vary the pace you are speaking at to focus attention on certain points

b) When you have delivered your report, ask a partner to give you feedback on each of these points. What did they notice you doing well? What could you do to improve?

Progress task 3: Talking to perform

You are pupils or teachers in one of the schools involved in the laptops project. The machines are popular but the scheme is very costly to run and more money is always needed to extend the benefits to other schools. You are asked to participate in a UK national charity event to raise more money.

Work in role to improvise a TV appeal for funds.

Assess to Progress

In this task you will be assessed on the way you:

- Use dramatic techniques to explore ideas and issues
- Develop and sustain a role through drama
- Evaluate the effectiveness of a performance and make changes as necessary.

1 In your group, think about the roles you could include in the appeal, for example:

   - a presenter giving information about the success of the project, how people can help, what more money is needed for.
   - pupils giving interview comments, telling their feelings, before and after the project
   - teachers giving their point of view on the benefits of the laptops

   What other roles could you choose? Decide on the role each member of the group will play.

2 Explore in role your feelings about the project and how you might show these in a TV appeal. Choose at least one dramatic technique to help you such as tableau, hot seating or role on the wall. Working as a group decide which technique best helped you develop your role.

3 Now discuss in your group how you will make your appeal persuasive. Think about how you will use your voice, movement and gesture to achieve this.

4 Look at this statement from a pupil at the school. Talk with your group and improvise how you would perform this in role.

a) How would the speaker's voice sound here?

b) How quickly would they be speaking?

c) What gestures or movement would they use?

Well, before we had the machines… the laptops… our lessons were not so good, y'know, like they were all the same and the teacher had to just tell us things 'cos, well, there weren't enough books for us all and I couldn't remember the work very good.
But the laptops, they changed all that. Now I can find things out for myself on the internet and I really enjoy learning. It'd be really bad if we couldn't keep them. Really bad.

d) How would you show that the pupil is really happy here? Think about the pace and fluency of the speaking. What gestures or movement would they use?

e) How has standard and non-standard English been used in this example?

5 Now you are ready to create your TV appeal. Develop your role using ideas from the different dramatic techniques you have tried. In your group:

- Plan the message you want to give
- Agree how to organise the contributions from each of the different roles you have chosen.
- Check that you are using your voice, gestures and movement to make the appeal persuasive.
- Take turns to listen to each section of the appeal and give feedback to each other.

Assess to Progress

You have completed three tasks: talking to others, talking to perform and talking with others. Rate yourself for each of the following skills by deciding where you would place yourself on the scale below.

1	2	3	4	5	6	7
I find this difficult.			I'm getting there.			I'm good at this.

- When talking with others, I can make sustained contributions in discussions, use questions to probe ideas and influence the direction of the talk
- When talking to others, I can develop ideas and reflect on feelings and also organise my ideas to have an impact on the audience
- When improvising I can use a variety of dramatic techniques to develop and sustain a role and evaluate performances.

Progress in ...
Reading

Progress in ... Reading and engaging with texts

LEARNING OBJECTIVES

- Choose from a range of reading strategies to engage with different types of text.
- Discuss your reading with others, giving informed opinions and making recommendations.
- Explore how readers' thoughts and opinions shape their responses to texts they read.

Activate your learning

1 a) Put the following types of text in order, starting with those you read most often, and ending with those you read least often.

manuals or 'how to' texts	autobiographies or biographies
novels	match reports or reviews
magazines	newspapers
web pages for school work	web pages about your interests
comics, graphic novels or manga	music, film or game reviews

b) Working with a partner, discuss your decisions and compare the types of text you read. What similarities do you notice in what you read? What differences are there?

2 Look at the five types of text you read most often. For each, discuss the following questions with your partner:

a) How much time per week do you spend reading this type of text?

b) When and why do you read this type of text?

c) What would your top five have been three years ago? Has this order changed or stayed the same? Why do you think this is?

Assess to Progress

Confident readers use a range of reading strategies to help them make sense of a wide range of texts, from fiction and non-fiction to internet and electronic texts. How many of the following reading strategies do you use?

Visualising	Using prior knowledge	Predicting
Speculating	Asking questions	Relating to your own experience
Evaluating	Empathising	Rereading
Relating to other texts you have read	Passing comments	
Scanning	Skimming	Close reading

Rate yourself for each of the following skills by deciding where you would place yourself on the scale below.

1 2 3 4 5 6 7

I find this difficult. I'm getting there. I'm good at this.

- I can choose from a range of reading strategies according to the type of text I am reading and my purpose for reading.

  Self-check: Which skills would you use if you were reading a magazine about your favourite band?

- I can discuss what I read with others, giving my opinion based on evidence and making recommendations.

  Self-check: You are researching a project in geography and have read some helpful information on the internet. Would you be confident in discussing this with others?

- I can explore how different readers' thoughts and opinions shape the texts they read.

  Self-check: You don't like horror films. How would you read a review of a new horror film in your local newspaper? Would your view of horror films affect your opinion of the review if it recommended the film?

Build your skills

When confident readers explore a text, they use a range of reading strategies to help them build up an understanding of the text and to think about their own opinions on what they read.

Read this opening of an article from the *Times* about safe computer use. Then follow the skill steps to see how you can use different reading strategies to help you decide on and express your own view about a topic.

Computer games to get cigarette-style health warnings

Video games will be forced to carry cigarette-style health warnings under proposals to protect children from unsuitable digital material.

The report, commissioned by the Prime Minister in response to a growing moral panic about video games, will conclude that they can harm the development of children's beliefs and value systems and desensitise them to violence. It will also recommend that retailers who sell video games to anyone under the age rating on the box should face a hefty fine or up to five years in prison, the *Times* has learnt.

Strategy 1 Relate to your own experience and knowledge

When you read a text, one strategy you can use is relating what you read to your own experiences. This can help you to form an opinion based on experience. Another useful strategy is using prior knowledge – what you already know about a topic – to develop your viewpoint on the text. Read these four readers' responses to the *Times* article:

I agree with this completely. Something needs doing about the stuff kids can get off the internet and in game shops.

That's ridiculous and pointless! They already have a warning system like DVDs, don't they? Does it work? No!

My children would just want it if they put a warning on it – it just makes them want it even more!

I think, by and large, warnings would work to help parents know what's suitable or not suitable.

1 Working with a partner, decide which readers have related their comments on the text to their own experiences. What do they say that shows this is their own viewpoint? Which readers have drawn on prior knowledge?

2 Discuss the opening of the article with your partner. Thinking about your own opinions and experiences, explore the following questions:

- Do you agree with the proposal to put health warnings on video games?
- In your experience, why do you think this proposal would work or not work?
- What can you pick out from your own life that will help you explain why you think as you do?

trategy 2 Evaluate

Evaluating a text means passing judgements on what you read, thinking about your reactions to what you are reading and why you are reacting that way. This could be commenting on the ideas and points of view in a text and the way these are presented. To use this strategy, you need to be able to pick out details from the text to respond to and evaluate the effects created.

1 Close read the next paragraph of the newspaper article below. Look at the details that Rifat has identified in this paragraph and how she has evaluated these. What do you think Rifat's view on this topic is based on the comments she has made? Discuss your ideas with a partner.

I'm not sure I believe a report written by just one person can be truly objective. However, it does say that she is a 'clinical psychologist' and 'parenting guru' which convinces you to listen to her views.

The report, written by Tanya Byron, the clinical psychologist and television parenting guru, is also expected to address the dangers of children's use of the internet. 'Parents are afraid to let their children out,' she said. 'So they keep them at home, but allow them to take risks online.'

This statement sounds very general. My parents might be afraid to let me out, but it doesn't mean they keep me in and lock me up! I think this exaggeration detracts from her argument.

2 Now read the next five paragraphs of the article. Pick out up to ten details that you want to pass judgements on, noting what you would say about each one.

She will call for a massive campaign to educate parents, teachers and child-carers about how to ensure that children get maximum benefit from the digital world without being exposed to its dangers.

This will include a drive for greater awareness of inappropriate content such as pornography. Parents will be encouraged to monitor children's online use and keep computers in living rooms rather than bedrooms. Dr Byron, a *Times* columnist who has two children aged 9 and 12, said that video and online games could have enormous benefits 'in terms of learning and development', but that there was too little awareness among parents about the associated risks they posed and how to manage those risks.

'You would not send your child to the pool without teaching them to swim, so why would you let them go online without teaching them to manage the risks?' she said.

Dr Byron said that the current classification system for video games was confusing and not tough enough. At present only games showing sex or gross violence require an age rating from the British Board of Film Classification (BBFC) and fewer than 2 per cent of titles carry an 18-certificate.

Support

Choose from a range of reading strategies, such as skimming and scanning, to identify the key points the writer makes in this report. What do you think about each point? Has the report changed or reinforced your point of view?

3 Evaluate the whole report with your partner and discuss its overall effect. Does it convince you of the need to give computer games health warnings? Share your comments and make sure your judgements are based on evidence from the text.

Reinforce your skills

In the next day's newspaper, a response was printed from Jack, a 14-year-old who wrote in to comment on what he had read. Read the article below and then work through the activities that follow to practise using a range of reading strategies.

Playing computer games has been only a benefit to me

Commentary: Jack Miller (aged 14)

I think that adult concerns about the dangers of video games and the internet to children are a bit exaggerated.

I spend about 13 hours a week playing games online and I have never come across any inappropriate material such as pornography.

In fact, I would say that the internet and computer games have only been of benefit to me. I am sure that one of the reasons that I'm in the top maths set at my school is because I used to spend so much time when I was younger playing. In the game *Heroes III*, you have a castle and you have to build up an army - I spent a lot of time sitting at the computer adding up.

I also use Wikipedia to help with my homework. I could survive without it, I would just go to the library, but it is really helpful. And I have just started to use a maths revision site to help with revision for my SATs tests next month.

My favourite game is *World of Warcraft*, in which you have to complete quests. I find it really satisfying. My brothers Harry, 16, and Max, 10, both play computer games too.

It is wrong to say that computer games can isolate children because we usually play games with our friends over the internet and it is a way of playing together just like in real life. I play shoot-'em-up games with a lot of killing, but that does not make me behave more aggressively because I know they are not real and it is not part of my real life.

The existing classification system for video games seems clear to me and to my parents, so I'm not sure it needs changing. But some change does need to happen.

1 a) Reread the text and note down any comments you would like to make in response to Jack's points.

b) Can you relate any of the points Jack makes to your own experience or prior knowledge? How does this influence your opinions? Record your comments and opinions in a table like the one below.

Evidence from the text	Comment and opinion
'Adult concerns'	It's only <u>some</u> adults and it's right. Children don't share these concerns, nor do most adults.

2 Working with a partner, evaluate the overall effects of Jack's commentary. Do you think he presents his arguments in a convincing way? Pick out details from the text to support your points.

3 Write a short statement that you would like to post in response to these articles. Think about whether you agree or disagree with what has been said and be sure to link your comments to points made in both articles.

Stretch

Research this topic further. Try to find a range of texts presenting different viewpoints and draw on these in your statement.

Extend your skills

When you read magazine or newspaper articles, leaflets, web pages or even novels, your own opinions and preferences as a reader affect your understanding of what you read.

1 Working with a partner, think about the intended audience of the texts opposite. Who do you think would be most likely to read each text? Give reasons for your choices.

2 Now discuss your own reactions to each text. What does the main headline used for each text make you think?

e.g. My reaction to the headline in the *Sun* is that this sounds like an interesting story, although I'd be worried that Beckham didn't have any management experience. The way they call it an 'Olympic footie dream' makes me think they're trying to convince me it would be a good idea, but I'm not sure.

3 Now think of three people you know, of different ages and with a variety of interests.

a) How do you think each person would respond to each text?

b) How might their responses be different from your own? Why? How are these views the same as or different from your own views and interests?

c) Choose one of the people and write a paragraph recommending the text you think will interest them most and explain why. Share your answers with a partner.

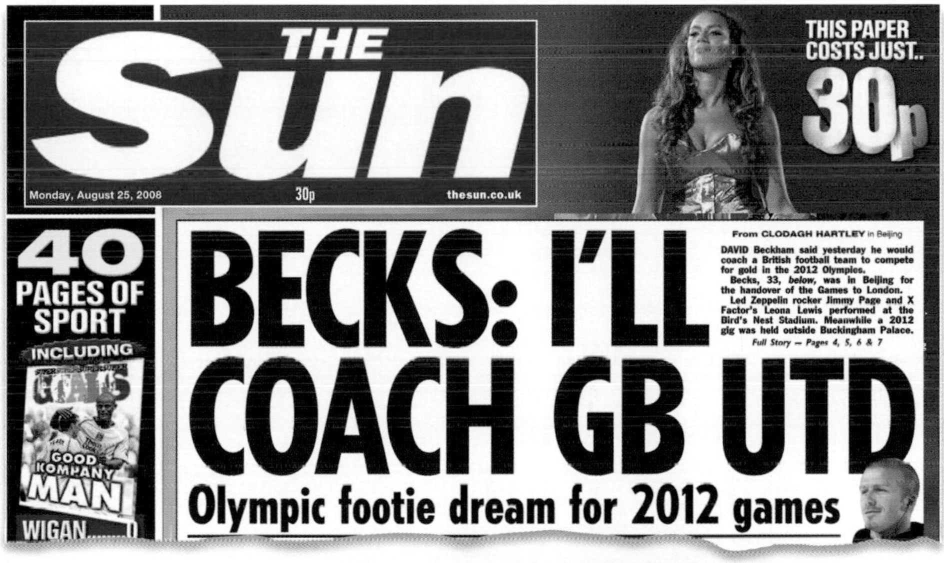
THE Sun
Monday, August 25, 2008 30p thesun.co.uk

THIS PAPER COSTS JUST.. 30p

40 PAGES OF SPORT INCLUDING GOALS GOOD KOMPANY MAN WIGAN

BECKS: I'LL COACH GB UTD

Olympic footie dream for 2012 games

From CLODAGH HARTLEY in Beijing

DAVID Beckham said yesterday he would coach a British football team to compete for gold in the 2012 Olympics.

Becks, 33, *below*, was in Beijing for the handover of the Games to London.

Led Zeppelin rocker Jimmy Page and X Factor's Leona Lewis performed at the Bird's Nest Stadium. Meanwhile a 2012 gig was held outside Buckingham Palace.

Full Story — Pages 4, 5, 6 & 7

Apply your learning

Task Use a range of reading strategies to explore the texts below and answer the questions about them opposite. The first text is a review of the novel *The Stuff of Nightmares* by Malorie Blackman; the second is the opening section of the novel.

Every horror story needs a monster, be it vampire, werewolf or serial killer. With most horror, however, as long as you're not naive enough to open the door behind which the monster lurks, you'll be fine. Even if you are that naive, you already know a stake and garlic will defeat a pesky vampire, a silver bullet will do away with a werewolf, and we can CSI pretty much any serial killer these days. Those monsters are getting a bit threadbare. The terror would really begin if the monster was already inside your head. What if the thing to be scared of was you? How do you defeat your own nightmares?

This is the life-or-death challenge facing Blackman's young protagonist. Kyle is a runner; he'd much rather pound the streets in an attempt to burn off his anxieties than stay home and confront the nightmare of what's happened to his family. But when the train carrying his class on a school trip crashes, he realises that this is one horror he can't outrun. It appears he's the only passenger still conscious after the accident, and as he moves around the wrecked carriage, checking on his friends, the novel shifts into more supernatural territory. Kyle discovers he's able to slip inside the minds of those around him and experience their secret nightmares and deepest fears.

These nightmares are 13 well-crafted short stories in their own right, reminiscent of episodes of The Twilight Zone or Tales of the Unexpected. They are striking in their range, from twisted dreams to chilling reality, from a woman who marries the devil to a soul crushed by apartheid.

There's something about running. Something ... well if you don't get it, you won't get it. Every time my foot smacks the pavement, it's like an echo of my heartbeat slamming inside me, telling me that 'I'm here, I'm now, I'm *alive.*' I don't jog – jogging is for posers showing off their latest designer gear. No, I *run.* Tunnels like the one down by the canal and dark places are best. Places where I can't see my shadow chasing me or tantalising me by running ahead. In tunnels and dark places there are no shadows, no ghosts. There's only me.

This morning was just right, mid spring cool rather than early spring cold, and the air tasted of the new and fresh instead of the usual diesel and dog poo, so I decided to run through the park, which was kind of a mistake, 'cause it wasn't long before I wasn't alone as I ran. *He* crept into my head, where he wasn't welcome. Sometimes, if ... *when* I inadvertently let my guard down, he does that.

I picked up the pace until I was sprinting just as hard as I could. But I couldn't escape. Instead I found myself running into the past ...

1 The writer of the review says that in horror stories 'monsters are getting a bit threadbare'. Using your own knowledge of this type of story, explain whether you think this is true.

2 How does the reviewer try to persuade you to read this novel? How effective do you think the review is?

3 What impression do you get of the main character Kyle? Draw on evidence from both texts to support your answer.

4 Kyle says, 'I wasn't alone as I ran. *He* crept into my head.' Based on what you read in the review, who do you think 'he' could be?

5 Who would you recommend this novel to? Write a paragraph making your recommendation and explaining why this reader would enjoy this book. Include details from the review and the extract and explain how they support your recommendation.

Assess to Progress

How confident are you now about using a range of reading strategies to help you understand and express your opinions about the texts you read? Look back at the ratings you gave yourself on page 55. Now rate yourself again.

SKILLS FOR LIFE

Your school librarian is collecting pupils' comments about giving books ratings to help her decide whether to introduce age rating in the school library. Read the following text, then answer the questions that follow.

Book bosses are planning to put age guidance levels on books

It will mean you can pick up a new paperback and see immediately what age it's meant for. But lots of top authors are against this. They're worried that doing this will put kids off reading as they'll be afraid to try books that are meant for older kids and scared of being teased if they want to read books for a younger age group.

1 What arguments are given for including age guidance levels?

2 What arguments are given against including age guidance levels?

3 What is the writer's viewpoint on this topic?

4 Do you think this is a good or bad idea? Give reasons for your answer.

Reading AF2

Progress in ... Developing active reading strategies

LEARNING OBJECTIVES

- Select from a range of reading strategies the most appropriate ways to locate, retrieve and compare information and ideas from texts.
- Research from a variety of sources, making relevant notes in a range of formats.
- Synthesise and summarise information from different sources or different places in the same text.
- Identify the main ideas and arguments in a text, using appropriate textual references and quotations to support these.

Activate your learning

Working with a partner, look at the information about the Nokia N82 phone and the iPhone 3G to see which one best suits your needs. You are looking for a phone that has a particularly good camera.

iPhone 3G 	**Nokia N82** 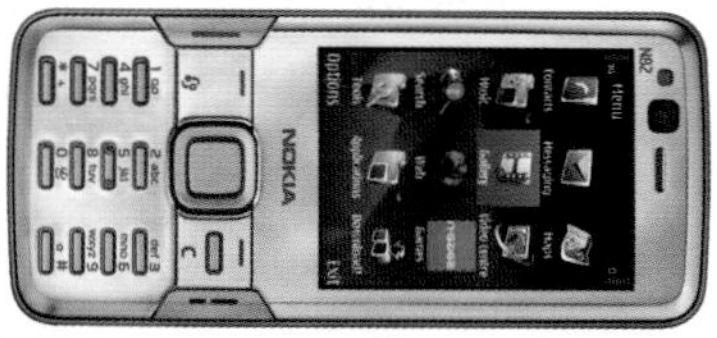
Good general phone performance	Many advanced features
Stunning appearance	Excellent multimedia player
Easy to use	Great camera
Impressive music player	Photos easily transferred to a computer
Long lasting battery	Especially simple menu system
Impressive operating and email systems	Easy to use
Great web browser	No space for dedicated multimedia keys
No radio	Keys aren't that large
Virtual keyboard takes some getting used to	iPhone-style sensor that changes the screen orientation
2Mp camera only average	Super-fast internet connections
Battery can't be removed	Not the most rugged of devices
Quite heavy	Camera has auto focus and Xenon flash
Expensive	Expensive

1. Skim, scan and close read to locate key information about the camera on each phone. Record your findings in bullet-pointed notes.
2. Summarise the information in a sentence outlining your choice of phone.
3. Your friend is not sure how to choose between the two phones and you have promised to help. Referring to the information in the chart, write a brief overview for your friend, giving information about the most impressive and the most disappointing feature of each phone. Include brief quotations to support what you think are the most important points your friend should be aware of.

Assess to Progress

How good do you think you are already at selecting, retrieving and comparing information from a range of texts? How good are you at making notes and selecting quotations to support your ideas? Rate yourself for each of the following skills by deciding where you would place yourself on the scale below.

1 3 4 5 6 7

I find this difficult. I'm getting there. I'm good at this.

- I can use a variety of reading strategies to locate, pick out and compare information from a variety of texts.
- I can make effective notes in a range of formats, including using diagrams, charts and grids.
- I can synthesise and summarise information from different sources and pieces of writing.
- I can use textual reference and effectively integrate quotations to support my ideas.

Build your skills

When you are reading and responding to a novel, reading strategies and note-making skills can help you find information and understand the text.

Look at the following extract from the novel *How I Live Now* by Meg Rosoff. This novel tells the story of Daisy who comes to live with her relatives in England. When the country is attacked and invaded, Daisy and her cousin Piper are taken prisoner. Here, after they have escaped, Daisy and Piper are trying to make their way home.

At sunset the sky cleared and turned orange and grey and pink and the temperature started to drop but to compensate there was a bright moon so we wrapped ourselves in our blankets and kept walking and following the map and what with all the stopping to hide and occasionally to rest it was nearly morning but still dark when we came through the deserted village, past the pub and the village shop, and started up the familiar long hill to the house. I expected the landscape to be barren and dead but it wasn't. The hedgerows sagged under the weight of life: berries and flowers and birds' nests. The optimism of it should have cheered me up a little but it didn't. It was like seeing a vision of some past life, a life so recent and so distant that I could remember the exhilaration without being able to remember what it felt like.

In my new incarnation I expected nothing, good or bad.

The house looked deserted, dark and silent, even the honey-coloured stone had the feeling of something abandoned. The old jeep was parked off to the side where we'd left it when the gas gave out. There were no signs of life.

No signs of death either.

I wish I could say my heart soared at the sight of it but it didn't. What heart I had left no longer felt like flesh and blood. Lead, maybe. Or stone.

Step 1 Use reading strategies to locate information and make notes to organise your ideas

You have been asked to answer the following question:

What is the mood and atmosphere of this passage?

Working with a partner, use a variety of reading strategies to help you to complete the following activities.

1. **Skim** the passage to get a general impression of what is going on.
2. **Scan** the passage for specific information that supports the general impression you have formed. Think about:
   - why Daisy and Piper are wrapped in blankets rather than wearing coats
   - what they could be hiding from
   - what impression is built up with the phrases 'deserted village', 'barren', 'dead', 'sagged under the weight of life'
   - which other words and details reinforce this idea
   - what impression you get of Daisy's 'past life'.

Shabana has begun to plan her answer to the main question. She has skimmed the passage and feels that, although it is not obviously about the horrors of war, it suggests that dreadful things have happened and are still happening. She has started to scan for details that helped her form this general impression. She is taking notes in a P-E-E-E-L grid to help her organise her ideas.

3. Look at the grid below. Then close read the text and add your own points to a similar table.

Point	Evidence	Explanation	Elaboration	Link
They don't seem to have proper clothes with them.	'we wrapped ourselves in our blankets and kept walking'	It could be cold. They may have lost their coats. They may have to carry the blankets. Did they leave in a hurry?	'our' blankets suggests these might also be used for bedding. Are they sleeping out in the open?	Linking these details with the fact that they are hiding suggests they are on the run and are frightened of getting caught.

Step 2 Synthesise information

Once you have made your notes, the next step is to synthesise these into a coherent response to the question. Remember to refer to the text and integrate quotations into your answer to support the points you are making.

1 Look at how Shabana has begun her paragraph:

The reader becomes aware of the mood and atmosphere of the text right from the start, as the opening sentence highlights how Daisy and Piper are walking through the night 'wrapped ... in our blankets', occasionally 'stopping to hide'. This suggests that ...

She uses a mixture of textual reference and short quotations, integrated into the flow of her sentence to support what she is saying. Notice how she has used quotation marks and that, to keep the grammar of the sentence right, she has used ellipsis (...) where she has left out the word 'ourselves'.

2 Using your notes, draft your own response to the question: What is the mood and atmosphere of this passage? Try to synthesise the points you have made, integrating quotations and referring to the text to support your ideas.

Support

Try using some of the following sentence starters:

- I think that the ... because ...
- It seems as if ... because ...
- At this point I noticed that ...
- It seemed as if the author wanted the reader to feel ... because ...

Reinforce your skills

The skills you practised in the previous section can also help you locate, compare and synthesise information and ideas from more than one text.

The headteacher of your school is worried that pupils don't know the laws about carrying knives. She has asked you to read the two texts below: the first presents information from the Criminal Justice Act; the second is from a BBC news report about knife law.

What the law says

Using a knife as a weapon or carrying a knife that can be used as a weapon in a public place is against the law.

- Any item or objects that could be used to inflict damage to another person, or threaten such actions, is classed as an offensive weapon. This could include things like hammers, corkscrews or even compasses.
- If you are caught carrying anything that could be seen as an offensive weapon in a public place, you will have to explain to a police officer why you are carrying it.
- If you cannot give a good reason why you should be carrying such an item, you may well be arrested.
- It is also an offence to bring any weapon onto school premises - this law was recently added in 2006.
- It is not legal to carry a knife for self-defence, and if you use it, then you could be charged with assault with intent, or even worse.
- It is also illegal for anyone under 16 to purchase a knife (and 18 for an air rifle or BB gun).

Young people and knives

If police think you are carrying an offensive weapon they can stop and search you.

- This doesn't always stop children from taking knives to school to 'defend' themselves or using them to threaten others.
- To help stop this, in 2007 teachers were also given powers to search children for knives at school.
- Metal detectors have also been introduced at some schools to prevent kids taking knives and other weapons into class.

1 Read both texts using a range of reading strategies to help you find out what the law says about penknives in school and about knives in general.

2 a) Discuss with a partner which method of taking notes will be the most useful for this task.

b) Make notes to help you retrieve the information you need for your leaflet.

Support

Remember to scan for specific information about knives in schools. Note key words and ideas using a QUADS or KWEL grid to help you.

3 Using your notes, write the text for a leaflet for pupils, presenting the important information they need to know about the law on carrying knives. You need to synthesise information from both texts and present this in an informative, easy-to-understand way. Make sure you refer to the texts and integrate short, relevant quotations as evidence to support the points you include.

Stretch

When you are researching a topic, always check where the information has come from. Some sources are more accurate and reliable than others. Read these comments from an internet discussion forum about carrying knives and answer the questions below.

Knives are really handy for nail breaks, snipping loose threads, cutting apples (I love apples but can only eat them if cut up), taking cuttings (with permission), putting the little screw back in my glasses (again!), cutting open the sellophane/tape on boxes ... so many things. I carry a Swiss Army knife with me or a Swiss Army pruning knife – both legal.

---

1 Why might this point of view be misleading?

2 Look at the sources of the two articles on the previous page. Compare them with the internet discussion above. Which of the three would be the most reliable?

3 What sort of source would be the least reliable? Why?

Extend your skills

When you are researching from a variety of sources, presenting different points of view, you need to be able to draw together and summarise the results into one coherent response. In this section you will be developing this skill by working with a variety of views on what should be done about knife crime.

Step 3 Combine and summarise information

1 Begin by discussing in a group of four why you think young people carry knives and how you think the law could prevent this.

2 Now close read the two texts on the next page. Copy the table below and note the main points and evidence from the different viewpoints about what could be done to address this problem.

Source	Main points	Quoted evidence
Group discussion		
Politicians' views		
Gang member's views		
Mother's views		

3 Now write a short essay explaining the points of view that people have on the issue of teenagers carrying knives and how they think this problem could be solved. Think about:

- how you could organise the paragraphs in your essay to explain these points, e.g. Could you contrast different points of view in the same paragraph?
- how to include relevant evidence and integrate quotations, e.g. Could you present one point of view and integrate quotations from more than one source to support this?
- how to end your essay with your own personal response to the issue, summarising the points made and presenting your own point of view.

Teenagers with knives may have to visit victims in hospital

The government will today unveil a battery of fresh powers to prevent the spread of youth and knife crime after another two men were stabbed to death at the weekend.

Teachers are to be given the power to search pupils for drugs and alcohol in schools, while teenagers arrested for carrying knives may be forced to visit victims of fights in hospital and perpetrators in jail.

The children's secretary, Ed Balls, has indicated, 'It will ensure that everyone knows that a teacher's authority in the classroom is unquestionable and teachers are clear about their right to use it.'

The home secretary's suggestion that teenagers arrested for carrying knives should be forced to confront the consequences of fights by visiting hospital wards and prisons is part of a wider youth crime action plan ... Jacqui Smith's proposals come in the face of opposition taunts that the latest measures are unlikely to curb violence unless those caught possessing a blade are given custodial sentences.

'I'm very keen we make people face up to the consequences of their actions,' Smith told Sky TV. 'It's a practical and tough approach to make young people understand the implications of carrying a knife.'

The visiting scheme will say that all the participants, including the families of victims, have to give their consent. No additional remission will be granted as a result, officials stress. Alongside reminders to the police and licensing authorities of the powers they possess to punish clubs, pubs and retail outlets that break the law on the sale of drink and knives, the action plan is designed to stamp out violent youth crime.

Members of gangs and their families spoke to researchers during a two-year research project

Mother of gang member: 'Social services, probation officers, all these do-gooders, mentors and whatever: it's a job, money coming in their pockets every month, it's nothing more than that. Nobody's interested to really do anything for anybody. They're just interested in making it all look good on paper, they're not really interested.'

Gang member: 'My parents told me, if someone hurts me, to hurt them two times back more. So I was always looking out for anybody who was trying to disrespect me, and then to get them back two times more was my plan. Do you understand me? And then so that just led me into trouble basically. And then trouble finds you around people who are getting into trouble themselves, and before long you're talking to people. I was 17 years old the first time I went to jail.'

Mother of gang member: 'Every time I've gone to court with my kids you go in there and there's all these solicitors and all these magistrates or judges or whatever. And all these people are snobs they have no real idea of our life, they have no real idea about being poor. Whether you're poor and white, whether you're poor and Asian, whether you're poor and black, they have no idea. They've no idea to know what it's like to wake up hungry and cold. They've no idea about having no clothes or shoes on your feet. They've no idea whatsoever. So all they see is a criminal. You've done something wrong, you've got to be punished. Do they not think they've been punished enough? What they need is help, not punishments.'

Apply your learning

Use the skills and strategies you have developed through the unit to help you complete the task below.

Task Working on your own, read the Wikipedia entries on the next page. The first entry is about George Sampson, who managed to overcome many social and physical disadvantages to win *Britain's Got Talent* when he was just 14 years old; the second is about Scheuermann's disease which George suffers from.

1. Explain in your own words what Scheuermann's disease is.
2. List four pieces of information about Scheuermann's disease.
3. Find information from both articles about how the disease could affect George and how it has already affected him. Include short quotations as evidence to support what you say.
4. Explain how this disease could affect George as he grows older. Use a combination of your own words, textual references and integrated quotations.
5. Is it true that people with this disease tend to be tall and thin? Write your answer in your own words and include quoted evidence.
6. Find one piece of information which tells you that George has a lot of determination. Find and copy a quotation which proves this.
7. How reliable do you think these sources of information are? Give reasons for your answer.
8. From reading both articles, do you think it is a good idea for someone who has Scheuermann's disease to continue break dancing? Justify your decision with evidence from both texts.

George Sampson is a street dancer from Warrington, and was the winner of *Britain's Got Talent* on 31 May 2008. Coming from a poor background, George had to dance on the streets in his home town in order to raise money to travel to London for auditions and to raise money for his family.

Sampson suffers from a rare condition called Scheuermann's disease, which affects developing bones in children and teenagers and can cause a curvature of the spine. The condition even caused him to go temporarily blind in one eye for two months around Christmas time, Sampson said to the *Sun* newspaper. 'The eye was all inflamed. I'd been using Deep Heat for my sore back, so at first I just thought I'd got it in my eye. But I ended up blind,' he said. 'The spinal nerves were trapped and it affected my optic nerves, I lost all my coordination and it was really hard to dance, as I didn't have my balance. I kept bumping into everything.' Although his eyesight was restored, doctors have said he must immediately go to hospital at the first sign of any soreness in his right eye. Despite the scare, Sampson went ahead to compete and win the talent show, and has said nothing will prevent him from performing.

Scheuermann's disease is a skeletal disorder of childhood which is also known as Sherman's disease (since some people have difficulties spelling Scheuermann).

It is found mostly in teenagers and presents a deformity (where) patients cannot consciously correct their posture. The sufferer may feel pain, which can be aggravated by physical activity and by long periods of standing or sitting; this can have a significantly detrimental effect on their lives as their level of activity is curbed by their condition and they may feel isolated or uneasy amongst their peers if they are children, depending on the level of deformity. Also, the decreased level of height will emphasise body fat around the intestines, making the person with (this disease) seem more heavy-set than normal.

The seventh and tenth thoracic vertebrae are most commonly affected. It causes backache and spinal curvature. In very serious cases it may cause internal problems and spinal cord damage. The curvature of the back decreases height, thus putting pressure on internal organs, wearing them out quicker than the natural ageing process. A possibility of organ failure increases with long periods of time.

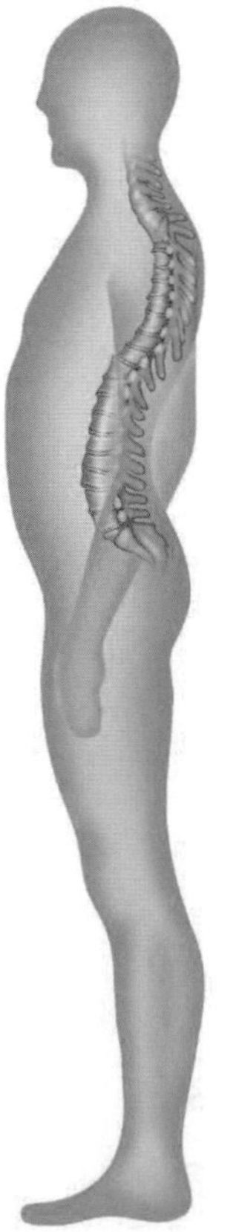

Assess to Progress

How good do you think you are now at selecting, retrieving and comparing information from a range of texts? How good are you at making notes and selecting quotations to support your ideas? Look back at the ratings you gave yourself on page 65. Now rate yourself again for each of the skills.

SKILLS FOR LIFE

Your friend wants to enter a talent competition but is not sure what is involved. You have found the following information which may help:

The age categories for the competition are under 18, and 18 and over (adults). The minimum age for the under 18s is 12 years old and those who are under 16 will have to be accompanied by an adult.

The judges will be looking primarily at ability and performance. Equally important is the image of the contestants in terms of presenting themselves as individuals and retaining an air of professionalism in performance and persona. Motivation is also essential.

On the day of the audition you will be asked to prepare a performance up to two minutes long in front of a professional judging panel. Upon entry each contestant will be allocated an audition time, which will reduce waiting times for competitors. The splitting of the competitors throughout the day should also mean you can queue indoors and not in the cold.

The audition can be a song or dance of the contestant's choice in any style or genre; in the case of vocalists it can be their own or a cover song.

1 What advice would you give your friend about the sort of skills the judges will be looking for?
2 Your friend is under 16, so do any special requirements apply?
3 What information can you give your friend who is worried about having to queue all day?
4 Write a note to your friend summarising the most important points about preparing for the audition.

Progress in ... Analysing and exploring different layers of meaning

LEARNING OBJECTIVES

- Use inference and deduction as part of a range of strategies to analyse and explore different layers of meaning within texts.
- Make detailed comments that are securely based in textual evidence.
- Consider the wider implications or significance of information, events or ideas in a text.

Activate your learning

The language used in advertising can convey meanings both **on the surface** and **beneath the surface** of the text. For example, 'great value' on the surface means that your money will be wisely spent, but reading beneath the surface it could mean that the product is poor quality or cheap.

1 Look at the following slogans from a magazine advertisement for a spot cream. Try to match each to the meanings below.

a) Get Clearasil – Get Confidence

b) Clearasil *may* cause confidence

c) Clear Confidence

d) Prove your confidence and you could win £2000

You have no confidence.

You need confidence.

You can buy confidence.

You might be more confident if you use Clearasil.

You will only be confident if you get rid of your spots.

There is a chance that Clearasil won't work.

The only important thing in the lives of teenagers is confidence.

2 Decide which of the meanings are on the surface, and which are beneath the surface. Use this example from an advertisement for a hair product to help you explain your choices to your partner.

> **Correct, protect and prevent frizz with Frizz-Ease.**
>
> **Surface meaning** – This product can stop your hair being frizzy.
>
> **Deeper meaning** – There is something wrong with frizzy hair and you need to buy this.

3 Now look at these sentences. Working with a partner, discuss how many meanings you can find for each.

- Cover that spot so no one need ever know.
- Get drop-dead gorgeous skin all year.
- Achieve visibly clearer skin in just three days – 'guaranteed'!

4 Working with a partner, design a layout for the spot cream advertisement using the sentences you have explored. Think about how you could use images such as graphs, cartoons or photographs to help create another layer of meaning.

Assess to Progress

How good do you think you are at inferring meanings and making deductions to explore different layers of meaning in the texts you read? Rate yourself for each of the following skills by deciding where you would place yourself on the scale below.

1 3 4 5 6 7

I find this difficult. I'm getting there. I'm good at this.

- I can identify and explore different layers of meaning in the texts I read.
- I can support my comments with textual evidence.
- I can consider the wider implications or significance of information.

Build your skills

The text opposite is an advertorial – an advertisement written in the style of an editorial or a magazine article. Working with a partner, read the advertorial and try to answer the questions around the text that will help you to use a range of reading strategies as you read. Then look at the skills steps below to help you to organise your ideas about the text.

Step 1 Identify layers of meaning

1 First of all, check that you understand the key points from the advertorial.

a) What product is being advertised?

b) How much does the product cost?

c) What does it look like?

d) What is its purpose?

e) Who is this advertorial targeting?

Now you need to explore and analyse the hidden meanings. How does the advertorial suggest that the Xbox will improve the target reader's life? You need to answer questions like this in a way that shows you can **read between the lines** of the text, e.g.
The advertorial suggests that the reader's life will improve because they will have a more united family that has fun together.

2 How else does it suggest that life will be better with an Xbox for the reader? Discuss your ideas with a partner.

Step 2 Secure your comments with evidence

You should use precise quotations to show your **inferences** are secured in the text.

1 How do you know from the text that this device offers a wide variety of entertainment? What does the writer imply it could do for a family? Copy and complete the following comment by choosing a precise quotation:

The Xbox has got something for everybody according to this advertorial. It's not just the innovative high-tech, online and wireless options, you can also play '__________', which suggests that someone who had never played a computer game could get involved.

2 Make a comment that explains how the advertorial suggests that the Xbox will allow parents to protect their children. Secure your comment by choosing precise quotations.

A family-size box of delights

The Xbox 360 is changing home entertainment in a direction that unites the family in a multimedia environment

Video games consoles are changing. The association with lone, male teenagers playing violent shooting games in their bedrooms is rapidly being replaced by something that actually brings families closer together. At the heart of this trend? A combination of high tech innovation and traditional family activity. Welcome to Microsoft's Xbox 360. With quizzes and karaoke, role-playing and skill-learning, wireless controllers and a wealth of online resources, it brings everyone together for some top quality entertainment.

One of a kind

The new generation Xbox 360 manages to combine the physical fun factor of Nintendo Wii, but with a much greater advantage – a truly high-definition format, and an unrivalled, exclusive emporium of online resources. No other game console has yet offered all of these attractions. The reason for Xbox 360's popularity, especially when hooked up to a broadband connection, is that it offers a new fusion of the family TV and home computer. Family photos and personal music can be combined with games. It's managed to change entertainment from simply staring at a screen to active involvement.

Xbox 360's online resources are revolutionising family culture. Live Arcade offers a huge selection of games – puzzles, traditional board games and classic arcade favourites – which can be downloaded and played on or offline. Live Marketplace is an online store of over 250 blockbuster and classic movies for download, plus hundreds of music videos, game demos and trailers too. Live Party allows families to play and chat with up to eight players, but more significantly, to do this with others across the globe. Wireless equipment allows simultaneous gaming with people as far afield as America or Australia. With Instant Messaging chat also easily accessed, the Xbox 360 is a great portal to bring together extended family and friends.

Another revolution has come with Xbox 360's family settings tools. Parents can limit what younger children see by setting age ratings on all downloaded content and other games formats, including access to Xbox Live. Passwords can override these settings, and a family timer facility can restrict children's' game time within blocks of 15 minutes.

A new form of expression

By Christmas, Xbox 360 will have up to 1,000 games to chose from. Some of the great new additions

include Lips, a karaoke singing game using a wireless, movement-sensitive microphone, where everyone can see their moves recreated on screen. The only way to really discover how much fun you can have, is to give it a go. Xbox 360 is one of those rare gifts that sits well on everyone's Christmas list.

*Xbox is available in three different guises, Arcade, Pro and Elite. Arcade, which comes bundled with five games, is a great entry level option for £129.99 *ERP.*

XBOX 360

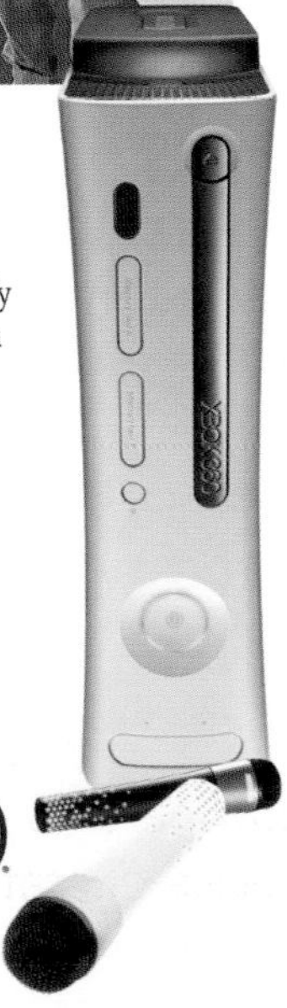

FAMILY GAMES

You're in the Movies

This unique, revolutionary game allows players to star in their own movie. Using the Xbox 360 live vision camera, become any role such as action hero, silent movie star, kung fu master, or even a zombie. Set up your own visual setting and script. Be guided by a director and get points for your performance. Bravo!

Age rating 3+ *(PEGI)*

a) What does the opening comment suggest about family relationships?

b) What does the writer think of the video games consoles of the past?

c) How have the advertisers tried to target a broadrange of readers in this text?

d) How much does an Xbox cost?

e) What effect do the images have on the reader?

Language

Step 3 Analyse layers of meaning

As you have seen, words can have a range of meanings and associations (**connotations**) linked to them. By choosing a particular word, a writer can set off a chain of associations in a reader's mind.

1 Why do you think the writer has included the following words and phrases?

changing | new generation | trend | innovation

yet | unrivalled | greater advantage | revolutionary

popularity | unique | much-loved | one of those rare gifts | swanky

2 a) Choose three words or phrases from the above list and for each one create a spider diagram listing all the connotations or implied meanings it has.

b) Write a paragraph explaining:

- Why the writer has chosen these words
- The layers of meaning they create

Support

Use a table like the one below to help you explore the connotations of each word, the way they could affect the reader and why the writer has chosen the word.

Word	Connotations	Effect on reader	Reason for word choice
trend	Fashionable Shift in direction Stylish	Makes readers think that everyone is getting one	Make readers think that they would be missing out if they didn't get one.

Reinforce your skills

In this section, you are going to practise your skills in exploring the different layers of meaning in a text by reading an extract from the novel *Here Lies Arthur* by Philip Reeve, a reworking of the legend of King Arthur. Most tales about Arthur tell how he was presented with a sword by the Lady of the Lake, who appeared by magic. In this extract, however, we see the sword's appearance from the lake from a different perspective. Gwyna, a young girl, is following the instructions of Myrddin, the famous magician.

I ducked under water, as I'd been told to. It was easy to stay down with the weight of the sword in my hands and no clothes to float me up. My bare feet sank into the thick dough of leaf mould on the bottom. I blundered forward with my eyes open, scrambling through the crown of an old drowned tree, slithering in its slimy, rotted bark, stirring up such a tumble of peaty flakes that for a moment I could see nothing at all. And then, close ahead of me, I saw the square gleam of Arthur's belt-buckle, the tower of armoured torso. I blinked the grit from my eyes and looked up and saw his head and shoulders high above me, out in the air. For a moment our eyes met. His were wide under the iron eyebrows of his helmet. Wide and filled with wonder and something that I did not recognise, because never in my life had anyone been afraid of me before.

'Do it slowly, gracefully,' Myrddin had told me. But when I tore the oilcloth wrapping from the sword it almost floated free, so I had to snatch it down and stuff it between my knees and poke the sword up with my spare hand. I felt it break the surface. My hand, out in the air, felt even colder than the rest of me. The sword was too heavy. I could feel it wobbling. My fingers were so numb that I knew I couldn't keep a grip much longer on the wet hilt. Why didn't he take it from me? Bubbles seeped from the corners of my mouth. Why didn't he take it?

He took it. I snatched my empty hand back into the world of fishes ...

I'd not thought to see Myrddin again. Why would he even remember me, now I'd served my purpose? Yet here he was. He must have thought of further uses for me.

'You played your part well. You should hear the stories they're already telling, our men and the Irishman's. How the lady beneath the lake gave Arthur a magic sword ...That hand raising out of the water ... Even Arthur believes it! He's used to my tricks, but he really thinks I conjured up the lady of the waters for him ...'

I wondered sleepily how anyone could have been fooled by my dirty, trembling hand, holding up a sword too heavy for it. I did not know then that men see whatever you tell them to see.

1 a) Working with a partner, reread the extract, then act out the scene up to the point where Arthur takes the sword. Work in role, with one of you playing Gwyna and the other Arthur.

b) Discuss what you were able to infer from the extract and how you showed this in your role play.

- What is the 'magical' lake like?
- How old are Arthur and Gwyna?
- Who has arranged for this to happen and why?

2 Now join with another pair to form a group of four. Use hot-seating to explore the feelings of Arthur and Gwyna in this extract. Use evidence from the text to back up your points, e.g. Gwyna feels in awe of Arthur. We see this when she describes him as 'the tower of armoured torso'.

3 a) Look at the details used to describe the lake at the start of the text. Do the words below create the magical atmosphere that the reader might expect or do they produce a different effect?

thick dough	**leaf mould**	**blundered**	**slimy, rotted bark**	**grit**

b) Look at the way the start of David's answer explores the word 'grit', integrating precise quotations. Continue the answer, exploring the connotations of the other words and integrating quotations.

The words used to describe the lake make it seem like a horrible place to be. There is no magic or beauty created as Gwyna rubs the 'grit' out of her eyes. The presence of 'grit' makes the scene seem dirty, uncomfortable and a bit like an ordinary dirty lake to the reader.

4 Discuss with your partner how the details included in the extract influence the way you feel about Gwyna, Myrddin and Arthur. Record your ideas using a table like the one below.

Details	Implied meaning	Overall picture of Gwyna
'as I'd been told to'	*Gwyna is obedient.*	*She does not have much power.*
'I blundered forward'	*This was a very difficult task.*	*She is brave to overcome her fears.*
'never in my life had anyone been afraid of me before'		

Extend your skills

You are now going to use skills of inference and analysis to explore different layers of meaning and some of the wider implications of the text. Look at the following comment which is taken from a review of *Here Lies Arthur*:

> 'Philip Reeve has given us not only wonderfully drawn characters, but also a more honest picture of life in medieval Britain.'

1 Working in a small group, discuss what you think the writer of this review meant by an 'honest picture of life in medieval Britain'. Is the reviewer implying that:

- many legends and myths are not truthful?
- life in medieval Britain was not quite what we are led to believe in stories such as many of those about King Arthur?

2 In your group, discuss and answer the following questions. Find quotations to support your answers.

a) Why does Gwyna think she is no more than a worthless slave to Myrddin? What does this suggest about the way young girls were treated in those days?

Support

Think about why Gwyna might be surprised to see Myrddin again after she has given the sword to Arthur. She thinks that she has 'served her purpose' – what does this suggest about her place in society?

b) Why have the spectators believed the story? Does this suggest that beneath lots of legends, facts lie undiscovered?

c) Why does Gwyna think that men can be manipulated so easily? She says 'men see whatever you tell them to see'. What are the wider implications of this statement?

3 Write a paragraph explaining how the extract gives an honest picture of life in medieval Britain.

Stretch

The title, *Here Lies Arthur*, has several possible meanings. Try to link the title to what you have read in the extract to infer one of the writer's overall themes.

Apply your learning

Use the reading skills and strategies you have practised in this unit to compete the following task.

Task Working on your own, read through the following text. It is a blog written by Charles Starmer-Smith, which runs online in response to news articles in the *Daily Telegraph* newspaper. Here the author gives his thoughts on the different ways people are trying to save the environment.

Ass of the week ...

First we are told to stop flushing at 30,000 feet in China, then I hear donkeys are replacing rubbish trucks in Sicily and now a chocolate-powered truck is driving from here to Mali, all in the name of saving our planet. All quite amusing, but doesn't it all smack of winning the skirmishes but not fighting the war?

A donkey: the latest weapon against global warming

So the Sicilian town of Castelbuono has replaced four of its garbage trucks with donkeys and claims to be saving money as well as helping to combat global warming. Meanwhile China Southern Airlines, one of the country's leading carriers, is encouraging passengers to use the toilet before they board flights and then cross their legs for the rest of the journey. It estimates that a single flush at 30,000 feet uses a litre of fuel.

And now two mad-cap Britons are driving 5,000 miles from the UK to Mali, West Africa, in a truck fuelled only by the remnants left from chocolate production, in a bid to raise awareness about global carbon emissions.

Sadly, new research shows that although we are flying more, few British people are prepared to offset their carbon emissions. But who can blame them? Most travel companies like to claim they have the best carbon calculators and offset schemes in to which you should invest more of your hard-earned money, without ever contributing a penny themselves.

1 How do you think Charles Starmer-Smith feels about the plans to:

a) reduce toilet flushing?

b) replace rubbish trucks with donkeys?

c) use chocolate as fuel to travel to Africa?

Try to explore the range of feelings he expresses and back up your answers with evidence from the text.

2 Charles Starmer-Smith says that the stories he has heard 'smack of winning the skirmishes but not fighting the war'. What can we infer from this quotation? Use evidence from the text to back up your points.

3 a) Explain the effect of the choice of the following words in the text:

claims	mad-cap	sadly	hard-earned

b) How does the writer's choice of words and phrases contribute to the overall effect of the text?

4 The blog ends with a criticism of travel companies.

a) Which words tell us that the writer is holding the travel companies responsible for the fact that 'few Britons are prepared to offset their carbon emissions'?

b) How does the final paragraph show us what the writer really feels about attempts to prevent global warming?

5 Look at the title, the image and the words used in the blog. Explain how the writer has used each one to explore his feelings about the ways that some people are trying to save the environment. Remember to support your points with evidence from the text.

Assess to Progress

How good do you think you are at inferring meanings and making deductions to explore different layers of meaning in the texts you read? Look back at the ratings you gave yourself on page 77. Now rate yourself again for each of the skills.

SKILLS FOR LIFE

You have been asked to check whether the sweets sold in the school canteen fit in with the school's healthy eating policy. You read the following information on a packet of 'Strawberry Pop' sweets:

Now with no artificial colourings or flavourings
The Healthy Option
Only 25 calories per sweet
Low in fat
Now with real strawberry juice
With added vitamins and minerals

Sugar	45%
Vegetable oil	10%
Natural flavourings	0.1%
Calcium	0.1%
Salt	0.1%
Strawberry juice	0.06%

1 Which exact word tells us that Strawberry Pops did not previously contain any strawberry juice?

2 What can you infer from the word 'real'?

3 What does the first sentence tell us about what was in the sweets previously?

4 What is the impact of the word 'only' in the third sentence?

5 Are you able to justify that the sweets are 'low in fat' or 'the healthy option' from this information? Write a comment to the school canteen manager, incorporating the details you have found.

Progress in ... Analysing how texts are organised and structured

LEARNING OBJECTIVES

- Analyse how meaning can be conveyed in different ways according to the form and layout of a text.
- Analyse how structural choices and organisation support a writer's theme or purpose.
- Comment on how a range of organisational features contribute to the effects achieved in a text.

Activate your learning

The text below is part of an advertisement for a deodorant spray for men which the advertisers claim provides 'Future-ready Protection'. The advertisement shows the designs of three weird and wonderful inventions that could be used to keep you cool in the future. The deodorant manufacturer is asking customers to design their own 'Future-ready Protection'.

1 a) Working in pairs, look at the images and discuss what you think these inventions are and what they do.

b) What presentational features are used to draw your attention to what is important?

c) How effective are the diagrams in communicating the fact that these inventions are linked with the need for a deodorant?

FUTURE VISIONS

Can you do better than these three innovative designs of pioneering future technology?

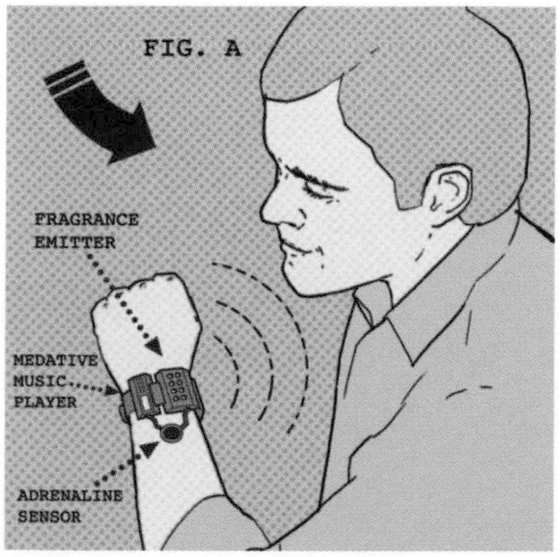

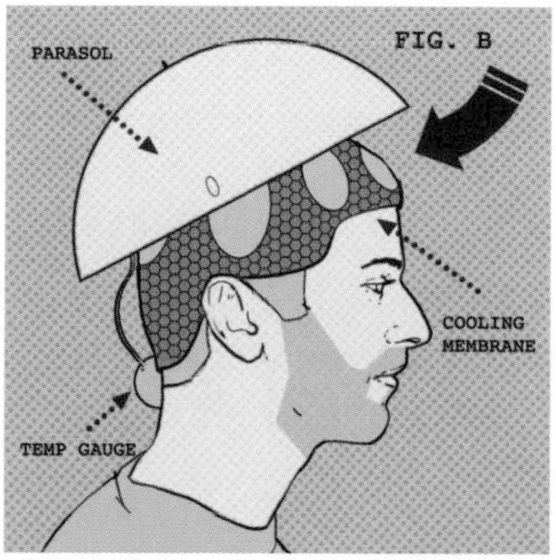

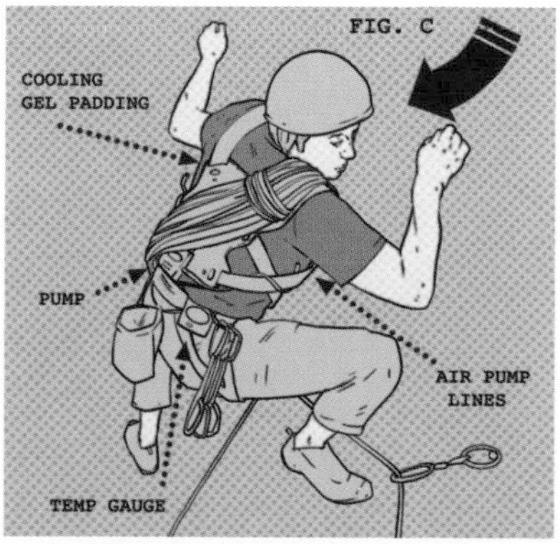

2 Now match the following sections of text to the appropriate image in the advertisement:

- **Cool-max climbing harness:** This compact device has a temperature gauge which detects when your body reaches sweating temperature, at which point it responds by pumping out shots of cool air.
- **De-stress sensory zone buster:** Responding to increased adrenaline, this device emits calming fragrances and meditative music when you experience a stress reaction. Not recommended for hot dates.
- **Igloo mark 1 hat:** When temperatures soar the stylish Igloo mark 1 hat, with inbuilt ice-cool panels, will keep you refrigerated so you never lose your head.

3 a) Discuss the links between these ideas and a deodorant for men. What does the text add to the purpose of the advertisement?

b) Now create your own invention. Decide how you would use different presentational features to communicate your idea effectively.

Assess to Progress

How good are you at analysing how the structure, form and layout of a text influences its meaning? Rate yourself for each of the following skills by deciding where you would place yourself on the scale below.

1	2	3	4	5	6	7
I find this difficult.			I'm getting there.			I'm good at this.

- I can analyse how meaning can be conveyed in different ways according to the form and layout of a text.

  Self-check: When reading a leaflet or an article, can you explain how the different ways information is presented have an effect on impact and meaning?

- I can analyse how structural choices and organisation support the writer's theme or purpose.

  Self-check: Do you understand why bullet points are effective at communicating information in bite-size chunks in a persuasive text.

- I can comment on how organisational features contribute to the effects achieved.

  Self-check: When reading a charity leaflet, can you recognise and comment on the way the writer organises the text to try to influence your response?

Build your skills

The way a writer presents and organises ideas, information or stories will always depend on the needs of the readers and the purpose of the text.

1 Working in pairs, look at the leaflet below and decide what its purpose and aim is.

Rhys has noticed several techniques that the writer of the leaflet has used, starting with the main heading. He has created the chart opposite to help him organise his ideas about the presentational techniques.

2 Copy and complete the chart to explain the effects of the following presentational features Rhys has spotted:

- The main title is white on blue.
- There is a mixture of lower case, block capitals and handwriting.
- The words are different sizes.
- The word 'ACTIVE' seems distorted or almost moving.

Technique	Effect produced
The main title is white on blue.	The blue reminds me of the blue sky of a summer's day and the white writing really stands out against this – almost like small clouds. This makes me feel that if I do any of these activities, the weather will be perfect.
There is a mixture of lower case, block capitals and handwriting.	

3 Now look at the images used in the leaflet on page 91. Working with a partner, discuss the following questions:

a) Why has the main picture been chosen as a background feature? How different would the leaflet be with a plain background?

b) Why do you think so many small, inset pictures have been used? Which of the following reasons do you agree with?

- Because there isn't room for bigger pictures.
- To give some active 'snapshots' of some of the activities to encourage people to take part.
- To illustrate some of the items in the list.

4 Why is there a bullet-pointed list rather than short sentences describing the activities? Give reasons why this list is in white lettering.

5 Now look at the bottom of the leaflet. What message is the reader given here? How does the way this message is presented support the overall meaning and purpose of the leaflet?

6 Work in a group of four. Discuss which presentational and layout choices you think have the most impact in supporting the persuasive purpose of the leaflet.

7 Write a short paragraph explaining how the layout and organisational choices help communicate the meaning and purpose of the text.

Support

You could use some of the following words and phrases to help you explain what you have identified:

- The writer uses ... to explain ...
- This technique makes the reader think ...
- ... is particularly successful because ...

Reinforce your skills

You are going to explore how the writer Tim Bowler has organised the ending of his novel, *River Boy* shaping *the writing to create meaning for the reader*. In this story, Jess's grandfather suffers a heart attack, but he insists that his family visit his boyhood home on the river so that he can finish his painting, 'River Boy'. At first, Jess finds it difficult to come to terms with her grandfather's impending death, but by the end of the book she has come to an understanding of herself, her grandfather, and of life and death. Here, she is remembering her grandfather after he has died.

1 Working with a partner, discuss your thoughts about what happens in this part of the novel.

And her thoughts ran back to Grandpa again, and she remembered his face as she had always known it, with its wicked eyes and laughing mouth, and she thought of his cussedness, his cantankerousness, his sense of humour and...

And all that he had been.

And somehow still was.

And she looked at the ashes and shook her head. The real Grandpa was not here. The real Grandpa was as free as wind and water and sky. He was feeling no pain over this and neither would she.

She tipped the urn and let a tiny portion of the ashes trickle into the water from the source. The water collected them and they started to run down with the current, some catching against the soft earth at the sides but most of them floating down like tiny seeds towards the greater stream.

Language

Rhys has started to explore the different organisational features and techniques the writer has used and how these help to shape meaning for the reader. He has created a table to help him organise his analysis.

Organisational feature	Reason for use	How it helps shape meaning
One long sentence in a paragraph of its own: 'And her thoughts ran back to Grandpa again, ... his sense of humour and ...'	To help the reader visualise Jess's Grandpa.	This sentence flows just like Jess's thoughts and new details are added like in a list as if she is just thinking of them. The ellipsis at the end suggests that she could just keep on going but remembers that he has died.
Two short sentences in paragraphs of their own: 'And all that he had been. And somehow still was.'	To sum up all that she has just described.	Starting with 'And', these sentences could have been joined on to the previous one, but separated like this they really stand out. The reader is reminded that he has died but in some way lives on. It almost has the ring of a prayer to it.
Many of the sentences start with 'And'.		
A very long sentence at the end.		

2 Working with a partner, copy and complete the table to explore the organisational features and develop your explanation of these. Discuss why you think the author has used the last two organisational features.

a) Why has the writer started so many sentences with the word 'And'? What is the effect of this repetition?

b) What is the effect of the long sentence at the end of the extract? How is this structure appropriate to what is being described?

c) The author describes the ashes 'like tiny seeds'. What effect does this have on you as a reader? How does this idea link to the previous paragraph?

3 Write a short paragraph explaining how the structural and organisational choices the writer has made help the reader to understand the ideas in this part of the novel.

Extend your skills

By comparing different text you can explore how structural and organisational choices create different meanings and effects.

The texts on this page describe the Gresford Disaster of 1934 in which 266 miners were killed in a gas explosion near Wrexham in Wales. Read the texts and think about the way in which the information is structured.

The Gresford Disaster

Work began at sinking the pit at Gresford in 1908 and was completed in 1911. The mine was one of the deepest in the Denbighshire coalfield with the Dennis shaft reaching a depth of about 2,264 feet and the Martin shaft about 2,252 feet.

By 1934, 2,200 coal miners were employed at the colliery, with 1,850 working underground and 350 on the surface.

On September 22 at 2:08 am a violent explosion shook the Dennis section of the mine, over a mile from the bottom of the shaft, and a fire took hold. At the time, a total of 500 men were working underground at the colliery on the night shift, which was unusually high because some men had worked double shifts that night in order to be able to attend a carnival and football match the following day.

Only six men managed to escape from the Dennis section by climbing from the pit bottom by ladder. All of the other 262 miners working in that section were killed.

THE GRESFORD DISASTER

You've heard of the Gresford disaster,
The terrible price that was paid;
Two hundred and forty-two colliers were lost,
And three men of a rescue brigade.

It occurred in the month of September;
At three in the morning that pit
Was wracked by a violent explosion
In the Dennis where dust lay so thick.

The gas in the Dennis deep section
Was packed like snow in a drift,
And many a man had to leave the coal-face
Before he had worked out his shift.

Down there in the dark they are lying,
They died for nine shillings a day;
They've worked out their shift and it's now they must lie
In the darkness until Judgement Day.

Farewell our dear wives and our children,
Farewell our dear comrades as well.
Don't send your sons in the dark dreary mine
They'll be damned like the sinners in Hell.

Language

When you are looking at how meaning is communicated in different forms of writing, such as an encyclopaedia entry and a poem, be aware that they rely on very different structural and presentational devices because they set out to do different things. A poem will include specific features, such as stanzas, rhyme, repetition and word patterns; that you would not expect to find in an information text such as an encyclopaedia entry.

1 Working in pairs, reread both texts and discuss how each writer structures the information about the disaster. How might this make the reader respond?

2 Copy and complete the following chart to help you to compare and contrast how the form and structure used in each text help to convey the meaning communicated to the reader.

Features of form and structure	**Encyclopaedia entry**	**Poem**
Text-level organisation: how the information is sequenced	The entry details the incident in chronological order; this has the effect of ...	The ballad begins by giving information about how many people died ...
Sentence-level organisation: sentence structures, repetition, etc.		
Paragraph / stanza structure	Four paragraphs, first and second setting the context and detail of the mine, e.g. 'By 1934, 2,200 coal miners were employed.' Third providing facts of the event and the fourth to consequences of the disaster.	

Stretch

Write about the two texts, comparing how they convey information about the disaster. You could try using some of these sentence starters in your writing:

- Where the encyclopaedia entry uses ..., the poem uses ... and this has the effect of ...
- The two versions are alike in that ...
- The encyclopaedia entry is different from the poem in the way ...
- It might be, on the other hand, that ...

Apply your learning

Task Working on your own, read the texts that follow. Both give an account of the funeral of the famous British sailor Horatio Nelson. The first is an information sheet from the National Maritime Museum; the second is an extract from the novel *Victory* by Susan Cooper.

Lord Nelson was a vice-admiral in the Royal Navy and was shot on the deck of his flagship *HMS Victory* by a French musketeer on 21 October 1805, when the Battle of Trafalgar was at its height. After more than three hours of agony, Nelson died with his friend Captain Thomas Hardy by his side.

The state funeral of Lord Nelson, 5–9 January 1806

Military escort

A huge procession made up mainly of soldiers escorted the coffin. The only naval people taking part were:

- Greenwich pensioners
- Nelson's fellow officers
- members of the *Victory*'s crew.

A simple service

The service was simple yet emotional...Then the coffin began to sink slowly into the crypt below. As it disappeared, the Chief Herald read out the full titles of the dead man. He ended with the words, 'The hero, who in the moment of victory, fell covered with immortal glory.' Then the Officers of Nelson's Household broke their staves and handed them to the Herald, to be thrown into the grave.

Mementos for his sailors

As they did so, the sailors were supposed to fold up the *Victory*'s shot-torn colours and place them on a table. But instead, the sailors ripped off a portion of one of the flags and divided it into smaller pieces to keep as mementos.

With music and high words the funeral service lasted for hours, inside St Paul's Cathedral. A great blaze of candles hung from the huge domed roof. At the very end, when the coffin was to be lowered into the ground, we seamen had been told to fold our ensign in ceremony and lay it on the top. But when Will Welmet, the bosun, and three of the older men took up that shredded white cloth, Will gave a kind of sob – and suddenly all the men were reaching for our flag and it came apart, and they stuffed pieces of it into their jackets. The coffin went into the crypt, under the stone floor, for ever.

The first four questions are about the fact sheet.

1 Which of the following statements best describes the purpose of this text? Give reasons for your choice.
   - The text gives straightforward information about Nelson's funeral.
   - The text gives a description of the funeral and those taking part.
   - The text gives an account of the funeral from the point of view of an eyewitness.

2 Look at the three bold subtitles in the text: **Military escort, A simple service, Mementos for his sailors**. Explain why the headings have been placed in this order.

3 What effect does the use of bullet points have when compared with how information is presented in the rest of the text?

4 Which part of the text best shares the emotion of the event with the reader?

The next three questions are about the extract from the novel.

5 How does the fact that this text is narrated in the first person, 'we seamen', add to its emotional impact?

6 How does the writer show that the funeral is a very important and grand occasion? Pick out details from the text that show this and explain how these details are structured to help create a sense of importance.

7 'The coffin went into the crypt, under the stone floor, for ever.' What effect does this last sentence have on the reader?

The last two questions are about both texts.

8 Although both describe the same event, they are in different forms and organised in different ways. Identify and describe two differences in their structure.

9 Which text has the most emotional impact on you as a reader? Explain your answer, commenting on:
   - the purpose and tone of each text
   - the overall structure of each text
   - the way sentences are structured.

Assess to Progress

How good do you think you are now at analysing how the structure, form and layout of a text influences its meaning? Look back at the ratings you gave yourself on page 88. Now rate yourself again for each of the skills.

Skills for Life

Your family is going on a canal boat holiday and you and your cousin have been told that you will be in charge of operating the lock gates. Look at this information and then answer the questions below.

Going downhill

Check that the far gates and paddles are closed and then fill the lock – if it's not already full – by opening the paddles at the end nearest to the boat. When the lock's full, open the gate and steer in. Close the gates and lower the paddles. Keep the back of your boat well clear of the cill on the top gates – cills stick out by up to 5ft (1.5ml) and you can only see them when the locks emptying.

Open the paddles in front to empty the lock, using your engine or ropes to keep the boat as still as possible.

When the water levels are equal, open the bottom gates and take the boat out.

Close the gates and lower the paddles before you move on, unless a boat coming from the opposite direction wants to use the lock.

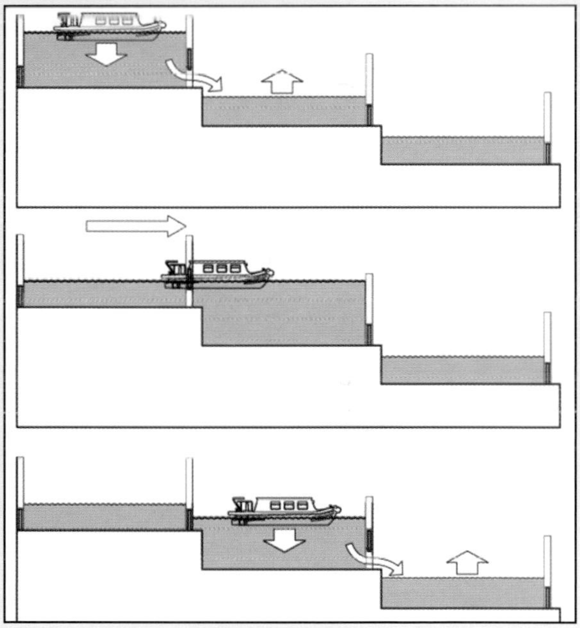

1. What are the most important points that you need to know about operating the locks? How does the layout emphasise these points?
2. How do the layout and organisation of the information support its purpose? Explain:
   - the ways the pictures support the message of the text
   - why the order of the information is important.
3. Explain another way you could organise and present this information.
4. Write an email to your cousin explaining in your own words what they need to know about operating lock gates. Remember to make sure you include all the important information including any safety points they need to be aware of.

Reading AF5

Progress in ... Analysing how writers use language to shape meaning

LEARNING OBJECTIVES

- Analyse in detail the way literary and rhetorical techniques and language features are used in texts.
- Explain the effect of those techniques and language choices on a text's meaning.
- Explore the potential impact of language choices on different readers.

Activate your learning

When you read a text can you recognise the way the writer has used words to create certain effects on the reader? When you hear a song's lyrics do you understand which words or images prompt you to feel sad or angry? If you are reading an advertisement do you recognise which words have been added to stir you up to really want that product – even though you can see it's not that great?

1 Look at the list of literary techniques below. Sort each of the terms into one of the following three categories:

- I know what this is and recognise it when it is used in texts.
- I have an idea of what this feature might be.
- I don't know what this term means.

personification · metaphor · simile · repetition · contrast

rhyme · alliteration · pun · exaggeration · sarcasm

vivid verbs · rhythm · stanzas · opposites

2 Working in a group, share your knowledge to create a poster giving definitions of each of the literary terms and giving an example of each one. Each person in your group may be an expert on the meaning of one or more of the terms.

Language

3 Referring to the class poster when you need help, match each of the examples below to the literary feature it demonstrates:

a) Remember Waqar's strut and Wasim's swagger? Remember Curtley's icy stare?

b) Sweat had salted my eyeballs like a tin of anchovies.

c) Difficult doesn't have many friends. But all that difficult wants is to make things better.

d) Because as I've discovered in my two-week tour of Britain's pretty bits, we may have lovely scenery, excellent cream teas and wonderful beaches. But our hotels make the average Moroccan jail look clean and comfortable.

e) The bed cannot possibly have cost more than 85 pence and couldn't have been more uncomfortable if it had been made from barbed wire.

Assess to Progress

How confident are you already at analysing in detail what effects a writer's use of language and choice of literary and rhetorical techniques have in a text? How readily can you explore what impact a writer's use of language may have on different readers? Rate yourself for each of the following skills below by deciding where you would place yourself on the scale below.

1 2 3 4 5 6 7

I find this difficult. I'm getting there. I'm good at this.

- I can recognise and comment on the way a writer is using language to create an effect.

  Self-check: Could you define the literary techniques listed on page 98, providing examples of each one and explaining the effects they create?

- I can analyse the impact a writer's language choice has on the way I understand and respond to a text

  Self-check: Could you understand and analyse how writers use language to influence your response to a text, such as in newspaper editorials arguing a particular point of view?

- I can explore in depth the possible impact a writer's language choices can have on different readers.

  Self-check: Could you explain how a writer's language choices in an advertisement might appeal to the target audience of young people but alienate older readers?

Build your skills

A writer needs to think carefully about the best way to use language to express ideas. But as a reader, how can you decide whether a writer's efforts have been effective or not? In the following extract, taken from the memoir *The Life and Times of the Thunderbolt Kid*, Bill Bryson describes his childhood growing up in small-town America. Read the text and then follow the skill steps to explore and analyse the writer's use of language.

I was enormously stupid. I mean really quite enormously. I remember when I was about six passing almost a whole movie picking some interesting sweet-smelling stuff off the underside of my seat, thinking that it was something to do with the actual manufactured composition of the seat before realising that it was gum that had been left there by previous users.

I was sick for about two years over what a grotesque and unhygienic activity I had been engaged in and the thought that I had then eaten greasy buttered popcorn and a large packet of Chuckles with the same fingers that had dabbled in other people's abandoned chewings. I had even – oh, yuk! yuk! – licked those fingers, eagerly transferring bucketloads of syphilitic dribblings and uncategorisable swill from their snapped-out Wrigleys and Juicy Fruits to my wholesome mouth and sleek digestive tract. It was only a matter of time – hours at most – before I would sink into a mumbling delirium and in slow, fevered anguish die.

Step 1 Think about the big picture

Language

You need to understand what the text is about before you can focus on the language the writer has used to communicate this and the effects this language creates. As you read a text for the first time, work out what is happening – what events and ideas are being described?

1 Working with a partner, prepare a flow chart showing the sequence of events and ideas in this text. Present your flow chart on the left-hand side of your page, beginning a new box each time you find a new point.

Look at the first column of the flow chart below to help you. You need to leave the right-hand two-thirds of the page free as you will add to the chart in the following steps.

Ideas/events	Use of language	Explanation
When he was six he was very stupid	Repetition – 'enormously'	Repeating builds the suspense for the readers – it makes you think: Just how stupid was he?
He pulled old chewing gum off the underside of a cinema seat and then licked his fingers	Alliteration … 'sweet – smelling stuff'.	All the 's' sounds make the gum sound slimy and sticky, which reinforces the picture you have in your mind of how disgusting it is that he later puts fingers that have touched that into his mouth!
	Contrast between sophisticated words used for 'actual manufactured composition of the seat' and 'gum that had been left there by previous users'.	The contrast builds up the idea that he thought it was a clever component of the seat, so it's written in more technical language. Then he reinforces the idea of how stupid he was by using very simple language to tell you it was just gum.

Language

Step 2 Pinpoint the way language is being used

This is where you need your knowledge of the different techniques a writer might choose, e.g. the use of contrasts, imagery and repetition.

1 Search each part of the text in turn and pinpoint how the writer has expressed the ideas. When you notice the writer using a particular technique, draw another box next to the relevant idea box in your flow chart. Note down the technique used and the quotation that shows this.

Support

Try to find examples of the following techniques:

- contrast
- imagery
- rhyme
- repetition
- onomatopoeia
- emotive language

Step 3 Analyse and explain how the techniques add meaning

Writers try to connect the way they write about something with the idea or event being expressed. To understand a text more fully, it is important to think about how a writer's use of a particular technique adds to the meaning they are trying to convey. Think about the ways the following effects can be created:

- Sound effects that reinforce or draw attention to the meaning of particular words, e.g. onomatopoeia, rhyme, alliteration
- Emphasis of a particular point, e.g. repetition, rhyme, alliteration
- Expansion of an idea by adding a different layer of meaning, e.g. imagery, personification
- Links between different parts of the text, e.g. rhyme, contrast, alliteration repetition
- Humour, e.g. puns, rhyme, imagery, unusual word choice, contrast.

1 Working with a partner, look at the explanation boxes on page 103 exploring what impact the use of different techniques has on the meaning. Discuss how the reader has developed their analysis of the techniques used and how effective their explanation is.

2 Note down your own ideas about how each technique you have spotted adds to the text's meaning. Add these explanations in boxes that link the quotation to the idea or event being expressed.

Reinforce your skills

You are now going to explore an extract from the naturalist Gerald Durrell's memoir *My Family and Other Animals*. Gerald is remembering something that fascinated him when he was young but which might not interest most readers. He has used several literary techniques to impress on his readers why it was so amazing.

Discoveries filled me with a tremendous delight so that they had to be shared, and I would burst suddenly into the house and startle the family with the news that the strange, spiky black caterpillars on the roses were not caterpillars at all, but the young of lacy-birds, or with the equally astonishing news that lacewing-flies laid eggs on stilts. This last miracle I was lucky enough to witness. I found a lacewing-fly on the roses and watched her as she climbed about the leaves, admiring her beautiful, fragile wings like green glass, and her enormous liquid golden eyes. Presently she stopped on the surface of a rose-leaf and lowered the tip of her abdomen. She remained like that for a moment and then raised her tail, and from it, to my astonishment, rose a slender thread, like a pale hair. Then, on the very tip of this stalk appeared the egg. The female had a rest, and then repeated the performance until the surface of the rose-leaf looked as though it was covered with a forest of tiny club moss. The laying over, the female rippled her antennae briefly and flew off in a mist of green gauze wings.

1 With a partner, prepare a flow chart showing the events described.

2 Join with another pair and reread the text. Work out which of the following literary techniques are used. Discuss each technique and explore how it adds to the meaning Gerald is trying to convey.

personification	metaphor	repetition	contrast
vivid verbs	alliteration	onomatopoeia	simile

3 Gerald Durrell went on to become a world-famous naturalist who collected, studied and helped to protect animal species. How does the way he has written this description show his attitude towards animals? Try to develop your analysis in detail.

Stretch

How might someone who was entomophobic – scared of insects – react to this description? Explain what effect the language choices would have on this person.

Language

Extend your skills

Not all readers will respond in the same way to a text. It depends on each reader's point of view and their interest in what the writer is telling them. Working out how a reader might respond to a text means you need to put yourself in their place and try to think from their point of view about what the text is saying.

The text on the opposite page is taken from the restaurant critic Michael Winner's review of a Chinese restaurant in London. Work through the activities below to help you explore the impact of the language choices on different readers.

1 a) As you read through the article, decide what impression Michael Winner is giving of the restaurant. Discuss your ideas with a partner.

b) Which literary techniques does he use to create this impression and how do they help him achieve this?

2 As well as informing his readers about the restaurant, Michael Winner also tries to make his review entertaining to read. Find three examples where he uses a literary technique to make his review entertaining.

To work out what effect a literary technique might have on a group of readers think about:

- what it makes readers **compare or contrast**
- how this might **surprise** those readers
- what **feelings** it might arouse in those readers
- what it makes those readers **picture** – how does that fit in with the idea being expressed?
- what it might **remind** those readers of
- what it might make those readers **wonder**.

3 Working with a partner, discuss how the following readers might respond to the language Michael Winner uses to describe his experience:

a) The owners and staff who work at the restaurant. Explain which details they might find annoying.

b) Wealthy readers who are used to eating out at expensive hotels. Which words or phrases would they find most entertaining?

4 Write a paragraph exploring the possible impacts of the language and the choices of literary techniques used in this review on different readers. Include the readers you thought about in the previous question as well as other audiences. Remember to integrate quotations from the review to support the points you are making.

Restaurant review: Michael Winner at Park in the Mandarin Oriental Hotel

Chris Rea, brilliant musician and lovely person (so's his wife but she can't play a note on anything), wanted Thai food. So I decided to try the Park. Worst decision of 2008. That leaves me a few months to make a lousier one. Which is unlikely.

The Park room is hotel-boring. The nice Polish waitress had her name, Monika, on a badge. That's in case she forgets it. She can look at her badge.

Chris ordered Asahi beer. 'It's Japanese,' he announced. The bottle label said it was brewed and bottled in the UK for Asahi Beer Europe Ltd, 17 Connaught Place, London W2 2EL. A very posh address for brewing beer.

I had pad thai – wok-fried noodles tossed with fried egg, beansprouts, chillies, tamarind sauce, crushed peanuts and fresh lime – with chicken. And a spring roll.

Everything was horrendous. The spring roll was old and tired, tasted as if it had been deep-frozen for ever. The dim sum were hard, rubbery and horrible. My main course chicken and noodles were also hard and dried out. We went for Sunday dinner. This rubbish tasted as if it was made on Wednesday and had been left freezing and stiffening. A total disgrace for a supposedly first-class hotel.

For dessert I tried apple crumble and ice cream. To describe it as moderate would be a compliment. That also tasted as if it had hung around far too long.

In the background, pleasing live saxophone music came from the bar. Later Chris Rea rang Geraldine and said, 'The saxophonist was better than the spring rolls.' A rotting horse would have been better than the spring rolls.

Language

Apply your learning

The texts you have read so far in this unit have all touched on the writer's memories of experiences, memories that were important or significant to them. The poem 'Lies' by Carol Ann Duffy seems to do the same – or does it?

Task Working on your own, use the reading strategies you have developed during this unit as you read the poem and answer the questions below. Remember to write in full sentences and use quotations to support your ideas.

1. In the first ten lines the writer chooses words and phrases carefully to impress on readers how aware she is of what she is doing. Pick out two words or phrases that create this effect and explain why they emphasise her awareness.
2. Read carefully the description of what it is like when the poem's narrator lies to the boy. Explain how the way the following phrases are written helps to suggest how much she enjoys the effect her lies have on him.
   a) 'his split strawberry mouth moist and mute'
   b) 'my weasel words'
   c) 'sparking the little lights in his spectacles'
3. Does Carol Ann Duffy make lying to the people at the bus stop seem enjoyable? Which literary techniques help to create this impression? Explain how they do this.
4. Now reread the third stanza where Carol Ann Duffy creates a contrast between other people's homes and hers. Which words or phrases does she use to create this contrast? What do they suggest about the difference between her home and other people's?
5. Look at how these two readers responded to the poem. Explain in detail which literary techniques that Carol Ann Duffy uses could have created this effect on each reader.

   Reader 1: It made me laugh. I thought she was totally mad!

   Reader 2: I think she wants the reader to feel really sorry for her – she makes her childhood sound really sad.

Lies

I like to go out for the day and tell lies.
The day should be overcast with a kind of purple,
electric edge to the clouds;
and not too hot or cold,
but cool. I turn up the collar of my coat
and narrow my eyes.
I meet someone –
a kid from school perhaps –
and give him five.
Then I start to lie
as we walk along Tennyson Drive kicking a can.
He listens hard,
his split strawberry mouth moist and mute;
my weasel words
sparking the little lights in his spectacles.
At the corner of Coleridge Place
I watch him run,
thrilled, fast, chasing his breath,
home to his mum.

Bus stops I like,
with long, bored, footsore, moaning queues. I lie to them
in my shrill, confident voice,
till the number 8 or 11 takes them away
and I stand and stare at the bend in Longfellow Road,
alone in the day.

At the end of the darkening afternoon
I head for home,
watching the lights come on in truthful rooms,
where mothers come and go
with plates of cakes,
and TV sets shuffle the bright cartoons.
Then I knock on the door of 21 Wordsworth Way,
and while I wait
I watch a spaceship zoom away overhead
and see the faint half-smile of the distant moon.
They let me in.
And who they want to know, do I think I am?
Exactly where have I been? With whom? And why?
The thing with me–
I like to come home after a long day out
and lie.

Assess to Progress

How confident are you now at analysing in detail what effects a writer's use of language and choice of literary techniques have in a text? How effectively can you now explore what impacts a writer's use of language may have on different readers? Look back at the ratings you gave yourself on page 99. Now rate your self again for each of the skills.

SKILLS FOR LIFE

Your older friend has received the letter below and is tempted to take out the loan it offers. Read the letter and then answer the questions below.

1 Pick out four persuasive words or phrases included in the letter. How does each one make the loan sound attractive?

2 Which facts suggest it is not a good idea for your friend to take out this loan?

3 Write a note for your friend explaining how the writer of this letter has used language to persuade.

£2000 is ready and waiting for you …

Dear Elliot Ross

Congratulations! As one of our valued existing customers, I'm delighted to let you know that we could offer you approval on a loan of £2000 over 1 to 5 years*. So, whether you're thinking of getting a new car, treating yourself to some stylish new clothes or taking a well-deserved holiday, one simple phone call is all it takes.

Approval on a loan in less than 30 minutes

The personalised amount shown above is just waiting for you right now provided your circumstances haven't changed since we selected you for this offer. An approval on a loan is so quick and easy and the money could be in your account in just a few days. £2000 is only a phone call away

What are you waiting for? Call us now on 0800 242445

* Typical 10.2% APR

Reading AF6

Progress in ... Understanding and responding to ideas, viewpoint, themes and purpose

LEARNING OBJECTIVES

- Analyse the ideas, differing viewpoints and themes in a range of linked texts, tracing the development of these.
- Develop an interpretation of a text, supporting points with detailed textual evidence.
- Respond to the ideas, viewpoints and themes presented in a text and explore how these are linked.

Activate your learning

Traditionally, the 'American Dream' is the belief that in America anyone can achieve wealth and success through hard work. Working in a group of four, discuss what you think about the 'American Dream' and share your thoughts and feelings about America. Then read the following text which describes the early history of the USA and answer the questions on the next page.

America has always been seen as a place of great hope, freedom and escape. From the first pilgrim settlers to the rush for land in the 1840s, America is 'the land of opportunity'.

The first pilgrims arrived in 1620, hoping America would be a safe haven, where they could practise their own religion without fear of persecution. They hoped they would escape Europe and find freedom. Battles with the native tribes, disease, famine and death soon showed life in America would not be easy, but nevertheless, millions of people over the next 300 years followed these early pilgrims in seeking out America as a place where their dreams could come true.

Famine, disease and poverty in Europe meant thousands of people crossed the Atlantic, searching for New Life in this New World. The California Gold Rush in 1849, the rush for oil in Texas in the early 20th century and the land runs in Oklahoma where thousands chased across the state to claim it as their own – all these events contributed to the view of America as the 'land of the free and the home of the brave'.

1 Look at the following ideas. Work with a partner to rate each statement as:

- definitely true – is clear evidence in the text
- probably true – hinted at in the text
- untrue, – factually incorrect
- not known – no evidence to support this.

The pilgrims were the first settlers in America.	America allowed anyone to immigrate into the country.
Many different nationalities emigrated to America.	Life in America isn't easy.
People emigrated to America to find safety and security.	Most people went to California because of the Gold Rush.
People emigrated to America to escape life in Europe.	People who went to America wanted gold, oil or land.

2 Look at the statements you identified as definitely or probably true. Why do you think people had these ideas about America? Discuss your ideas in a group.

Assess to Progress

How well can you understand and respond to the ideas, viewpoints and themes presented in different texts? Can you explore how similar ideas are treated in different texts? Rate yourself from 1 – 7 (with 1 being 'I find this difficult' and 7 being 'I'm good at this') for each of the following skills.

- I can analyse the ideas, differing viewpoints and themes in a range of linked texts and trace their development.

  Self-check: Can you think about how the same news story is reported in different newspapers and understand how writers show their differing viewpoints?

- I can develop an interpretation of a text, supporting points with detailed textual evidence.

  Self-check: Can you develop an overall understanding of a text, supporting the points you make with relevant details from the text?

- I can respond to the ideas, viewpoints and themes presented in a text and explore how these are linked.

  Self-check: Can you explain how a particular point of view is developed in a text and compare this with the view presented in another text?

Build your skills

In this unit, you will explore a range of texts that are linked by ideas and themes. The text below is taken from Frank McCourt's autobiography *Angela's Ashes*, which describes his childhood in Limerick, Ireland in the 1930s. Here, Frank's father is talking to him on a Sunday morning about his future.

Read the text and follow the skill steps to explore the ideas and themes.

He tells me school is easy now, you don't have to sit in a ditch learning your sums or the glorious history of Ireland. I should be good in school and some day I'll go back to America and get an inside job where I'll be sitting at a desk with two fountain pens in my pocket, one red and one blue, making decisions. I'll be in out of the rain and I'll have a suit and shoes and a warm place to live and what more could a man want? He says you can do anything in America, it's the land of opportunity. You can be a fisherman in Maine or a farmer in California. America is not like Limerick, a gray place with a river that kills.

If I were in America I could say, I love you, Dad, the way they do in the films, but you can't say that in Limerick for fear you might be laughed at. You're allowed to say you love God and babies and horses that win but anything else is a softness in the head.

Step 1 Trace the ideas in a text

When you read a text, you need to work out what ideas are established and how they develop over the text. In this text, Frank McCourt establishes the idea that Ireland is cold and damp, and that life is hard. He also establishes the idea that 'America is not like Limerick'.

1 Look at the following quotations and explain how each one helps to build up the idea that life in America is different from life in Ireland.

- 'You don't have to sit in a ditch learning your sums'
- I'll get ... 'get an inside job where I'll be sitting at a desk with two fountain pens in my pocket ... making decisions'
- 'I'll be in out of the rain'

2 Now reread the second paragraph. What details here help to develop the main ideas? Discuss your thoughts with a partner.

3 a) Frank McCourt writes, 'If I were in America I could say, I love you, Dad, the way they do in the films.' How does this suggest that his and his father's view of America might not be realistic?

b) Pick out any other details from the text that suggest that his father's view of America is not realistic.

Step 2 Explore the themes in a text and interpret the key message or purpose

Themes are the big ideas that run across a text, often including a message or an idea. When identifying how ideas link together to become themes, you will need to be able to use evidence from different parts of the same text.

Read the following passage from the end of *Angela's Ashes*, where Frank is older. Here, he has finally saved up enough money and is sailing to America.

I'm on deck the dawn we sail into New York. I'm sure I'm in a film, that it will end and lights will come up in the Lyric Cinema. I can pick out the Statue of Liberty, Ellis Island, the Empire State Building, the Chrysler Building, the Brooklyn Bridge. There are thousands of cars speeding along the road and the sun turns everything to gold. Rich Americans in top hats, white ties and tails must be going home to bed with the gorgeous women with white teeth. The rest are going to work in warm comfortable offices and no one has a care in the world.

Alex has picked out a detail from the second extract that links back to a detail from the first passage on page 113. He then explains the idea that links them.

Detail from passage 2	Detail from passage 1	Explanation of the idea that links them
'I'm sure I'm in a film'	*'the way they do in films'*	*Frank has seen so many films that it doesn't feel real. It's almost as though he doesn't believe that he's finally realised his dream of going to America and that his life is going to be different now – more like a film than his life in Ireland.*

1 a) Working with a partner, identify evidence from this passage and the one on page 113 that links together. Look for similar words, phrases or ideas. Copy the table above and add these details.

b) Discuss your ideas about how the details link together. Then add your explanation to the table.

2 Think about how the theme of America as a promised land to escape to is continued in the second extract. Look at the detailed evidence you have collected from both passages and discuss your ideas with your partner.

Step 3 Develop an interpretation based on your own point of view

When we develop an interpretation of a text, we add our own thoughts about the ideas and themes it explores, explaining our own viewpoint and relating it to the text.

1 Look back at your table of evidence picking out the ideas and themes you have identified. Working with a partner, develop your own interpretation of the text you have read.

2 Write a paragraph giving your interpretation of the text. Remember to support the points you make with detailed evidence from the text and integrate quotations into your response.

Reinforce your skills

You are now going to explore the ideas and themes in a poem called 'America the Beautiful' and build your own interpretation of this text. It was written by Katherine Lee Bates in 1893 and later turned into a patriotic song.

1 Read the poem. As you read, note down what ideas and beliefs it gives about America.

GLOSSARY

thoroughfare – road
alabaster – white stone

O beautiful, for spacious skies,
For amber waves of grain,
For purple mountain majesties
Above the fruited plain!
America! America! God shed His grace on thee,
And crown thy good with brotherhood, from sea to shining sea.

O beautiful, for pilgrim feet
Whose stern, impassioned stress
A thoroughfare for freedom beat
Across the wilderness!
America! America! God mend thine ev'ry flaw;
Confirm thy soul in self control, thy liberty in law!

O beautiful, for heroes proved
In liberating strife,
Who more than self their country loved
And mercy more than life!
America! America! May God thy gold refine,
'Til all success be nobleness, and ev'ry gain divine!

O beautiful, for patriot dream
That sees beyond the years,
Thine alabaster cities gleam
Undimmed by human tears!
America! America! God shed His grace on thee,
And crown thy good with brotherhood, from sea to shining sea!

Work with a partner to discuss the following questions:

2 a) Katherine Lee Bates tries to create the idea that America is like the Garden of Eden, where food is plentiful and life is easy. Pick out details from the poem that support this idea.

b) She also believes that Americans would die for their country. What evidence can you find to support this idea?

3 What is the poet's view of America? Write a paragraph developing your interpretation of the text and the view it presents. Remember to support your points with evidence from the text.

Support

Think about the writer's purpose in writing the poem. Katherine Lee Bates wrote this poem on a train journey she took to Colorado Springs in 1893 and several of the sights she saw on the trip are mentioned in her poem. The poem was published two years later on the fourth of July to commemorate Independence Day.

As well as responding to ideas within a text, it is important to be able to compare, analyse and respond to ideas and viewpoints presented across related texts. This poem and the passages from *Angela's Ashes* offer views and ideas about America.

4 Working with a partner, compare and contrast the ideas, themes and views from both texts. Record your ideas in a diagram like the one below, placing similar ideas or views where the circles overlap.

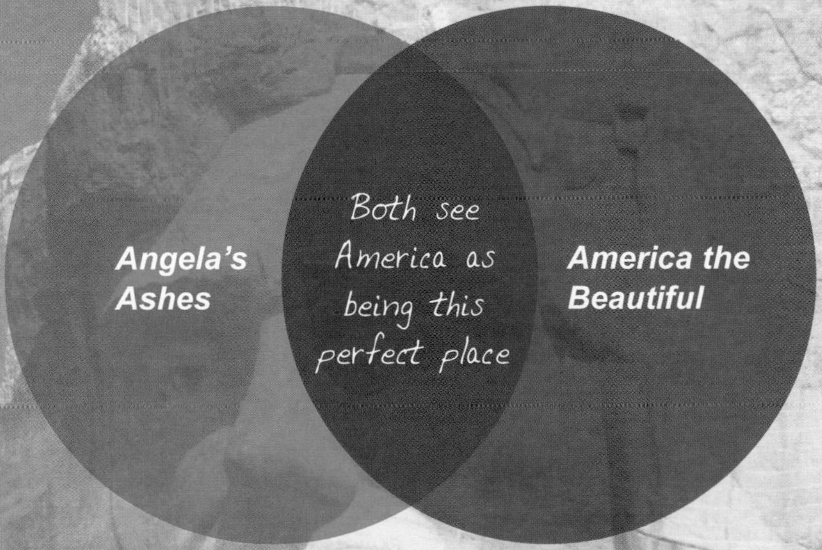

Extend your skills

Sometimes, exploring other texts will give you a different viewpoint on the same ideas and themes.

Read the following passage from the novel *Daughter of Fortune* by Isabel Allende, which is set in the middle of the 19th century. Two travellers arrive in America for the first time, landing at San Francisco at the time of the Gold Rush – Tao Chi'en, a Chinese doctor, and Eliza Sommers, who has come to find her fiancé who had left for San Francisco in search of gold.

Gold fever left no one unaffected: smiths, carpenters, teachers, doctors, soldiers, fugitives from the law, preachers, bakers, revolutionaries, and harmless madmen of various stripes who had left family and possessions behind to traverse half the world in search of adventure. 'They look for gold, and along the way lose their souls,' Captain Katz had repeated tirelessly in the brief religious services he imposed every Sunday on the passengers and crew of the *Emilia*, but no one paid any attention, blinded by the dreams of the sudden riches that would change their lives. For the first time in history, gold lay scattered on the ground, unclaimed, free, and plentiful, within the reach of anyone with the will to go after it. Argonauts came from distant shores: Europeans fleeing wars, plagues and tyrannies; Americans, ambitious and short-tempered; blacks pursuing freedom; Oregonians and Russians dressed in deerskin, like Indians; Mexicans, Chileans, and Peruvians; Australian bandits; starving Chinese peasants who were risking their necks by violating the imperial order against leaving their country. All races flowed together in the muddy alleyways of San Francisco.

GLOSSARY

traverse – travel

Working with a partner, discuss and answer the following questions:

1 The narrator's viewpoint is that gold 'fever' could affect anyone – good or bad. How does the writer establish this view?

2 The writer also establishes the idea that the American Dream comes at a price. What does she write that shows this?

3 The passengers are described as being 'blinded by the dreams of the sudden riches that would change their lives'. How realistic does the writer make these dreams seem? How does this idea compare with the earlier texts?

4 The writer also describes the people who came to America at this time: 'Europeans fleeing wars, plagues and tyrannies ... blacks pursuing freedom ... All races flowed together'. How do these words and phrases link to the other texts you have read in this unit?

Now read the next paragraph from the novel, which describes San Francisco at the time of the Gold Rush.

Everything was a shambles of temporary dwellings, barracks, shacks of sheet metal, wood, or cardboard, canvas tents, and straw roofs. The recent rains of winter had turned the dock into a swamp; any vehicle that had ventured there sank hub-deep in mire, and planks were laid across ditches deep in garbage, thousands of broken bottles, and other refuse. There were no drains or sewers, and the wells were contaminated; cholera and dysentery reaped scores of lives. Shouts from fights and accidents added to the din of hammers, saws, and picks. Shots rang out with terrifying frequency, but no one was affected by one more dead man; on the other hand, the theft of a box of nails immediately drew out a crowd of indignant citizens ready to mete out justice with their own hands. Property was much more valuable than life; any robbery over a hundred dollars was paid for on the gallows.

5 Discuss with a partner, what impression you get of what life was really like in San Francisco at this time. Pick out details to support your points.

6 How do the ideas and views in this text contradict views and ideas presented in the poem 'America the Beautiful'? Copy and complete the table below explaining why you think the writers' views are different and how this is shown. Pick out quotations from each text that explore similar ideas and contrasting ideas.

Evidence from 'America the Beautiful'	Evidence from Daughter of Fortune	Exploration of the contrasting ideas and views shown
'For amber waves of grain, For purple mountain majesties Above the fruited plain!'	'the muddy alleyways of San Francisco'	America isn't just rural and like Eden; it is real. It has real cities, with the same problems all cities face. The reality is different from the imaginary 'picture postcard' view of America.

Stretch

Think about the impact on readers with different attitudes or from different cultures as you interpret a text. How might an American reader's response to Isabel Allende's description of San Francisco differ from their response to the poem 'America the Beautiful'? Explore how specific details could affect different readers.

Apply your learning

Use the reading skills and strategies you have developed during this unit as you complete the following task.

Task Read the two extracts below, which are taken from the American writer John Steinbeck's novel *East of Eden*, a story about two families in California at the beginning of the 20th century. Then answer the questions on the opposite page.

The Salinas Valley is in Northern California. It is a long narrow swale between two ranges of mountains, and the Salinas River winds and twists up the center until it falls at last into Monterey Bay.

I remember that the Gabilan Mountains to the east of the valley were light gay mountains full of sun and loveliness and a kind of invitation, so that you wanted to climb into their warm foothills almost as you want to climb into the lap of a beloved mother. They were beckoning mountains with a brown grass love. The Santa Lucias stood up against the sky to the west and kept the valley from the open sea, and they were dark and brooding – unfriendly and dangerous. I always found in myself a dread of west and a love of east.

From both sides of the valley little streams slipped out of the hill canyons and fell into the bed of the Salinas River. In the winter of wet years the streams ran full-freshet, and they swelled the river until sometimes it raged and boiled, bank full, and then it was a destroyer. The river tore the edges of the farm lands and washed whole acres down; it toppled barns and houses into itself, to go floating and bobbing away. It trapped cows and pigs and sheep and drowned them in its muddy brown water and carried them to the sea.

The narrator then talks about his grandfather, Samuel Hamilton, who had come from Ireland to settle in the valley.

He came to the Salinas Valley full-blown and hearty, full of inventions and energy. In the dusty business of ranching he seemed always immaculate. His hands were clever. He was a good blacksmith and carpenter and woodcarver, and he could improvise anything with bits of wood and metal.

If the land had been any good the Hamiltons would have been rich people. But the acres were harsh and dry. There were no springs, and the crust of topsoil was so thin that the flinty bones stuck through. Even the sagebrush struggled to exist, and the oaks were dwarfed from lack of moisture. From their barren hills the Hamiltons could look down to the west and see the richness of the bottom land and the greenness around the Salinas River.

1 Pick out two details from the text that show America in a positive light. Explain your choices.

2 The writer ends the passage with the idea that life in America can be hard. Track how this idea is developed through the text. Identify five details or quotations from the extracts and explain how they help to develop this idea. Record your answer in a table like the one below.

Evidence that life in America can be hard	Explanation of how this evidence contributes to the idea

3 a) In this text the writer presents the viewpoint that dreams are never fulfilled and reality is always different from how we imagine it. Explain how he creates this viewpoint and refer to evidence from the text to support your explanation.

b) The writer also hints that Americans think there are always better things to be had. Find evidence from the text to explain this view.

4 Across all the different texts you have read in this unit, you have explored different ideas and views on the theme of the American Dream. Write a personal response, developing your interpretation of the texts and the way they have explored this theme. You may wish to use the following prompts to support your response.

- The American Dream is ...
- The writers who tell us about the American Dream include ...
- The first writer says the American Dream is ...
- The second writer thinks the American Dream is ...

Assess to Progress

How well can you understand and respond to the ideas, viewpoints and themes presented in different texts now? How confident were you about exploring how similar ideas were treated in different texts? Look back at the ratings you gave yourself on page 110. Now rate yourself again for each of the skills.

SKILLS FOR LIFE

You have read the following review of the classic film *Jaws* and you are trying to decide whether it is worth renting.

> It left a generation of schoolkids afraid to go into a swimming pool, let alone back into the water. Wunderkind Spielberg's story is all the scarier for hardly ever showing the Great White that is most of the characters' nemesis.
>
> The cast is top-notch. Scheider is police chief Brody, a hydrophobe taking up his new posting on Amity Island off America's East Coast. His buddies in battling the killer fish are rich-kid ichthyologist Hooper (Dreyfuss) and maverick fisherman Quint (Shaw). The film has political undertones but also owes a debt in its theme of self and mutual reliance to those twin classic 1950s westerns: *High Noon* and *Rio Bravo.*

1 How does the reviewer suggest that this film is a classic?

2 Your friend is worried that the violence in the film might be too graphic. What detail from the review might reassure them?

3 The reviewer describes the director, Stephen Spielberg, as a 'Wunderkind'. What does this suggest?

4 Pick out two other details that show the reviewer thinks this film is worth watching. Explain how each shows the reviewer's point of view.

Progress in ... Relating texts to their historical and cultural contexts

LEARNING OBJECTIVES

- Develop an understanding of how ideas, experiences and values are portrayed in texts from different cultures and traditions.
- Understand how the contexts in which texts are written and read can affect their meaning.
- Explore the textual conventions and features used by writers from different periods and consider the ways in which the English language has changed over time.

Activate your learning

On the next page are two sets of school rules. One set rules is from a modern-day school, but the other set was written 250 years ago.

1 Working in pairs, read both sets of school rules and discuss:

- how the pupils are expected to behave
- any clues you can find about when these rules were written
- what you can tell about the society these schools are part of, e.g. what the relationship between pupils and teachers was like, what beliefs people about how pupils should behave had.
- the language used and what effect this has.

2 Now join with another pair to make a group of four. In your group, discuss:

- how school life was different then and now
- the different ways language is used
- which school you would prefer to go to and why.

School Rules

1. School uniform is to be worn correctly according to the list published, and articles of clothing should be clearly marked with the owner's name.
2. Dangerous items or any article likely to cause harm (such as knives, aerosols, lighters) must not be brought to school.
3. Pupils must adhere to the Mobile Phone Policy (available on the Website).
4. Pupils should not wear nail varnish, jewellery or make-up (see uniform list).
5. Pupils must not have cigarettes, alcohol, solvents, or drugs in school, nor with them on their way to and from school. Abuse of this rule may result in permanent exclusion.
6. Pupils must remain on school premises at all times.
7. Money, bus contracts, valuables etc. must not be left in the pockets of clothing in the cloakrooms or changing rooms. Valuable items should not normally be brought to school, but if this is unavoidable, they should be left with form tutors or in the School Office.

Of Behaviour in the School

1. Bow at coming in, putting off thine hat. Especially if the Master or Usher be present.
2. Loiter not, but immediately take thine own feet: and move not from one place to another, till school time be over.
3. If any stranger come into the school, rise up and bow, and sit down in thy place again, keeping a profound silence.
4. Interrupt not the Master while a Stranger or Visitor is with him, with any question, request or complaint; but defer any such matter till he be at leisure.
5. At no time talk or quarrel in the school, but be quiet, peaceable and silent: Much less mayest thou deceive thyself by trifling away thy time in play.
6. Bawl not aloud in making complaints: A boy's tongue should never be heard in school but in answering a question or repeating his lesson.
7. Go not rudely home through the street, stand not talking with boys to delay thee, but go quietly home, and with all convenient haste.

Assess to Progress

How good are you already at identifying how texts might describe life, ideas, experiences and values that are different from your own, perhaps because they represent beliefs from a different country or because they have been written at some time in the past? Rate yourself for each of the following skills by deciding where you would place yourself on the scale below.

1	2	3	4	5	6	7
I find this difficult.			I'm getting there.			I'm good at this.

- I understand and can explore how texts from different times or cultures can show the ideas, experiences and beliefs people felt were important.

  Self-check: Do you know how to explore what life was like by looking at features in a text such as how people are described, the sorts of thing they did and believed in, how they were expected to behave and the kind of language used?

- I understand how the views in my own time and culture can affect the way readers now respond to texts from different times or cultures.

  Self-check: When you read the old school rules you thought these rules sounded very strict and pupils wouldn't follow them, but did you realise you thought this because pupils are treated differently nowadays?

- I understand some of the ways the English language has developed from different historical periods up to the present day.

  Self-check: When you compare the language in both sets of school rules, I can you explore the changes that have taken place over time in such things as spelling, grammar and formality?

Build your skills

To help you explore the ideas, experiences and beliefs in texts, it can help to look for clues about when and where something was written. You might find these clues from the main ideas in the text, in the type of language used and in the attitudes held by the people being described.

Read this extract from the novel *Hard Times*, written by Charles Dickens more than 150 years ago. It describes a school teacher, Thomas Gradgrind, and demonstrates how he teaches his class.

Thomas Gradgrind, sir. A man of realities. A man of facts and calculations. A man who proceeds upon the principle that two and two are four, and nothing over, and who is not to be talked into allowing for anything over ... With a rule and a pair of scales, and the multiplication table always in his pocket, sir, ready to weigh and measure any parcel of human nature, and tell you exactly what it comes to ...

In such terms Mr. Gradgrind always mentally introduced himself, whether to his private circle of acquaintance, or to the public in general ... Thomas Gradgrind now presented Thomas Gradgrind to the little pitchers before him, who were to be filled so full of facts.

Indeed, as he eagerly sparkled at them ... he seemed a kind of cannon loaded to the muzzle with facts, and prepared to blow them clean out of the regions of childhood at one discharge ...

'Girl number twenty,' said Mr. Gradgrind, squarely pointing with his square forefinger, 'I don't know that girl. Who is that girl?'

'Sissy Jupe, sir,' explained number twenty, blushing, standing up, and curtseying.

'Sissy is not a name,' said Mr. Gradgrind. 'Don't call yourself Sissy. Call yourself Cecilia.'

'My father as calls me Sissy, sir,' returned the young girl in a trembling voice, and with another curtsey.

'Then he has no business to do it,' said Mr. Gradgrind. 'Tell him he mustn't. Cecilia Jupe. Let me see. What is your father?'

'He belongs to the horse-riding, if you please, sir.'

'... Very well, then. Describe your father as a horsebreaker. He doctors sick horses, I dare say?'

'Oh yes, sir.'

'Very well, then. He is a veterinary surgeon, a farrier, and horse-breaker. Give me your definition of a horse.'

(Sissy Jupe thrown into the greatest alarm by this demand.) 'Girl number twenty unable to define a horse!' said Mr. Gradgrind.

Language

1 a) Working in pairs, create a list of questions about the text that you would like to have answered. Add these questions to a table like the one below.

b) Join with another pair to discuss your responses to the questions and record your ideas in the table.

Question	Response
What does it mean when he is described as 'a man of facts and calculations'?	*This gives you the impression that Mr Gradgrind believes that everything can be exactly quantified and he has time only for academic acheivements.*
What is a pitcher? Why are the pupils called 'little pitchers'?	

2 Now look again at the following part of the text:

> 'Girl number twenty,' said Mr. Gradgrind, squarely pointing with his square forefinger, 'I don't know that girl. Who is that girl?'
>
> 'Sissy Jupe, sir,' explained number twenty, blushing, standing up, and curtseying.

a) What are the details here that show that the expected behaviour in this classroom is different from that in a classroom today?

b) Find two other details in the text which show that experiences in this class are different from your own and explain how they differ.

3 a) Scan the text for clues that show you that the story was written in the past, looking for examples of archaic vocabulary and the type of language and sentence structure used. Working with a partner, discuss the examples you find and record your comments in a table like the one below.

Examples	Comments on language
'With a rule and a pair of scales, and the multiplication table always in his pocket, sir, ready to weigh and measure any parcel of human nature, and tell you exactly what it comes to ...'	*This is a long and complicated sentence using lots of commas. Is 'a rule' is the same thing as a ruler? I think it must be because the writer goes on to say that Gradgrind is 'ready to measure' human nature with it.*

b) When you have completed your table, choose two examples and write a paragraph explaining how the language gives clues about when the text was written.

Looking at particular details in a text can help you explore the point of view the writer has about the experiences and values being shown.

For example, Dickens chooses the name Gradgrind for his teacher. A dictionary gives the following definitions for the word 'grind':

- To reduce to fine particles.
- To oppress, torment or crush.
- To rub harshly.

4 a) How does the word 'grind' link to the teaching methods Mr Gradgrind uses? Discuss your ideas with a partner.

b) Now look at the following details about Mr Gradgrind from the text. What do these quotations suggest about the type of teacher he is?

- 'A man of facts and calculations ... With a rule and a pair of scales, and the multiplication table always in his pocket'
- 'he seemed a kind of cannon loaded to the muzzle with facts, and prepared to blow them clean out of the regions of childhood at one discharge ...'

c) Do you get the impression that the author thinks this is a successful way of teaching? Explain your reasons, referring to the text.

Support

Try to develop your explanation by referring to details from the text and incorporating these into your answer. Look at how the following response does this:

'He seems to believe that everything can be measured and weighed precisely. The fact that he keeps "a rule and a pair of scales" in his pocket shows he is always ready to weigh and measure.'

At the time when this story was written, most schools taught a very limited timetable with a heavy emphasis on religion. The text opposite is from a letter written to a local newspaper in 1887. The writer is complaining that pupils ought to be taught something more useful.

5 Working in a small group, read the letter and then discuss the following questions:

a) How does the range of subjects mentioned in the letter compare with the subjects taught in your school?

b) How are the attitudes to what boys and girls should be taught different from today?

The worthy clergymen have got a bad habit of educating lads as if every one of them were to be brought up to the Ministry. The consequence is that the study of dead languages, Bible history and theological subjects gets more than a fair share of attention to the practical exclusion of the essentials of a commercial training. It is nice to know the 119th Psalm by heart but bread and cheese are positively indispensable. Our girls ought to be taught baking and boiling, sweeping and sewing, and otherwise trained to become useful servants and wives in place of merely ornamental nonentities. More practical teaching so the boys grow up into useful artisans and workmen of various kinds, instead of turning them all out in the same mould, and only fit to prop up street corners or wear stand up collars and tight trousers bought at somebody else's expense. Schoolmasters should remember that the average lad's business in life is to become a wage-earning machine. He must get money before even he can enjoy the privilege of going to church.

6 Write a response exploring what education was like in the Victorian era when these two texts were written. Think about the similarities and differences between the details included in the letter and those in the extract from *Hard Times*. You might also want to contrast this with attitudes about education now. A planning grid like the one below could help you organise your ideas.

Views about education	Main points	Sentence starters
Hard Times	• Strict teachers • Focus facts	• The curriculum in Hard Times seems to be based on ... • It seeme as if the author wants the reader to feel ...
Letter	• Limited range of subjects studied	• However, the newspaper letter is ... because ... • In the same way ...
Your own school	• Wide choice of subjects	• I think that the ... in my own school, however ...

Reinforce your skills

You are now going to use the skills and strategies you have just practised to explore the ideas, experiences and values in a story from a different culture.

The extract below is taken from the novel *The Kite Runner* by Khaled Hosseini, and tells of 12-year-old Amir's life in 1970s Afghanistan. Here, he is taking part in a kite-flying tournament in his local town.

1 Begin by discussing in a small group what you know about Afghanistan and its culture. Then read the extract.

I had never seen so many people on our street ... Kite fighters were huddling with their spool holders, making last-minute preparations ... Already rooftops were jammed with spectators reclining in lawn chairs, hot tea steaming from thermoses, and the music of Ahmad Zahir blaring from cassette players. The immensely popular Ahmad Zahir had revolutionised Afghan music and outraged the purists by adding electric guitars, drums and horns to the traditional tabla and harmonium ...

... I still hadn't made up my mind about God. But when a Koran ayat I had learned in my diniyat class rose to my lips, I muttered it. I took a deep breath, exhaled, and pulled on the string. Within a minute, my kite was rocketing to the sky. It made a sound like a paper bird flapping its wings ...

At least two dozen kites already hung in the sky, like paper sharks roaming for prey. Within an hour the number doubled, and red, blue, and yellow kites glided and spun in the sky ... Soon the cutting started and the first of the defeated kites whirled out of control. They fell from the sky like shooting stars with brilliant, rippling tails, showering the neighbourhoods below with prizes for the kite runners ...

I kept stealing glances at Baba sitting with Rahim Kahn on the roof, wondered what he was thinking. Was he cheering for me? Or did a part of him enjoy watching me fail? ... I snapped my gaze back to the sky. A red kite was closing in on me – I'd caught it just in time. I tangled a bit with it, ended up besting him when he became impatient and tried to cut me from below.

2 Working with a partner, try to work out exactly what is taking place here.

a) Are there any details that suggest similarities between Amir's life and your own?

b) Are there any details that suggest Amir's lifestyle is different from your own?

c) Think about the ideas you shared about your knowledge of Afghanistan and its culture. Did any details in this passage surprise you? Why?

3 a) Scan the text for clues that show you where the story is set. Working with a partner, discuss the examples you find and note these down in a table like the one you used for question 3 on page 125.

b) What words in particular give you an idea about where this story might be set? What do you think the words 'ayat' and 'diniyat' could mean from the context of what is taking place in that paragraph?

4 In this extract, the writer describes how people listened to music to entertain themselves as they waited for the kite fighting to begin.

a) How is Ahmad Zahir's music different from the traditional music of the country?

b) What could it mean when it says that his music 'outraged the purists'? What might this tell you about the beliefs of some people in this country at this time?

5 Working with a partner, pick out other details from the text and explore how each one helps you understand something about the life and beliefs of the people being described. Use a table like the one below to record your ideas.

Detail from text	What this shows us
'I had never seen so many people on our street'	*Kite fighting is an important activity – one that the whole community is interested in.*

6 Write a paragraph explaining what you have understood about the society this story is set in. Include details from the text to support your points.

Stretch

Do some research to find out more details about this novel and what life was like in Afghanistan at the time it was set. Think about how you can incorporate your findings into your response.

Language

Extend your skills

Reading texts from a very long time ago can be difficult because some of the words and sentence structures are different from the ones we use today.

In the 14th century, Geoffrey Chaucer wrote a series of poems about a group of people travelling from London to the shrine of Thomas Becket in Canterbury. These travellers were pilgrims who believed that visiting the shrine was their duty as Christians. To pass the time on their journey, each member of the group agreed to tell a story. Chaucer introduces each of the pilgrims in turn – in the text on the next page he describes the Miller.

Read Chaucer's description of the Miller and see how many words and phrases you can understand.

As you will see, this is English, but it is not the same as the language we speak today! Some words are the same; some lock look similar to modern words but may have different vowels or vowels in a different order. Other words are very different and no longer exist. Another main difference in this description is that sometimes the word order is different from what you might expect. Despite all these differences, it is possible to have a really good idea of what Chaucer was writing about.

1 Try rereading the passage aloud to see if this helps you to work out what is meant.

2 Working in a pair, list all the words that look similar to or remind you of modern English words. Record your ideas in a table like the one below.

Words	How the word differs from modern English
'short-sholdred'	

3 a) With your partner, read the text again and write some questions you would like to have answered about any words or phrases you still don't understand. Then join with another pair to exchange questions and explore possible answers and ideas.

b) Can you see a pattern in the way that some of the words have changed?

4 a) Use the details about the Miller's appearance, behaviour and character to write a short description of him using modern English.

b) Write an accompanying commentary explaining the language changes you have made in your description.

Ful byg he was of brawn, and eek of bones.
…
He was short-sholdred, brood, a thikke knarre;
Ther was no dore that he nolde heve of harre,
Or breke it at a rennyng with his heed.
His berd as any sowe or fox was reed,
And therto brood, as though it were a spade.
Upon the cop right of his nose he hade
A werte, and theron stood a toft of herys,
Reed as the brustles of a sowes erys;
His nosethirles blake were and wyde.
A swerd and bokeler bar he by his syde.
…
A baggepipe wel koude he blowe and sowne,
And therwithal he broghte us out of towne.

GLOSSARY

eek – also
thikke knarre – heavy-set man
nolde – could not
harre – hinges
cop – top
bokeler – small shield
bar – carried/wore
therwithal – with all that

Apply your learning

Use the skills you have developed through this unit to help you complete the following task.

The text opposite is taken from the novel *Paddy Clarke, Ha, Ha, Ha* by Roddy Doyle, which is written from the point of view of Paddy, a 10-year-old boy growing up in Ireland in the 1960s. Here, he is describing events at his school.

Task Working on your own, read the text, then answer the questions below.

1 Find three details from the passage which give you clues about where the story is set. For each detail, explain the clue it gives.

Clues about *where* the story takes place	Explanation
a)	
b)	
c)	

2 Now find three details from the passage which give you clues about when the story is set. For each detail, explain the clue it gives.

Clues about *when* the story takes place	Explanation
a)	
b)	
c)	

3 What does the narrator's of the story use of language suggest about his age and behaviour?

4 What can you tell from the passage about what life in this school is like? Write a paragraph explaining how the writer shows his experiences and exploring the similarities to and differences from your own experiences.

5 Compare this passage with the extract from *Hard Times* on page 124. What similarities and differences do they have? In your answer, you should comment on:

- the way the teachers act
- the way the pupils respond
- the view of education the writer gives
- the language used in both extracts.

All the desks smelt the same, in all the rooms. Sometimes the wood was lighter because the desk was near a window where the sun could get at it. They weren't the old-fashioned desks where the top was a lid on hinges that you lifted and there was a place for your books under it. The top was screwed down on our desks; there was a shelf under it for books and bags. There was a hollow for your pens and a hole for the ink well. You could roll your pen down the desk. We did it for a dare cos Henno hated the noise when he heard it. James O'Keefe drank the ink.

... When there was a knock at the door, or if it was a master coming in or Mister Finnucane, the headmaster, or Father Moloney, we had to stand up.

–Dia duit, (Hello/God be with you) we said ...

... Some Fridays we didn't have proper school after the little break; we went to the pictures instead, in the hall. We were warned on Thursdays to bring in threepence to get in, but Aidan and Liam forgot their threepences once and they still got in; they just had to wait until everyone else had gone in. We said that it was because Mister O'Connell didn't have sixpence to give them – I thought it up – but they brought in the money on Monday. Aidan cried when we kept saying it.

Henno was in charge of the projector. He thought he was great. He stood beside it like it was a Spitfire or something. The projector was on a table at the back of the hall, in the middle between the rows of seats. For a dare when the lights were turned off, we crawled out into the aisle and got up a bit and made shapes with our hands in the path of the light that the projector made ... That was the easy part. The hard part was getting back to your seat before they turned the lights back on. Everyone would try to stop you, to keep you trapped in the aisle. They'd kick you and stand on your hands when you were crawling under the seats. It was brilliant.

–Take out your English copies, said Henno.

We waited.

–Anois. (Now)

We took them out. All my copies were covered in wallpaper that our Auntie Muriel had left over when she was doing her bathroom and she gave my da about ten rolls of it.

Assess to Progress

How good are you now at identifying how texts might describe life, ideas, experiences and values that are different from your own, perhaps because they represent beliefs from a different country or because they have been written at some time in the past? Look back at the ratings you gave yourself on page 123. Now rate yourself again for each of the skills.

SKILLS FOR LIFE

Your school is going to bury a time capsule to be opened in 50 years' time. The idea is that it captures a moment in time for future generations to see. You have been given a newspaper article to read before you decide what you should include in your capsule. It describes a time capsule that was found recently.

Builders to rebury time capsule

A glass time capsule dating back 107 years has been found by builders working on a former Leicester church.

The capsule contains historical items including the *Leicester Post* and a London paper and details of the finance behind the building of the church … The historical papers show it was possible to rent a home in Fosse Road North for £30 a year. 'Some things never change' historian Cynthia Brown said. 'There is a letter complaining about young people hanging around the streets because they have got little else to do!' It also explains how the church moved home to make way for the Great Central Railway …

1 What items were buried in the capsule?

2 Explain how the items found in the capsule give information about the society of the time.

3 Working in a group, discuss what items you would include in a time capsule to give an idea of what life is like in the 21st century. Choose five items and write an email to the headteacher explaining your choices.

Reading
Assessing your Progress

TARGETS FOR PROGRESS

- Include appropriate quotations or references when commenting on texts.
- Compare how ideas and feelings are presented across texts.
- Explore the way whole texts are organised to support the writer's purpose.
- Make detailed comments on how the writer's choice of language contributes to the effect on the reader.
- Explain how the writer's viewpoint can affect meaning.

Working through this unit will give you the opportunity to show the progress you have made in your reading skills as you read and explore chapters from an autobiography.

Activate your learning

1 Food programmes are very popular on TV and there are lots of celebrity chefs on our screens. One TV cook is Nigel Slater. Use these questions to explore some information about him:

- Nigel Slater's autobiography is called *Toast – the story of a boy's hunger.* He has also written a recipe book called *Nigel Slater's Real Food*. What do you think these titles suggest about the sort of food he likes to eat and cook?
- Nigel Slater is a food writer, and describes himself as a cook rather than a chef. What do you think the difference is?

2 You are going to read some chapters from Nigel Slater's autobiography, which is about growing up in Wolverhampton in the 1960s. Why do you think people write autobiographies? What sort of things do you expect Nigel Slater's autobiography to include?

Build your skills

The way Nigel Slater describes food in his autobiography shows how important it is to him.

1 Look at the table, which lists dishes mentioned in his book. With a partner, talk about:

- which foods you already know about
- how you can work out what the others are by thinking about the language more closely
- how the writer makes some of the dishes vivid.

honeydew melon	wonderful, fat golden chips	slices of home-made ginger cake
little anchovy puffs fresh from the oven	salmon with dill sauce	chicken liver paté
fat olives the colour of a bruise	toasted teacakes	chicken baked with Pernod and cream
lamb with rosemary and apricots	veal paupiette ... the size of a Cornish pasty and with dark, sticky sauce flecked with matchsticks of tongue, parsley and gherkins	pommes dauphinoise – potatoes thinly sliced and baked in cream with the subtlest hint of garlic
lemon meringue	flapjacks	Welsh rarebit

In the chapter from *Toast* opposite, Nigel Slater narrates an episode when he was in his last year at catering college. He was probably about 20 years old and full of ideas for his future life as a chef. As you read, notice how the descriptions show his growing passion for food and his discovery of a dish called pommes dauphinoise.

2 Read the whole extract then look closely at the section from 'White wine came in tall glasses ...' to '... a thousand miles away from anything I had made at college'. Identify the words and phrases that refer to the senses: smell, touch, sight and taste.

Pommes Dauphinoise

When my father was alive our eating out had been confined to the Berni Inn in Hereford. We usually skipped starters (I think we once had the honeydew melon but Joan said it wasn't ripe) and went straight to steak, fat ones that came on an oval plate with grilled tomatoes, onion rings, fried mushrooms and wonderful, fat golden chips. We drank lemonade and lime except for Joan who had a Tio Pepe, and then had ice cream for afters. Sometimes my aunt would take me to the Gay Tray in Rackham's store in Birmingham where we would queue up with our gay trays and choose something hot from the counter, poached egg on toast for her, Welsh rarebit and chips for me. There had been the odd afternoon tea taken in seaside hotels (two-toasted-teacakes-and-a-pot-of-tea-for-two, please) and tea taken at garden centres (four-coffees-with-cream-and-four-slices-of-coffee-cake, if you would) and, once, a memorable tea eaten in Devon with slices of home-made ginger cake, scones, cream and little saucers of raspberry jam. But that was it really. Eating out was something other people did …

During his last year at catering college, Nigel meets Andy Parffrey. They become friends and Andy introduces Nigel to new foods and new restaurants, one of which is Thornbury Castle …

White wine came in tall glasses with long, thin stems, tiny beads of condensation frosting the outside; little anchovy puffs arrived fresh from the oven with a dish of fat olives the colour of a bruise. We sat on chairs at either side of the fireplace, admiring the tapestries, the jugs of lilies and the polished panelling. The handwritten menu offered familiar things: chicken liver paté and onion soup, but also things that were new to me: chicken baked with Pernod and cream, salmon with dill sauce, and lamb with rosemary and apricots. I chose chicken with tarragon sauce. Andy had the veal paupiette, which arrived the size of a Cornish pasty and with a dark, sticky sauce flecked with matchsticks of tongue, parsley and gherkins. The food was like that Joe Yates had talked of, food from another world.

Then something came along that was to change everything. It was the simplest food imaginable, yet so perfect, so comforting, soothing and fragrant. The dish contained only two ingredients. Potatoes, which were thinly sliced and baked in cream. There was the subtlest hint of garlic, barely present, as if it had floated in on a breeze. That pommes dauphinoise, or to give its correct title pommes à la dauphinoise, was quite simply the most wonderful thing I had ever tasted in my life, more wonderful than Mum's flapjacks, Joan's lemon meringue, and a thousand miles away from anything I had made at college.

3 The title of this chapter is 'Pommes Dauphinoise', the food Nigel Slater discovers at the restaurant. With a partner, suggest at least one reason why you think this discovery might have been so important to him.

Reinforce your learning

1 Now read the extracts below from the chapters 'Toast 1' and 'Christmas Cake'. These chapters are from earlier in the autobiography and tell us a great deal about Nigel's mother. Think about the connections between these extracts and the first extract you read.

Toast 1

My mother is scraping a piece of burned toast out of the kitchen window, a crease of annoyance across her forehead. This is not an occasional occurrence, a once-in-a-while hiccup in a busy mother's day. My mother burns the toast as surely as the sun rises each morning. In fact, I doubt if she has ever made a round of toast in her life that failed to fill the kitchen with plumes of throat-catching smoke. I am nine now and have never seen butter without black bits in it.

It is impossible not to love someone who makes toast for you. People's failings, even major ones such as when they make you wear short trousers to school, fall into insignificance as your teeth break through the rough, toasted crust and sink into the doughy cushion of white bread underneath. Once the warm, salty butter has hit your tongue, you are smitten. Putty in their hands.

Christmas Cake

Mum never was much of a cook. Meals arrived on the table as much by happy accident as by domestic science. She was a chops-and-peas sort of cook, occasionally going so far as to make a rice pudding, exasperated by the highs and lows of a temperamental cream-and-black Aga and a finicky little son. She found it all a bit of an ordeal, and wished she could have left the cooking, like the washing, ironing and dusting, to Mrs P., her 'woman what does'.

Once a year there were Christmas puddings and cakes to be made. They were made with neither love nor joy. They simply had to be done. 'I suppose I had better DO THE CAKE,' she would sigh. The food mixer – she was not the sort of woman to use her hands – was an ancient, heavy Kenwood that lived in a deep, secret hole in the kitchen work surface. My father had, in a rare moment of do-it-yourselfery, fitted a heavy industrial spring under the mixer so that when you lifted the lid to the cupboard the mixer slowly rose like a corpse from a coffin. All of which was slightly too much for my mother, my father's quaint Heath Robinson craftsmanship taking her by surprise every year, the huge mixer bouncing up like a jack-in-the-box and making her clap her hands to her chest. 'Oh heck!' she would gasp. It was the nearest my mother ever got to swearing …

However much she hated making the cake we both loved the sound of the raw cake mixture falling into the tin. 'Shhh, listen to the cake mixture,' she would say, and the two of us would listen to the slow plop of the dollops of fruit and butter and sugar falling into the paper-lined cake tin. The kitchen would be warmer than usual and my mother would have that I've-just-baked-a-cake glow. 'Oh, put the gram on, will you, dear? Put some carols on,' she would say as she put the cake in the top oven of the Aga. Carols or not, it always sank in the middle. The embarrassing hollow, sometimes as deep as your fist, having to be filled with marzipan.

2 Working with a partner, answer these questions for each chapter and record your ideas in a table like this:

	Pommes Dauphinoise	Toast 1	Christmas Cake
How old is the narrator?	About 20? He's at catering college.		
What do we know about his family?			
What is his interest in food and cooking?		He describes an early memory of his mother burning toast.	
How does he appeal to our senses?		His description of hot buttered toast shows that he was already interested in food.	
What do we notice about his sense of humour?	He mimics the person ordering tea at the seaside ('four-coffees-with-cream')		

3 Now read the rest of the 'Christmas Cake' chapter on the next page. Working with a partner, complete the comparison table by adding ideas from this section of the text.

Forget scented candles and freshly brewed coffee. Every home should smell of baking Christmas cake. That, and warm freshly ironed tea towels hanging on the rail in front of the Aga. It was a pity we had Auntie Fanny living with us. Her incontinence could take the edge off the smell of a chicken curry, let alone a baking cake. No matter how many mince pies were being made, or pine logs burning in the grate, or how many orange-and-clove pomanders my mother had made, there was always the faintest whiff of Auntie Fanny.

Warm sweet fruit, a cake in the oven, woodsmoke, warm ironing, hot retriever curled up by the Aga, mince pies, Mum's 4711. Every child's Christmas memories should smell like that. Mine did. It is a pity that there was always a passing breeze of ammonia.

Cake holds a family together. I really believed it did. My father was a different man when there was a cake in the house. Warm. The sort of man I wanted to hug rather than shy away from. If he had a plate of cake in his hand I knew it would be all right to climb up on to his lap. There was something about the way my mother put a cake on the table that make me feel that all was well. Safe. Secure. Unshakeable. Even when she got to the point where she carried her Ventolin inhaler in her left hand all the time. Unshakeable. Even when she and my father used to go for long walks, walking ahead of me and talking in hushed tones and he would come back with tears in his eyes.

When I was eight my mother's annual attempt at icing the family Christmas cake was handed over to me. 'I've had enough of this lark, dear, you're old enough now.' She had started to sit down a lot. I made only marginally less of a mess than she did, but at least I didn't cover the table, the floor, the dog with icing sugar. To be honest, it was a relief to get it out of her hands. I followed the Slater house style of snowy peaks brought up with the flat of a knife and a red ribbon. Even then I wasn't one to rock the boat. The idea behind the wave effect of her icing was simply to hide the fact that her attempt at covering the cake in marzipan resembled nothing more than an unmade bed. Folds and lumps, creases and tears. A few patches stuck on with a bit of apricot jam.

I knew I could probably have flat-iced a cake to perfection, but to have done so would have hurt her feelings. So waves it was. There was also a chipped Father Christmas, complete with a jagged lump of last year's marzipan round his feet, and the dusty bristle tree with its snowy tips of icing. I drew the line at the fluffy yellow Easter chick.

Baking a cake for your family to share, the stirring of cherries, currants, raisins, peel and brandy, brown sugar, butter, eggs and flour, for me the ultimate symbol of a mother's love for her husband and kids, was reduced to something that 'simply has to be done'. Like cleaning the loo or polishing the shoes. My mother knew nothing of putting glycerine in with the sugar to keep the icing soft, so her rock-hard cake was always the butt of jokes for the entire Christmas. My father once set about it with a hammer and chisel from the shed. So the sad, yellowing cake sat around until about the end of February, the dog giving it the occasional lick as he passed, until it was thrown, much to everyone's relief, on to the lawn for the birds.

Extend your learning

Now look at this question, which needs a longer answer.

What impression does Nigel Slater give of his parents in the first section of 'Christmas Cake'?

- impression: This asks you to infer
- Nigel Slater: Think about the viewpoint of the writer
- parents: The focus on both his mother and his father
- first section: From 'Mum was never ...' to 'filled with marzipan'

When you write a longer answer to explore a text, you need to make a **point**, support it with **evidence** from the text and develop an **explanation**.

1 You can develop this approach by linking several points together and then giving an explanation. Your evidence could be a direct quotation or a reference to details in the text. Look at this example and identify each **point**, **evidence** and **explanation**.

> *Nigel Slater states that his mother was not a very good cook – she was a 'chops-and-peas sort of cook'. His father tried to inspire her by making her a special gadget for her food mixer but she was obviously overwhelmed by it and was shocked every time it appeared. Nigel and his father seem keen for her to be more creative in the kitchen but she is clearly not particularly interested in cooking.*

2 Another point you could make about the impression Nigel Slater gives of his mother is that she didn't like cooking. Choose one or two quotations or references to the text to support this point. Make another point linked to this, supported by some evidence from the text. Then extend an explanation of this whole point that she didn't like cooking.

Progress task

Working on your own, you are now going to answer some more questions on extracts from Nigel Slater's autobiography. Remember that the chapter 'Pommes Dauphinoise' comes at the end of the book.

Start by rereading the extracts from 'Toast 1' and 'Christmas Cake'. Think about:

- the way the writer appeals to our senses
- the way the writer links food and cooking to memory and feelings
- the humour of his observations of people and events.

Question 1 is about 'Toast 1'.

1 What do we learn from these two paragraphs about the writer's mother and his feelings for her? Make two points and support each one with a short quotation. Try to use a PEE answer for each point.

Questions 2 and 3 are about *Christmas Cake*.

2 Reread the paragraph below, in which Nigel suggests for the first time that his mother is ill. Why does he use the words highlighted and what is the effect?

> Cake holds a family together. I really believed it did. My father was a different man when there was a cake in the house. Warm. The sort of man I wanted to hug rather than shy away from. If he had a plate of cake in his hand I knew it would be all right to climb up on to his lap. There was something about the way my mother put a cake on the table that make me feel that all was well. Safe. Secure. Unshakeable. Even when she got to the point where she carried her Ventolin inhaler in her left hand all the time. Unshakeable. Even when she and my father used to go for long walks, walking ahead of me and talking in hushed tones and he would come back with tears in his eyes.

3 Nigel brings his memories to life by appealing to our senses. An example has been given below.Choose another example from **either** sound **or** smell and complete the table.

Example	How this appeals to our senses
'her attempt at covering the cake in marzipan resembled nothing more than an unmade bed'	*This appeals to our sense of sight, by helping us to see the cake as a messy, bed. The marzipan on the top of the cake must have looked like crumpled sheets, not smooth and flat as it should have been.*
	This appeals to our sense of _________ by ...

Before you answer the remaining questions, read the extract on the next page. This extract, focuses his attention on Nigel's father.

Question 4 is about 'Christmas Cake' and 'Smoked Haddock'.

4 From your reading of these two chapters, what might you **infer** about when and how the writer's mother died? Write a paragraph to explain how you know this.

Questions 5 and 6 are about 'Smoked Haddock', in which Nigel cooks supper for his father.

5 Explain how the writer's choice of words shows how Nigel and his father are feeling. One example has been done to help you.

Smoked Haddock

I may have rolled the pastry for a mince pie or fingered the butter, flour and sugar crust for a crumble, but at nine years old I had yet to cook an entire meal. My cooking had been confined to things I could do unsupervised, safe things. So protective had my mother been of her son's precious fingers I had yet to turn an oven on or light the gas ...

Since my mother had gone, my father's evening meals had been an almost steady stream of toasted cheese and Cadbury's MiniRolls. He had his pipe, of course, but I wasn't sure if that constituted a meal or not. He would come in, weary and smelling of oil, and then fiddle around making my tea. Every meal was seasoned with guilt. His. Mine. 'You might at least do the plates.' He said it just once. From then on I washed up after every meal, standing on a stool to reach into the deep steel sink.

I was never sure if he expected me to make my own tea as well. There was nothing said. Just his disappointment hanging in the air like a deflated Yorkshire pudding. His favourite meal – tripe and onions – was a recipe known only to him. His way with the venous and quivering sheets of blubber was a mystery I had no intention of unravelling. Smoked haddock, his runner-up, held no such trepidation. It looked as easy as making a cup of tea.

If a boy saves his pocket money up for three days he can buy enough smoked haddock to feed a tired and hungry man. My savings weren't quite enough, I was a few pennies short, but the man in Mac Fisheries gave it to me anyway. 'It goes under the grill, doesn't it?' He came round to the front of the counter and put his arm around my shoulders. He told me to warm the grill first, to rub some butter on the fish and cook it for about ten minutes. Then he warned me not to get fancy with it. He led me out of the shop, still with his arm around me. 'He'll enjoy that, your dad.' ...

A fillet of smoked haddock takes about five minutes to cook under a domestic grill. You rub it with butter, shake over some black pepper, but no salt, and let the flames do the rest.

The haddock lies saffron yellow under the grill. The butter glistens on the fat flakes of fish. All is plump, sweet and juicy. It never looked like this when Mum cooked it.

Where is he? He is always here by six o'clock. It's now ten past. I cut two slices of bread and butter them. I have never known him eat more. Twenty past, half past. Where is he? The haddock is starting to curl up at the edges. The butter has set to a grainy slime, the fish is now dull with a milky residue that has trickled down and into the grillpan.

The fish is turning the colour of a pair of old stockings, the edges have buckled like a dead frog in the sun. My father's beloved smoked haddock is stone cold.

I hear the purr of my father's new Humber in the driveway. His fish looks more like roadkill than supper. Perhaps I should just chuck it in the bin so he won't know. Then he wouldn't feel bad about being late. But the pong hanging in the kitchen gives me away. Damn Auntie Fanny, if she hadn't just died I could blame her.

My father comes in, his face a bit red, his hair newly cut. Aftershave. His piece of fish is now on the table, sandwiched between two glass plates. 'Where have you been? It's ruined.'

'No it's not, it's just how I like it.'

As he sits down and starts to eat I leave the room. It was supposed to be such a treat. Why be late tonight of all nights? He hasn't had smoked haddock for tea since Mummy died. Suddenly, the tears come from nowhere, they just well up. A great hot wave. Later, I walk into the kitchen to see if he has finished. He is sitting with his head in his hands. He's crying.

GLOSSARY

saffron yellow – saffron is a spice with a golden yellow colour.

Example	How the language shows how Nigel and his father are feeling
'Every meal was seasoned with guilt'	The use of the word 'guilt' instead of salt and pepper makes us feel that they both felt uncomfortable at every meal. Sorrow and regret was mixed in with every meal.
'Just his disappointment hanging in the air like a deflated Yorkshire pudding' 'His fish looks more like roadkill than supper'	

6 Read the last part of the chapter again, from 'The haddock lies saffron yellow under the grill' to the end. In your own words, explain why you think Nigel Slater chose to end the chapter in this way. How does he want the reader to feel?

Question 7 is about all four texts.

7 These four chapters come from a much longer autobiography. What do you notice about the way the chapters are arranged in the book? You should write about: the chapter titles; the order of the chapters; how the rest of the book might be organised.

Assess to Progress

1 Think about the different reading skills you have used in this unit. Which questions did you feel most confident answering? Which questions did you feel less confident answering?

2 Rate yourself for the following skills by placing yourself on the scale below.

1 2 3 4 5 6 7

I find this difficult. — I'm getting there. — I'm good at this.

- Comparing how ideas and feelings are presented across texts.
- Explaining hoe the writer's viewpoint can affect meaning.

3 What have you learnt throughout the reading units? Discuss your ideas with a partner.

Progress in ... Writing

Progress in ... Generating ideas, planning and drafting

LEARNING OBJECTIVES

- Plan different types of writing and develop your ideas using different forms and conventions to contribute to the impact and effectiveness of your work.
- Link your ideas and planning choices to your task, purpose and audience to increase the effectiveness and individuality of your writing.
- Establish and sustain an individual writing voice and viewpoint by selecting appropriately from the techniques and devices used by other writers.

Activate your learning

A student has gone missing on the way home from school and the police are trying to piece together what has happened by studying a variety of documents.

1 Look at the extracts opposite and the list below of features included in each text type. Copy and complete the table.

Document	Features of the text type
A Police notes from an interview with a friend, attached to the full incident report	
B The student's diary for the last few days	
C A text message arranging a meeting with friends after school	
D A letter from the headteacher to the student's parents asking them to make an appointment urgently	
E A magazine article about eating disorders	

Features of text type

- Text-speak and abbreviations
- Present tense; non-chronological order; focus on groups of things; impersonal, third person; connectives stress sequence, cause and effect, comparison
- Mixture of past and present tense (for impact); chronological order; doing/action clauses; formal tone
- Informal tone; incomplete sentences
- Formal, polite tone; set layout; modal verbs

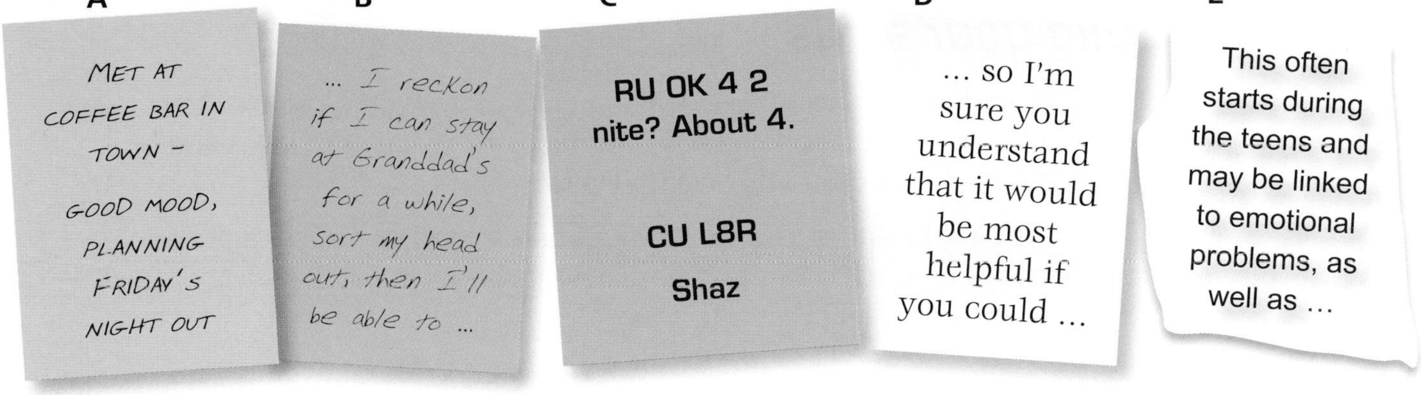

2 Work with a partner to compare your completed tables. Did you disagree on the features of any text types? Discuss which of these types of text you have had experience of writing and the features you used.

Assess to Progress

How good do you think you are at planning and developing different types of writing? Can you link your ideas and plans clearly to the task, purpose and audience and create an appropriate voice and viewpoint in your writing? Rate yourself for each of the following skills by deciding where you would place yourself on the scale below.

1 2 3 4 5 6 7

I find this difficult. — I'm getting there. — I'm good at this.

- I can plan my writing and develop my ideas, using different forms and conventions appropriately.

  Self-check: Can you plan and write a variety of texts (e.g. letters, reports, instructions) and choose the right style and conventions?

- I can make planning choices that are appropriate to what I have to write.

  Self-check: Can you choose from planning devices (e.g. mind maps, spider diagrams, bullet points, timelines) when they are appropriate to your writing?

- I can find and maintain a writing voice that suits the task.

  Self-check: Can you adapt the style and sound of your writing depending on what the task is and who the reader will be?

Build your skills

When you are reporting on other people's points of view on a complex topic, you need to use the appropriate text conventions to shape your ideas and write about them in a clear and balanced way.

As part of a healthy eating campaign, your science teacher has set a project in which pupils research and report back developments in food production that are both healthy and cost-effective.

You have been asked to read the following information about hydroponics (growing plants using liquid mineral foods instead of soil) and write a report giving an overview of the arguments for and against its large-scale use, as well as your own point of view.

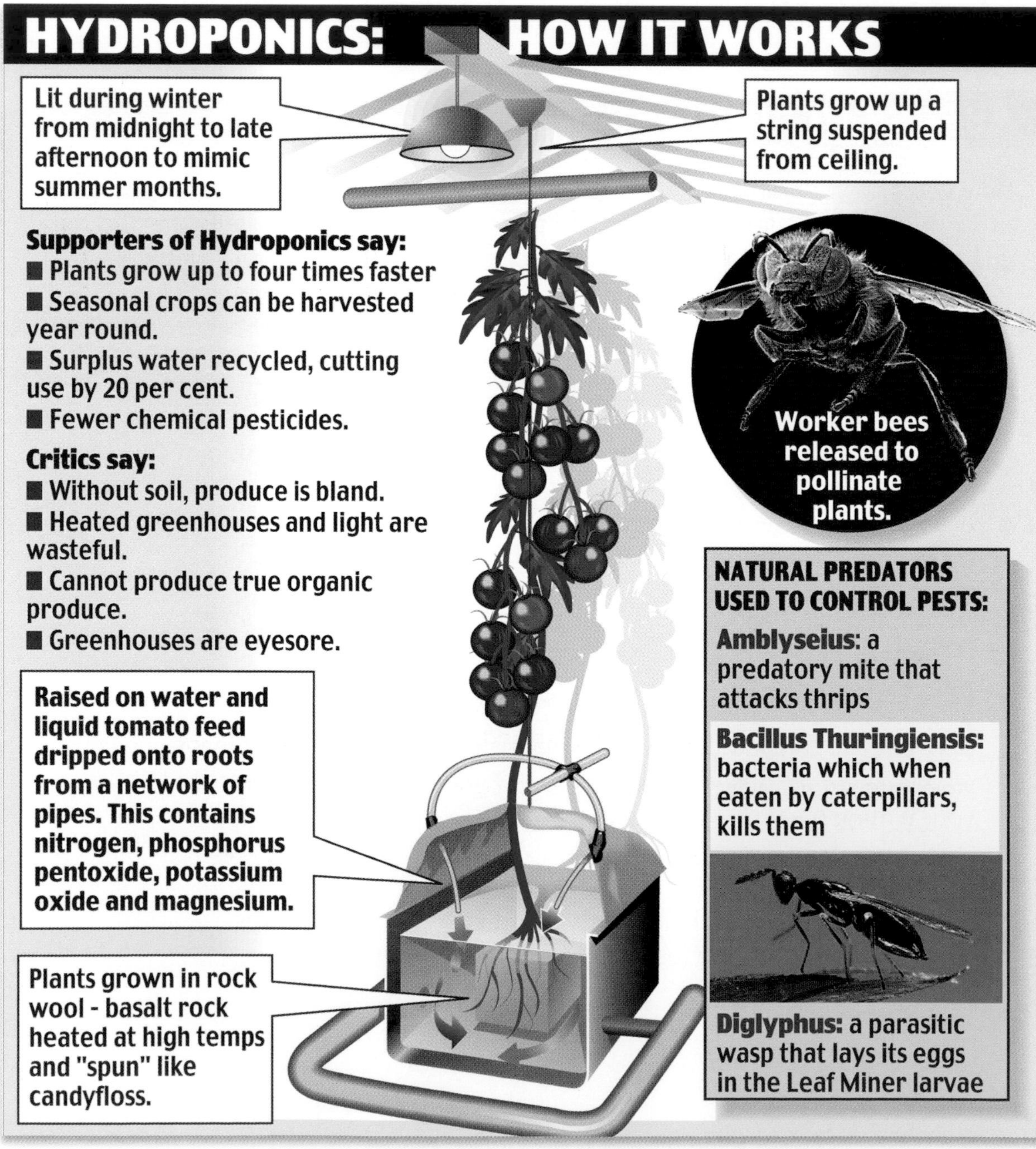

Step 1 Choose a planning format

1 Work in pairs. Read the information carefully to make sure you understand what hydroponics is and what people think about it.

2 Decide how you will plan your report, remembering that you need to give a balanced view of all the issues and opinions. You will need to plan the sequence in which you will present the information as well as shaping your ideas in more detail.

a) Discuss which of the following would be most appropriate to help you plan the sequence of your writing: mind maps, spider diagrams, flow charts, bullet points, timelines or headings.

b) Now discuss and choose the format that will best help you organise your ideas and notes: diagrams, sketches, columns or grids.

Millie has decided to use a flow chart to plan the sequence of her writing.

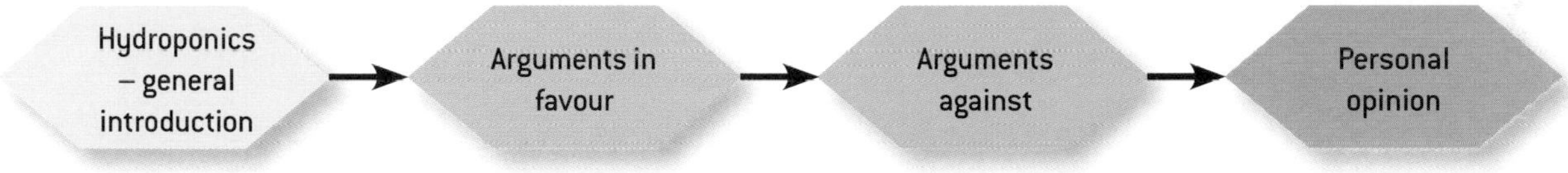

She then uses bullet points in a grid to help her organise her ideas.

Hydroponics – general introduction	Arguments in favour	Arguments against	Personal opinion
• Method of growing plants using liquid foods instead of soil	• Plants grow faster	• Greenhouses are eyesores	• I think that hydrophonics could benefit ...

3 Using the planning format you have decided is the most appropriate, start assembling and shaping your own ideas prior to writing your report. Think about:

- how you could begin and end each paragraph so that you link ideas in a way that will help your reader understand the issues
- where you could give examples to support the points you include, e.g. 'Hydroponics isn't as new an idea as we might think, as similar techniques were used to create the ancient Hanging Gardens of Babylon'
- where you could make comparisons, use statistics, quote expert opinions or include other helpful details.

Language

Step 2 Adapt text conventions to suit audience and purpose

Before you begin to draft your report think about other examples of this type of writing you have read, what techniques and features they include and how you can use these in your own writing.

1 Working with a partner, read through the list of text conventions below and discuss and decide which ones you would use in your writing to help you to create an effective report.

Conventions

- Headings and sub-headings to sort information clearly
- Tables, diagrams, illustrations to add information and break up the text
- Presentational devices (e.g. different fonts/sizes, bullet points, boxes) to guide your reader through the text
- A general statement at the start (e.g. 'Hydroponics is a method of growing plants ...'), followed by more specific information in sections (e.g. 'Plant food', 'Support', 'Protection')
- Clear, factual style which does not include the writer's opinions or feelings
- Use of the third person (i.e. 'he', 'she', 'it', 'they')
- Use of present tense (e.g. 'Surplus water is recycled ...'; 'Plants are grown ...')
- Use of both passive and active voice to avoid repetition (e.g. 'They grow up a string ...'; 'a string is suspended from ...')
- Short sentences for clarity and conciseness
- Connectives to emphasise quantity, cause and effect, comparison or contrast
- Technical and specialist vocabulary (e.g. 'pesticides', 'phosphorus', 'predators').

Millie has started to draft the opening of her report and is trying to use some of these conventions in her writing.

General statement at the start.

Hydroponics is a method of growing plants using liquid mineral foods instead of soil. Plants are grown all year round in greenhouses which are artificially lit through the winter to copy the pattern of summer sunlight.

Use of present tense 'plants are grown'.

Clear, factual style.

2 Now draft the opening of your report. Annotate your writing to highlight the conventions and techniques you are using. Swap your writing with a partner and give constructive feedback on their opening.

Step 3 Maintain a consistent style and viewpoint

Using language that fits the task means not only choosing an appropriate style but making sure it stays the same throughout your writing. Millie has written the first draft of her report but her teacher says it needs to sound more impersonal and knowledgeable and that she needs to sustain this style consistently. She advised Millie to think about:

- the words and expressions she chooses
- the way her sentences are constructed
- the way each paragraph will develop to emphasise a key idea
- whether these choices stay the same throughout the report.

1 Working with a partner, look at this section from Millie's report. In the light of her teacher's advice, discuss how appropriate her choices are.

> *Pesticides won't be used and instead the growers will be using natural methods to control pests. They're going to use bacteria that kill caterpillars, but I think that sounds really gross.*

2 Redraft Millie's paragraph about controlling pests. Try to follow the teacher's advice to create a more impersonal style.

3 Now complete your own draft report. Remember to create an appropriate voice and viewpoint and use the conventions and techniques you have explored to help you achieve an effective and balanced report.

Support

__Firstly__, plants grow up to four times faster with the use of hydroponics and __in addition__ … __Therefore__ …

Here the words 'Firstly' and 'in addition' indicate that a reason is about to be given, and the word 'Therefore' flags up that a conclusion will follow.

List as many reason indicators and conclusion indicators as you can and think about how you can use these in your own report.

Language

Reinforce your skills

You are now going to use the skill steps help you to create a distinctive character and voice in a piece of fiction writing.

The extract below is from the science fiction novel *The Day of the Triffids* by John Wyndham. After a meteor shower, genetically modified plants called triffids have become man-eaters, with the ability to uproot themselves and move around, hunting their prey with deadly, whip-like poisonous stings. Here, Bill Masen and his friend Josella are trying to escape from the triffids.

As we turned the corner Josella gave a cry, and ran forward. A figure was lying on the gravel, chest downwards, but with the head turned to show one side of its face. The first glance at it showed me the bright red streak across the cheek.

'Stop!' I shouted at her.

There was enough alarm in my voice to check her.

I had spotted the triffid now. It was lurking amongst the bushes, well within striking range of the sprawled figure.

'Back! Quick!' I said.

Still looking at the man on the ground, she hesitated.

'But I must –' she began, turning towards me. Then she stopped. Her eyes widened, and she screamed. I whipped round to find a triffid towering only a few feet behind me.

In one automatic movement I had my hands over my eyes. I heard the sting whistle as it lashed out at me – but there was no knockout, no agonised burning even. One's mind can move like lightning at such a moment: nevertheless, it was more instinct than reason which sent me leaping at it before it had time to strike again. I collided with it, overturning it, and even as I went down with it my hands were on the upper part of its stem, trying to pull off the cup and the sting. Triffid stems do not snap – but they can be mangled. This one was mangled thoroughly before I stood up.

Josella was standing in the same spot, transfixed.

'Come here,' I told her. 'There's another in the bushes behind you.'

1 This extract has been written from Bill's point of view using the first person voice. Working with a partner, reread the passage and discuss the techniques the writer uses to create Bill's character. Think about:

- the way the dialogue and action gives an impression of his character
- how the writer shares Bill's thoughts (inner reflection) and comments with the reader.

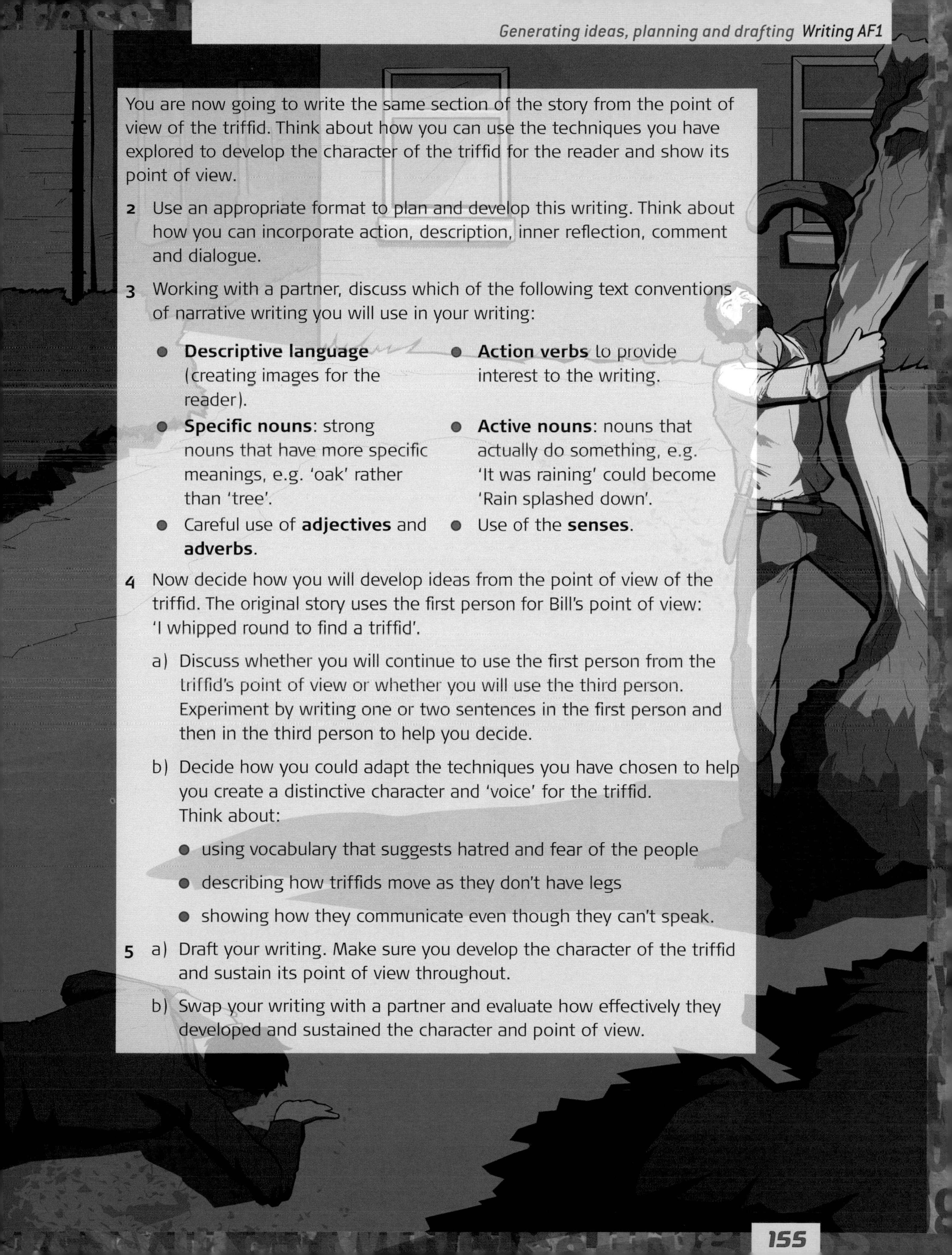

You are now going to write the same section of the story from the point of view of the triffid. Think about how you can use the techniques you have explored to develop the character of the triffid for the reader and show its point of view.

2 Use an appropriate format to plan and develop this writing. Think about how you can incorporate action, description, inner reflection, comment and dialogue.

3 Working with a partner, discuss which of the following text conventions of narrative writing you will use in your writing:

- **Descriptive language** (creating images for the reader).
- **Specific nouns**: strong nouns that have more specific meanings, e.g. 'oak' rather than 'tree'.
- Careful use of **adjectives** and **adverbs**.
- **Action verbs** to provide interest to the writing.
- **Active nouns**: nouns that actually do something, e.g. 'It was raining' could become 'Rain splashed down'.
- Use of the **senses**.

4 Now decide how you will develop ideas from the point of view of the triffid. The original story uses the first person for Bill's point of view: 'I whipped round to find a triffid'.

a) Discuss whether you will continue to use the first person from the triffid's point of view or whether you will use the third person. Experiment by writing one or two sentences in the first person and then in the third person to help you decide.

b) Decide how you could adapt the techniques you have chosen to help you create a distinctive character and 'voice' for the triffid. Think about:

- using vocabulary that suggests hatred and fear of the people
- describing how triffids move as they don't have legs
- showing how they communicate even though they can't speak.

5 a) Draft your writing. Make sure you develop the character of the triffid and sustain its point of view throughout.

b) Swap your writing with a partner and evaluate how effectively they developed and sustained the character and point of view.

Extend your skills

In autobiography it is important to develop your own individual writing voice to help the reader understand your character and viewpoint. The extracts below are the openings to four different autobiographies: *Long Walk to Freedom* by Nelson Mandela, a former president of South Africa; *Anything Goes* by John Barrowman, an actor and performer; *Being Jordan* by Katie Price a model and TV personality; *The Autobiography of Martin Luther King, Jnr* by the civil rights campaigner.

1 Read each extract and discuss in pairs who wrote which opening.

A
The scene opens with a high shot of Covent Garden. Tourists are clustered around a street performer who has a sword balanced on his forehead and tea plates spinning on a tray in each hand. The weather is unseasonably warm for June, so a few of the foreign tourists wandering in the crowded, cobbled square are carrying colourful umbrellas for shade …

Enter our leading man stage left.

That would be me.

B
I was born in the late twenties on the verge of the Great Depression, which was to spread its disastrous arms into every corner of this nation for over a decade. I was much too young to remember the beginning of this depression, but I do recall, when I was about 5 years of age, how I questioned my parents about the numerous people standing in breadlines. I can see the effects of this early childhood experience on my present anticapitalistic feelings.

C
My family are the most important people in my life. I love them all to bits. Through the bad times and the good times they have always been there for me, especially my mum. It is something the press has managed to twist over the years. The way some journalists have described my background, you would think I had the most miserable and unstable childhood, which couldn't be further from the truth.

D
Apart from life, a strong constitution and an abiding connection to the Thembu royal house, the only thing my father bestowed upon me at birth was a name, Rolihlahla. In Xhosa Rolihlahla literally means 'pulling the branch of a tree', but its colloquial meaning more accurately would be 'troublemaker' … In later years friends and relatives would ascribe to my birth name the many storms I have both caused and weathered.

2 Discuss each extract with your partner picking out features that create the writer's individual 'voice'. Think about the register (how formal the writing is), tone (is it light-hearted, playful, solemn?), content (what is being described) and the language used.

3 Write the opening paragraph of your own autobiography. Decide which features you will use to develop your own individual voice.

Stretch

What kind of voice would you need to create if you were completing a job application form and describing your personality? Draft a letter of application adapting the techniques you have explored.

Apply your learning

Task Write the opening of a story where something unexpected happens with disastrous consequences. The story is aimed at readers who enjoy adventure series like *Doctor Who* or *Harry Potter*. You could use the following sentence as a jumping-off point for your writing:

> A minute before, the sun was glowing in the sky, the birds were singing, the world was at peace, but then all the lights seemed to go out …

Choose an appropriate planning format to help you generate, develop and organise your ideas. Then draft the opening of the story. Think about:

- the relevant conventions you need to draw on and adapt
- how you will link your ideas into a paragraph sequence
- using relevant techniques to create and sustain a convincing voice
- maintaining a first person or a third person viewpoint throughout.

Assess to Progress

How good do you think you are now at planning and developing different types of writing? Have you linked your ideas and plans clearly to the task, purpose and audience and created an appropriate voice and viewpoint in your writing? Look back at the ratings you gave yourself on page 149. Now rate yourself again for each of the skills.

Skills for Life

Your friend is interested in growing a Venus flytrap. You have carried out some research and found the following information:

- Simple needs
- Lots of water
- Grow naturally in wet environments
- Plenty of light
- Windowsill
- Originally grew in poor soil
- Developed flesh-eating habit to get necessary food.

Write an email to your friend explaining what they need to know to look after these plants properly. You could also give your own point of view and explain whether you think growing one is a good idea.

Progress in ... Writing to suit your reader and purpose

LEARNING OBJECTIVES

- Write fluently, sustaining your use of standard English appropriately for a wide range of audiences and purposes.
- Draw on the conventions of different types of writing to contribute to the effectiveness of the texts you create.
- Understand when and how to use a range of formal and informal styles of writing to enhance and emphasise meaning.
- Make judgements about the effectiveness of the writing techniques you use and their effect on the reader.

Activate your learning

1 Look at these six scenarios. Match each scenario to the form of writing you think you should use.

You lost your wallet at the sports centre and a man handed it in. You want to thank him.

Your tent was stolen at a rock festival. You want to warn other people about it for next year.

You are planning a surprise 25th wedding anniversary party for your mum and dad and you want to invite all their friends and relatives.

The screen on your new phone cracks days after the warranty runs out. You want to complain to the manufacturer.

You have really enjoyed taking a lead part in the school play. You want to thank your drama teacher for all the time spent on rehearsals and preparation.

You want to do work experience at a local bank. You have been advised to request the support of the managing director.

Write a letter	**Send a card**	**Write a formal invitation**
Send an email	**Make a speech**	**Post a message on a website**

2 Pick one of the scenarios and write the text. Select the appropriate conventions for this form of writing. Spend no longer than two minutes.

Language

3 Share your text with a partner.

a) Compare your choices of scenario and the decisions you made to construct your text.

b) Discuss the likely response to your text from your intended audience and any changes you think are needed.

Assess to Progress

How good do you think you are already at writing in formal and informal styles and choosing these appropriately according to the audience and purpose of your writing? Can you use and adapt techniques and conventions in your writing to elicit appropriate responses from readers? Rate yourself for each of the following skills by deciding where you would place yourself on the scale below.

1 2 3 4 5 6 7

I find this difficult. — I'm getting there. — I'm good at this.

- I can judge when it is appropriate to use standard English and know how to sustain the use of this effectively in my writing.

  Self-check: Do you know which scenarios would require the use of standard English?

- I am confident at using and adapting the conventions of different types of writing to help me create effective texts.

  Self-check: Do you select the appropriate conventions to help your writing?

- I can make decisions about specific techniques to use in my writing based on my awareness of how to generate different responses from my readers.

  Self-check: Can you explain your choice of techniques based on your reader's response?

- I can use a wide range of formal and informal styles to enhance and emphasise meaning in my writing.

  Self-check: Can you make the right decision about the level of formality to use in different types of writing and think about how the style can affect the meaning of you text?

Build your skills

Whatever type of text you are writing, it is important to make sure that you meet the needs of your audience and your purpose for writing. To help you to do this, you need to:

- identify the conventions used in this form of writing
- think about the needs and expectations of your readers
- decide on the level of formality you should use.

Read the text below, then follow the skill steps to explore how the writer has tried to meet the needs of the audience and the purpose of the text.

A DIY guide for the under 30s
Changing a plug fuse

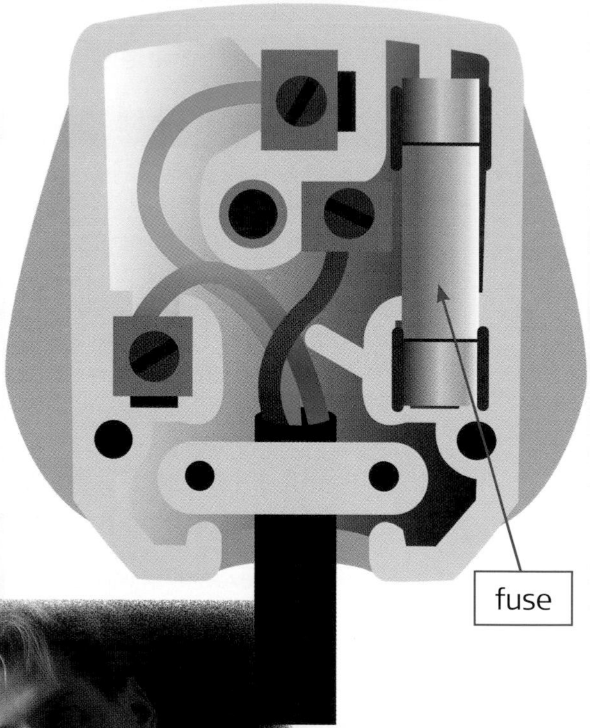

Most appliances now come with plugs. Occasionally, however, the fuse inside will go, at which point most young people will run out and buy a new toaster. But changing the fuse is a simple procedure: unscrew the big screw on the face of the plug and remove the back. The fuse is the little cylindrical thing pinched between two metal clamps. Prise it free with a screwdriver. It will be labelled 3A or 5A, or something else. Don't worry about what this means; just make sure the replacement fuse matches. Fuses are widely available, but you probably have an abundant supply of them sitting in the plugs of redundant appliances in your cupboards. Press the new fuse into clamps, screw the plug back together and plug it in. If the toaster still doesn't work, well, it could be a lot of things. Have some cereal.

Language

Step 1 Select conventions that suit your audience, purpose and text

1 Working with a partner, make an initial judgement on this text's purpose and audience. Think about:

- who might be informed by this text
- who you think would be entertained by this text
- how formal the language is
- how you would describe the tone.

2 Work in role, taking turns to act as the writer of the text and an interviewer. Interview the writer about the conventions and techniques used in the text and how these match the audience and purpose. Use the following questions to get you started:

- Why did you state the obvious so much in this article? e.g. 'most appliances now come with plugs', 'it could be a lot of things'
- Why did you use technical language mixed with very simple language? e.g. 'little cylindrical thing'
- Have you used complex sentences and a range of punctuation to sound formal or is there another reason? Is this part of the humorous approach?

3 Make a list of the features and conventions you have found in this text. Which ones did you expect to find in an informative text? Which ones made you think the purpose of the text was to amuse or entertain?

Support

Reread the text and look for the features of writing included at word, sentence and whole text level. Think about:

- what type of vocabulary is used
- what tense of verb is usually used
- what types of sentence and sentence structure are used
- whether the text is written in the first or third person
- how ideas are developed and linked.

Language

Step 2 Choose techniques to provoke a particular response

It is important to think about the effect the techniques you use will have on your intended reader.

1 With your partner, work in role as a reader who is under 30 and a reader who is over 30. Improvise their likely response to the article. Use the questions below to get you started:

To the under-30-year-old:

- Did you find it helpful to find out how to change a fuse in this way?
- Did you find the writer's opinion of young people fair?
- Were you amused at the very basic level of detail such as 'Don't worry about what this means'?

To the over-30-year-old:

- Did you find the presentation of young people funny?
- Did you think that the writer appreciated that you were more knowledgeable than young people are today?
- How old do you think the writer is?

2 Reread the text and pick out examples of specific techniques that might have evoked these responses. Working with a partner, discuss the examples you have found and your ideas about how different readers would respond to these.

Language

Step 3 Use the appropriate level of formality and standard English

In this text, the writer has chosen language similar to that used in other instructional texts. The writer uses standard English to ensure that the instructions are clear for a wide audience, e.g.

> But changing the fuse is a simple procedure: unscrew the big screw on the face of the plug and remove the back.

However, this text has also been written to entertain and make fun of the idea that young people don't know how to do DIY or change the fuse on a plug. When the writer includes details that we wouldn't usually expect to see in instructional writing, this adds to the humour, e.g.:

> If the toaster still doesn't work, well, it could be a lot of things. Have some cereal.

1 Look at the next section of the text where the writer explains how to bleed a radiator.

> *First you will need a radiator key, a small tool that _______ to a little square nut normally found on a valve at the top of the right _______ of a radiator. On some radiators it's at the back. The reason for bleeding is that sometimes radiators get _______ air in them, which stops them getting hot. _______ your radiator key to the nut in question and turn it _______ until you hear a satisfying hissing sound ...*

a) First choose the right vocabulary from the box below to fill the gaps. Make sure that your choices help to create a formal tone.

corresponds	**flank**	**side**	**excess**	**apply**	**fix**
anticlockwise	**round**	**matches**	**a bit of**	**loads of**	**whack**

b) Then write your own sentences to complete the instructions. Make sure you maintain the use of standard English and match the level of formality created.

Reinforce your skills

You are now going to write your own set of instructions for the over 30s.

1 Choose one of the ideas below:

- Using a social networking site, e.g. Once upon a time, young people had penpals. In the modern age, they have virtual friends ...
- Predictive texting, e.g. The modern world is all about speed; everyone wants things done yesterday ...
- Using an iPod, e.g. Imagine if you had a tiny gramophone that you could carry around in your pocket and listen to wherever you went ...

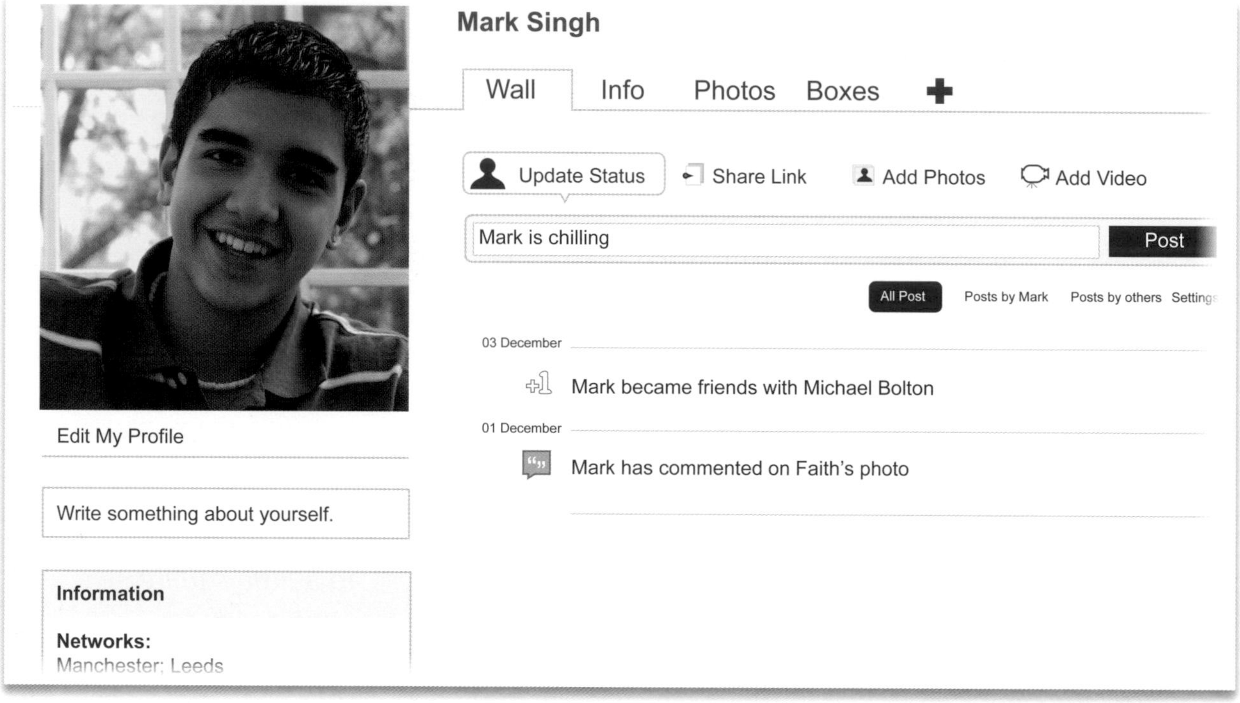

2 Choose an appropriate planning format to help you generate and organise ideas. Think about what your reader will need to know and how you will present this information in a humorous and entertaining way.

3 Now think about how you can use the features and conventions you have explored in your own writing and add these to your plan.

- Which **conventions** can you use to meet the needs of the audience and purpose?
- Are there any **techniques** that you think are suitable, bearing in mind the intended audience response?

4 Swap your plan with a partner. Compare the way you intend to draw on different techniques and conventions in your writing. Discuss how readers would respond to the techniques you plan to use.

Language

Support

Standard English means using grammar, spelling and vocabulary in a way that is accessible to most people. Try to avoid:

- incorrect grammar such as double negatives, which may cause confusion, e.g. *When you're not doing nothing else*
- slang or regional dialect words.

Remember, it is about making your writing understandable to the widest range of people – not formality. The sentences 'The man's tired' and 'The gentleman feels fatigued' are both standard English.

5 Draft your writing. Remember to think about the level of formality you want to achieve and use standard English appropriately.

6 Share your writing with your partner. Working together, make annotations to explore the way you have used different conventions and techniques and the effects these have. Check that you have maintained an appropriate level of formality and sustained your use of standard English.

Follow the example below to help you annotate your text.

> *Once upon a time, young people had penpals. In the modern age, they have virtual friends. These people are real, although some information you get about them might be pure fabrication. Don't worry, your friends won't be miniaturised and uploaded to the internet, a Facebook page just allows you to ...*

I have chosen 'fabrication' as it is more formal than 'made up' and it sets the right kind of formal tone.

I've added this more light-hearted comment using an imperative sentence to exaggerate the misunderstandings older people might have.

Language

Extend your skills

Being able to draw appropriately on the conventions of different types of writing can help you create unexpected but powerful effects for your readers. Skilful writers are able to craft their writing, using specific techniques to shape how a reader will respond to the text.

1 a) Working with a partner, make a list of the features you would expect to see in a piece of scientific writing.

b) Now make a list of the features you would expect to see in a piece of poetic or descriptive writing.

The text below is written by Rachel Carson, a marine scientist, and describes how the seashore is affected by different forces. Even though the writer is a scientist, the language she uses to explain the process creates a personal and poetic style.

The edge of the sea is a strange and beautiful place. All through the long history of the earth it has been an area of unrest where waves have broken heavily against the land, where the tides have pressed forward over the continents, receded, and then returned. For no two successive days is the shore line precisely the same. Not only do the tides advance and retreat in their eternal rhythms, but the level of the sea itself is never at rest. It rises or falls as the glaciers melt or grow, as the floor of the deep ocean basins shifts ... or as the Earth's crust ... warps up or down in adjustment to strain and tension. Today a little more land may belong to the sea, tomorrow a little less. Always the edge of the sea remains an elusive and indefinable boundary.

The shore has a dual nature, changing with the swing of the tides, belonging now to the land, now to the sea. On the ebb tide it knows the harsh extremes of the land world, being exposed to heat and cold, to wind, to rain and drying sun. On the flood tide it is a water world, returning briefly to the relative stability of the open sea.

GLOSSARY

ebb tide – outward tide
elusive – difficult to find
flood tide – inward tide

Language

2 a) Look back at the list of features you expected to see in a piece of scientific writing. Can you find any of these in this piece of writing?

b) How has the writer created a more personal and poetic style? What features has she used to achieve this? Discuss your ideas with a partner. Think about:

- the choice of vocabulary
- the sentence structures
- the use of imagery.

c) Pick out an example of a specific technique used in the text and explain how this helped you understand what the writer was describing.

3 Now look at the following description of an experiment demonstrates the process of refraction. Using the techniques you have just explored, write your own explanation of the process in a poetic way, bringing the idea to life for the reader.

1. Cut two narrow vertical slits 2 cm apart at one end of a shoe box.
2. Place a sheet of white paper in the bottom of the shoe box.
3. Place a jar full of water in the shoe box. Align the jar with the two slits.
4. Place a torch over the two slits so that the beam of light goes straight through to the jar of water.
5. Observe how the jar of water bends the light, causing the rays to meet.

Explanation: Light moves more slowly through water than through air. When the light goes through the water, it slows down and bends. As the light re-enters the air, the beam of light speeds up again. This process is called refraction.

4 Annotate your writing to explain the choices you made to elicit a specific response from the reader. Swap your writing with a partner and discuss the effectiveness of the techniques you have used.

Stretch

Write a description of an everyday event, such as asking a boy or a girl out on a date, in the style of a science experiment. How can you adapt the conventions and features of this type of writing to create an entertaining piece of writing for your readers?

Apply your learning

Task Read the text below, taken from a 1950s women's magazine, giving advice on how a wife should look after her husband. Imagine you were living at this time. You are going to write a formal letter to the magazine giving your opinion on the views expressed in the article and explaining what advice you think husbands and wives should be given. Work through the activities at the top of the opposite page.

The good wife's guide

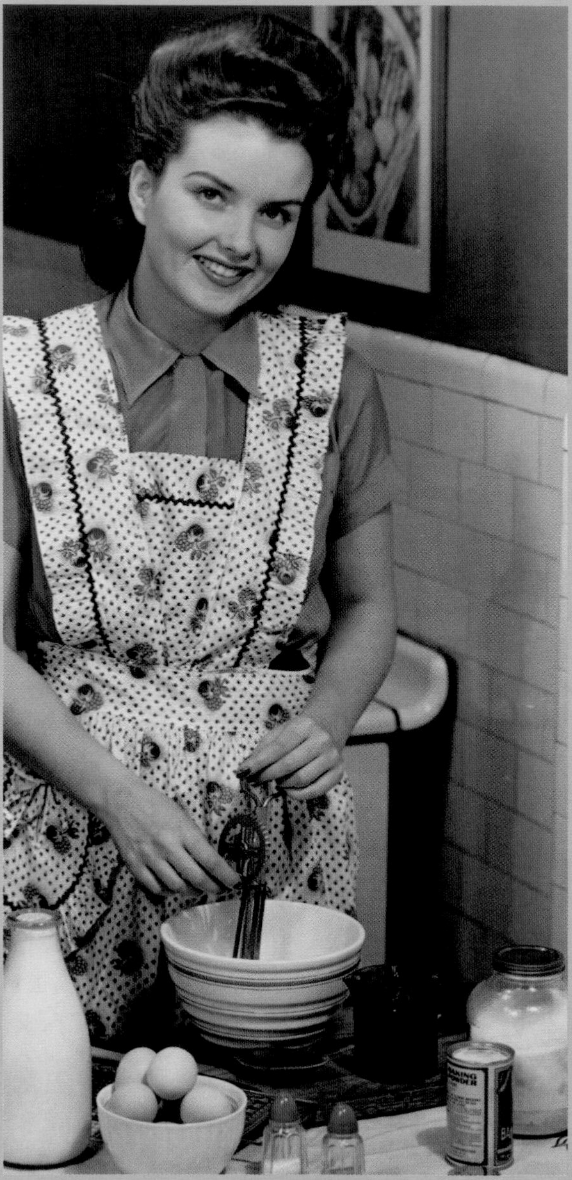

- Have dinner ready. Plan ahead, even the night before, to have a delicious meal ready, on time. This is a way of letting him know that you have been thinking about him and are concerned about his needs. Most men are hungry when they come home and the prospects of a good meal (especially his favourite dish) is part of the warm welcome needed.
- Prepare yourself. Take 15 minutes to rest so you'll be refreshed when he arrives. Touch up your make-up, put a ribbon in your hair and be fresh looking.
- Be a little more interesting for him. His boring day might need a lift and one of your duties is to provide it.
- Clear away the clutter. Make one last trip through the main part of the house just before your husband arrives.
- Gather up schoolbooks, toys, paper etc and then run a dustcloth over the tables.
- Over the cooler months of the year you should prepare and light a fire for him to unwind by. Your husband will feel he has reached a haven of rest and order, and it will give you a lift too. After all, caring for his comfort will provide you with immense personal satisfaction.
- Prepare the children. Take a few minutes to wash the children's hands and faces (if they are small), comb their hair and, if necessary, change their clothes. They are little treasures and he would like to see them playing the part. Minimise all noise. At the time of his arrival, eliminate all noise of the washer, dryer or vacuum. Try to encourage the children to be quiet.
- Be happy to see him.

1 Working in role with a partner, discuss how you as a reader respond to the ideas in the article. Note the pieces of advice you would like to respond to in your letter or points you would like to make.

2 Use an appropriate planning format to organise and shape your ideas. Think about what conventions you will need to use in a formal letter and how you could use different techniques to show your point of view and influence your reader's response.

3 Write your letter to the magazine. Remember to use standard English and sustain an appropriate level of formality.

Assess to Progress

How good do you think you are now at writing in formal and informal styles and choosing these appropriately according to the audience and purpose for your writing? Did you use and adapt techniques and conventions in your writing to elicit appropriate responses from readers? Look back at the ratings you gave yourself on page 159. Now rate yourself again for each of the skills.

Skills for Life

You and your friends have been given permission by your headteacher to organise a surprise party for a pupil who has been selected to play for the county cricket team. There are strict conditions though. You must:

- write a letter to the community centre warden asking for permission
- leave a note for the playgroup organiser to explain that you will need the hall to be cleared of toys
- send an email to the school technician to ensure that the sound and lighting equipment is set up and checked on the day of the event
- put a flier on the community notice board to reassure local residents that the music will stop at 10pm
- send an email to everyone in your year group advertise that the party, mentioning the date, time and venue.

1 Working in a group of five, select a text each to draft. Remember to think about which conventions and techniques you will use and how you will create the appropriate level of formality.

2 Discuss the texts as a group. Give constructive feedback to each writer and agree on any improvements that could be made to the text.

Writing AF3

Progress in ... Presenting texts in ways that create impact and engage the reader

LEARNING OBJECTIVES

- Consider the purpose and audience for your writing when structuring and sequencing your ideas.
- Control and shape the content of your writing to have an impact on the reader and achieve particular effects.
- Use a range of features to signal the overall direction of your writing.

Activate your learning

You have been asked to write a magazine article about 'data mining' – the way that companies and the government collect and store data about our lives, e.g. electoral registers, census information, passports.

1 a) Working with a partner, look at the following ideas about this issue. Discuss the best order to present these in the article. Decide which sections you want to start with, which you want to end with and which link well together.

b) Explain your order to another pair. Compare the choices you made and discuss any differences.

Explanation about how little privacy we have any more

Explanation about how data mining works

Explanation about how the government uses data to stop benefit fraud and terrorism

Pros and cons: comments from two people involved in data mining, one for and one against gathering data on people in this way

Explanation about how data mining started

Advice on how to protect your privacy so that you don't give away more than you'd like

Information about the different ways we are tracked throughout our day

Explanation about the benefits of logging and analysing all the data in our lives

A jargon-buster explaining some of the scientific language used in the article

2 What presentational features could you use in the article? Think about features that could help to explain ideas or emphasise particular points. Explain your choices to your partner.

3 The editor wants a punchy headline to grab readers' attention and give them an outline of the article. Which of the following headlines would you choose? Explain your choices to another pair.

Data mining

Big Brother is watching you

Who's watching you?

Are you sure you want everyone to know your dirty little secrets?

Assess to Progress

How good are you at structuring, organising and presenting texts in ways that create impact and engage the reader? Can you shape the structure of your writing to match its audience and purpose? Rate yourself for each of the following skills by deciding where you would place yourself on the scale below.

1	2	3	4	5	6	7
I find this difficult.			I'm getting there.			I'm good at this.

- I consider the purpose and audience when I sequence and organise my ideas and I use presentational features effectively.

  Self-check: Can you re-order the ideas in the task differently to persuade the reader rather than just informing? Which presentational features will use you to emphasise the information?

- I can control and shape the content of my writing to have an impact on the reader.

  Self-check: Do you think about how the reader will respond as you plan your writing. Can you create an impactful, attention-grabbing opening?

- I use a range of features to signal the overall direction of my writing.

  Self-check: Do you use connectives when writing to build the reader up to the conclusion? Do you sequence your paragraphs so that they build up to the final information?

Build your skills

A skilful writer can structure the ideas they choose to write about in a way that suits their purpose and sequence and shape their writing to have a particular impact on the reader. The opinion column opposite was written by the education journalist Hilary Wilce in response to the following news story:

Psychologists say lessons in happiness should be on the school curriculum

Read the article, then work through the skill steps below to explore how the writer has structured and organised the ideas in the text.

Step 1 Sequence ideas to suit the purpose, audience and task

1 a) Look at the headline. What do you think the 'greatest gift of all' is?

b) How does the headline suggest the writer's point of view? Will the writer be for or against introducing lessons in happiness?

2 Look at the ideas below that Josie has picked out from the article. Working with a partner, find these ideas in the text and reorder Josie's list to show how they are sequenced.

Lots of young people think the only way to be happy is to be famous.

It is more important to teach self-awareness to pupils as this can help them to be happier.

The people who criticise the idea of teaching happiness think the time would be better spent teaching the traditional subjects they used to study in school.

It would be helpful to teach children about happiness: what great thinkers have said about it and how pupils can evaluate what will make them happy.

It isn't possible to teach children how to be happy as teaching feelings doesn't fit into the school curriculum.

The pressures of the school curriculum mean that there isn't time for activities that give pupils time for self-reflection.

One primary school introduced daily meditation sessions to give pupils time for self-reflection.

3 Sum up what the writer's point of view is. How does the way the writer has sequenced her ideas help persuade the reader to agree with her point of view? Discuss your ideas with your partner.

The greatest gift of all

It was predictable, of course, that as soon as someone raised the idea that happiness could be taught in schools, along would come the usual army of Eeyores to tut-tut and bang the drum for a return to studying Greek grammar or the Punic Wars or whatever else they think will turn today's wishy-washy kids into fine, upstanding adults just like themselves.

But for once these dreary nay-sayers were right. It is as ridiculous to think you can teach happiness as it is to think you can teach fear or courage, or gloominess or amazement. Feelings are feelings, and don't readily lend themselves to being stuck on anyone's school syllabus.

However, something does need to be done to help our poor, deluded youngsters consider what happiness is all about, since so many now seem to believe that the only route towards it lies in becoming a footballer, pop star, or Big Brother celebrity - and also since, career advisers tell us, so many of them fervently seem to believe that that is what they will become.

There is plenty you can teach children about happiness. You can, for example, teach them what great minds have had to say about the subject.

Gandhi thought it was about serving others, while Freud thought it was all to do with love and work. You can teach them to consider what true happiness actually consists of - is it pleasure, contentment, or a sense of fulfilment?

And to think about how those things that they think will make them happy - another computer game; those new jeans; that week of excess in Ibiza - probably won't. Or not for very long.

Above all, you can get them to see how their minds are the most powerful tool they have in shaping their own happiness, and how we all create our own reality, every minute of every day, by the assumptions we start from, the thoughts we feed ourselves, and the conclusions we reach. In fact, many schools are already discovering that teaching self-awareness reaps happier children, better behaviour and higher achievements.

Children seem to enjoy getting to know themselves, and to sense instinctively its importance. One teacher at a small Kent primary school recently asked her class if they would like to try meditating. It would help them to settle their thoughts, she told them, and learn how to feel more peaceful inside.

All they would have to do was sit quietly for five minutes, either with their eyes closed, or else looking at the flame of a candle she would light for them. OK, they said, doubtfully. We don't mind giving it a go. Later in the term, however, she was forced to give up these daily sessions as the pressure of the national curriculum began to breathe more hotly down her neck.

But her pupils were distraught. They had come to love this small oasis of calm in their busy day, and the way it allowed them to tune out the world, and tune into themselves.

Their teacher had to promise them they would start again the following term, but then she somehow never got round to it. When she thinks about that broken promise now, she says, it makes her very unhappy.

Step 2 Shape language to achieve particular effects and reader reactions

Once you have chosen ideas that fit your purpose for writing, you need to shape the way you express and link these with the reader in mind.

Look back at the opening two paragraphs of the article on page 173 and then read the comments below that Josie has made about the way the writer has shaped and linked her ideas.

In the first paragraph, the writer starts by describing the people who are against the idea of teaching happiness as 'the usual army of Eeyores' who would prefer pupils to study obscure old-fashioned subjects such as 'Greek grammar or the Punic Wars'. This makes them sound like they are against progress and makes you think the writer will be for the idea of teaching happiness.

However in the following paragraph, the writer challenges our assumption by stating that 'for once these dreary nay-sayers were right' and it is 'ridiculous to think you can teach happiness'. This surprises the reader as the writer is now agreeing with the people who are against the idea, but the fact that she still describes them as 'dreary nay-sayers' suggests that she will have a different reason for her view.

1 How do these opening paragraphs engage the reader's interest? How does the writer try to influence the reader's opinion of the different points of view?

2 Reread the next paragraph where the writer gives her point of view about what people need to know about happiness and why? What effect does introducing this idea here have?

3 Now look at how the writer develops this idea in the following paragraphs. How does the writer use language to encourage the reader to agree with her point of view?

Look at the concluding paragraph of the article:

Their teacher had to promise them they would start again the following term, but then she somehow never got round to it. When she thinks about that broken promise now, she says, it makes her very unhappy.

4 What effect does ending the article with this idea have? How does it link back to the other ideas in the text?

Reinforce your skills

You are now going to use the skill steps you explored to help you plan, organise and shape your own piece of writing in response to the idea of introducing lessons in happiness into the school curriculum.

1 Work with a partner to discuss the information in the table below about happiness. Then put each piece of information in order according to how useful it would be when:

a) writing to persuade adults that we are happier than we have ever been – how could you use this information to support your ideas?

b) writing to argue that happiness is something we could never really 'possess' – how could you use the information to express a critical view on trying to achieve happiness?

c) writing an information text about happiness for a general audience.

Happiness is an emotion ranging from mild enjoyment through to intense joy.	We are too busy being bothered about being happy in the future to enjoy what we have now.
Scandinavian countries and Canada are the happiest. England was 41st out of 178 in the 'Satisfaction with Life' global survey.	Primary school children rate themselves as happier than secondary school pupils.
In the past, people didn't think of being 'happy' or not. The Victorians, the Edwardians, England at War – they didn't have time to think about whether they were happy or not. Happiness is a luxury.	Happiness is very selfish. It's more important to make others happy. If we all spend our time trying to make ourselves happy, it will make someone else somewhere else miserable.
We all have the potential to be more happy.	Happiness depends on both your genes and your lifestyle.
Scientists believe being happy is one factor in a long, healthy life.	Even though we have more now, we were happier 50 years ago. It's true that money doesn't buy you happiness.

You have been asked to write an article for a youth magazine responding to the idea of including lessons in happiness in schools.

2 Discuss your thoughts about this idea with a partner. What would be the benefits of lessons in happiness? What could be the arguments against?

3 Choose a planning format to record the ideas you want to include, e.g. a two-column table to note the arguments for and against.

4 a) How can you arrange your ideas so that they have a powerful effect on the reader? Try three or four different ways of organising your ideas, noting the effect different orders have, before deciding on the best one.

b) Comment your plan explaining why you have sequenced the ideas in this way. Look at the comments Fayaaz has added to his plan:

Idea	Explanation
What is life about if it isn't about being happy?	I put this question first to give the reader something to think about. I'm planning on answering it as I go through the article and then using the summary paragraph to explain the importance of lessons in happiness.
America has 'happiness' written into their laws.	I put this next because we like to compare ourselves with America. I want the reader to think, 'If they can be happy, why can't we?'
England is 41st in the Satisfaction with Life survey.	I'm going to give some of the countries that are happier than us, to make it seem like we're the only ones in the world who aren't happy and stress the importance of these lessons.

5 Now draft your writing. Think about how you can shape your ideas to:

- create an opening that engages the reader's attention
- links and develops ideas to achieve specific effects
- create an effective ending.

6 Design a layout for your article, choosing presentational features that will create impact and help to deliver the points you want to make to the reader. Then choose a headline for your finished article.

Support

Think about the presentational devices you can use to:

- make information clear, e.g. short paragraphs or sections
- signpost the reader to help them to follow your points, e.g. sub-headings
- draw attention to key points, e.g. bold text, font style and size
- present information visually, e.g. charts, graphs, tables.

Extend your skills

You can also use organisational features to signal the direction that your writing will take. In the following passage, the writer Norman Lewis recounts a bullfight in Spain.

Read the first paragraph, then look at the comments to explore how the writer signals what might happen in the text.

The writer uses the title to suggest that this is an extraordinary bull. He then focuses on the picadors and the other fighters.

There are details that make the reader think that this bull is different, signalling that the outcome may be unusual.

The Intelligent Bull

The first picador was carried off to the infirmary with concussion, a limp and broken figure on a board; while the others, refusing to play their part, clattered out of the ring – an almost unheard-of action – receiving, to my surprise, the public's full support. Most of the two or three thousand spectators were on their feet waving their handkerchiefs in the direction of the president's box and demanding the bull's withdrawal.

The writer also adds a detail about how unusual it is for the bullfighters to leave the ring.

The bull itself, monstrous, watchful, and terribly intact, had placed itself in front of the burladero, behind which Cardeno and his three peons had crowded, wearing the kind of expression that one might expect to see on the faces of men mounting the scaffold. Occasionally one of the peons would dart out and flap a forlorn cape, and the bull would chase him back, groping after him round the corner of the burladero with its horn, without violence, like a man scooping unhopefully with a blunt finger after a whelk withdrawn into the depths of its shell.

In the next day's newspaper report this bull was amazingly classified as 'tame', although it was the most aggressive animal I have ever seen in my life. When any human being appeared in the line of its vision it was on him like a famished tiger, but tameness was apparently the professional name for the un-bull-like quality of calculation which caused this bull not only to reject the cape in favour of the man but to attempt to cut off a man's flight by changing the direction of its charge. Physically this bull was in tremendous shape, and although half an hour had passed, the third episode of the fight, sometimes referred to in Spanish as 'the Luck of Death', had not yet begun.

GLOSSARY

picador – one of two horsemen who pierce the bull's neck and tire it in preparation for the matador

burladero – wooden barrier shielding the bullfighters from the bull

peons – the matador's helpers

1 Work with a partner to discuss whether you think the bull or the matador will win the fight. Pick out details from the first paragraph that signal this to the reader.

2 Think about a confrontation you can recount, e.g. a sporting event. Write the opening paragraph of your recount, adding details to signal the outcome to the reader.

3 With your partner pick out details from the second and third paragraph that suggest the outcome. What techniques does the writer use to signal this?

4 Write the next section of your recount. Use the techniques you have explored to suggest the outcome to the reader. Remember, you could deliberately mislead them or make it clear what the real outcome will be.

Stretch

Think about how you can control the flow of information you give to the reader. Can you include details early in your writing to tantalise the reader and grab their attention and then develop these later?

Apply your learning

Working on your own, use the skills you have developed through this unit to complete the following task.

Task Do you ever feel like you are missing out at school? That you should have a chance to learn Mandarin Chinese, or how sound studios work, or how to use a digital video camera? Should school just be preparing you for the world of work, or should it prepare you for the world of play as well? Now is your chance to have your say.

You have been asked to write an editorial in the school newspaper to explain what lessons you would like to see on the school curriculum. Think about your purpose and the audience who will read your editorial.

Before you begin, you will need to:

- choose an appropriate planning format to help you generate and organise your ideas
- think about how you can structure and sequence your text to make your explanation clear and persuade your reader that the subjects you are writing about should be added to the curriculum
- make sure your ideas are tightly linked and that you have thought about how to shape and structure these to achieve particular effects and signal the direction of your text
- decide how to create an engaging opening that grabs the reader's attention and then build to an effective ending
- add details about layout and presentation after you have decided on the overall structure of your writing.

When you have completed your plan, draft the text for the editorial. Remember to follow your plan and keep the structure of your text in mind as you write.

Assess to Progress

How good are you now at structuring, organising and presenting texts in ways that create impact and engage the reader? How well can you shape the structure of your writing to match its audience and purpose? Look back at the ratings you gave yourself on page 171. Now rate yourself again for each of the skills.

1	2	3	4	5	6	7
I find this difficult.			I'm getting there.			I'm good at this.

- I consider the purpose and audience when I sequence and organise my ideas and I use a range of presentational features effectively.
- I can control and shape the content of my writing to have an impact on the reader.
- I use a range of features to signal the overall direction of my writing.

SKILLS FOR LIFE

Your school is taking part in a volunteer reading scheme. It will involve pupils working with younger pupils either in your school or in a local primary school. As part of this, you have been asked to create a web page and leaflet to encourage other pupils in your school to take part.

Design and write the leaflet and web page, which will be displayed in form rooms and on your school website. It should include the following information:

- Volunteers will not need to be 'excellent' readers, just willing to work with others.
- Volunteers will need to give up about an hour a week of their time.
- This helps children develop a love for reading.
- Reading is one of the most important skills you will ever learn.
- The project aims to make reading enjoyable and fun.

Writing AF4

Progress in ... Shaping and crafting cohesive paragraphs and texts

LEARNING OBJECTIVES

- Plan texts so that the flow of ideas is logical and coherent.
- Plan and write well-organised paragraphs.
- Use different ways of linking paragraphs and sentences to 'glue' your text together.
- Craft your paragraphs to achieve effects and emphasis that suit your purpose.

Activate your learning

The Fastforward Trust gives money and support to young people so they can achieve their full potential. It is making £1000 available to the pupil who writes the most persuasive letter about how they would make best use of the money to improve their future.

In the past money has been awarded to teenagers wanting to:

- learn a new skill to improve their chances of getting a job in their chosen field
- buy equipment to take part in a trek or challenge that will stretch them
- research and run a social project such as setting up a cyber café.

1 Work with a partner. Discuss what you would most like to do with £1000 and why it would be a good use of the Trust's money: perhaps learn a new skill, prepare to start a small business in the future, learn or improve at a sport or hobby, invest in some equipment, or change something about where or how you live.

2 Plan and write your letter. Then swap your letter with a partner and discuss how well you think each letter would convince the Fastforward Trust to award the money.

Assess to Progress

How confident are you already at organising a text so that the ideas flow logically? Do you know how to signal the way paragraphs and sentences belong together and follow on from each other? Do you know how to shape the language in your paragraphs to support your purpose for writing? Rate yourself for each of the following skills by deciding where you would place yourself on the scale below.

1 2 3 4 5 6 7

I find this difficult. I'm getting there. I'm good at this.

- I can plan a text so that the flow of ideas is easily understood.

  Self-check: Look at the plan you just wrote. How easy is it for readers to understand how your ideas follow on from each other?

- I can use different ways of linking paragraphs and sentences to 'glue' my text together.

  Self-check: Look at the words and phrases you used to start each paragraph. How varied are they? Do you use words that show readers how one paragraph follows on from the next?

- I know how to shape my paragraphs to fit my audience and purpose for writing, using language to create particular effects or emphasis.

  Self-check: Look back at the paragraphs in your letter. How did you choose language to present your ideas in a persuasive way?

Build your skills

When you plan a non-fiction text you need to make it clear to readers how your ideas follow on from each other. Follow the skill steps below to explore how writers plan and structure their paragraphs.

Step 1 Decide on the purpose of your text

Knowing why you are writing should help you decide on the best way to organise your text. Working in a pair, read the text opposite and then complete the activities below.

1 Decide what the text's purpose is. Then make a flow chart showing the main point made in each paragraph.

2 Join with another pair and compare the flow charts you have made. Discuss how placing the points in this order helps the writer to achieve their purpose.

3 You are going to plan an argument to persuade the owners of the local sports centre to introduce lessons for young people about how to practise parkour safely. Make a list of main points you would keep from the text opposite and any points you would need to add to create an effective argument.

Step 2 Organise your points to achieve your purpose

Think of your text as a journey your readers' minds will take and decide what route is best for them to follow. Key parts of any non-fiction text are the introduction and the conclusion. These show where your readers start off from and where you want them to end up. The paragraphs between mark the route the readers' mind will travel.

1 What points were the start and the end of the readers' journey in the text opposite?

2 Draw a flow chart showing **how** the rest of the writer's points lead readers from the beginning to the end.

e.g. First he explains ...

3 Plan your text using a similar flow chart to show how you will make points that take your readers from the start point to the end point:

- **Start point:** the sports centre owner may not know what parkour is and already offers young people a range of other physical activities.
- **End point:** classes teaching how to practise parkour safely would attract more visitors and benefit young people.

WHAT IS PARKOUR?

Parkour is an art form of human movement, focusing on uninterrupted, efficient forward motion over, under, around and through obstacles (both man-made and natural) in one's environment. Such movement may come in the form of running, jumping, climbing and other more complex techniques.

The goal of practising *le parkour* is to be able to adapt one's movement to any given scenario so that any obstacle can be overcome with the human body's abilities.

According to founder David Belle, the 'spirit' of parkour is guided in part by the notions of 'escape' and 'reach', that is, the idea of using physical agility and quick thinking to get out of difficult situations, and to be able to go anywhere that one desires.

However, fluidity and beauty are also important considerations; for example, Sébastien Foucan, a *traceur* who trained with David Belle during the infancy of the art, speaks of being 'fluid like water', a frequently used metaphor for the smooth passage of barriers through the use of parkour.

Similarly, experienced traceur (*parkour practitioner*) Jerome Ben Aoues explains in the documentary *Jump London* that:

'The most important element is the harmony between you and the obstacle; the movement has to be elegant …If you manage to pass over the fence elegantly – that's beautiful, rather than saying, "I jumped the lot. What's the point in that?"'

To some people (particularly non-practitioners), parkour is an extreme sport, to others a discipline more comparable to martial arts. Some consider it a combination of the two, recognising similarities between parkour and the stunts and techniques of Hong Kong martial arts star Jackie Chan, whose fight and chase scenes take place in industrial or urban environments. Still others see it as an art form akin to dance: a way to encapsulate human movement in its most beautiful form. Parkour is often connected with the idea of freedom, in the form of the ability to overcome aspects of one's surroundings that tend to confine – for example, railings, staircases or walls.

The practice of parkour requires considerable physical and mental dedication, and many adherents describe it as 'a way of life'. Parkour is art in motion.

GLOSSARY

scenario – situation

encapsulate – to capture the essence of something

confine – act as a barrier

Step 3 Signal to readers the route they are following

Opening words and phrases can signal to a reader how a paragraph or sentence fits in with the one that they have just read and what direction they are heading in. To give helpful signposts you need to be aware of why you are writing your next paragraph or sentence. Then pick words and phrases to open your sentence that will show readers your intention.

1 Pick out any words or phrases the writer of the text on page 183 used to signal his route to readers. Then use the chart below to help you decide **what** he was signalling to readers about the point that was to follow.

2 Work with a partner and use this chart of useful linking words and phrases to create example sentences you could use in your argument to persuade the owners of the local sports centre to introduce Parkour classes.

How the points are linked	Useful words and phrases to achieve this
The next point follows on in time from the last point.	then, after that e.g. *After that young people will be fitter and healthier*.
The next point follows on in order of importance.	firstly, secondly, thirdly ... e.g. *Firstly, there are few or no expensive equipment costs so this would be a cost-effective way for the sports centre to attract new users*
This next point adds on to the last point.	also, furthermore, moreover, in addition, besides, in the same way, again, another, similarly.
This point opposes (goes against) the last point.	but, yet, however, nevertheless, still, though, although, whereas, in contrast, rather
This point shows what the effect of the last point is.	therefore, so, consequently, as a consequence, thus, as a result, hence, it follows that, because, since, for.
The last point was quite general and this point is a more specific idea about the same topic.	for example, for instance, after all, an illustration of, even, indeed, in fact, it is true, of course, specifically, to be specific, that is, to illustrate, truly
I made the last point but now I'm willing to consider the other side.	admittedly, I admit, true, I grant, of course, naturally, some believe, some people believe, it has been claimed that, once it was believed, there are those who would say

Reinforce your skills

Now practise the skills you have developed as you plan and write a web page for the sports centre to reassure people who are interested in taking up parkour that the classes will be safe and fun for them. Make sure you decide what route your readers will follow and which words and phrases you can use to signal the direction your paragraph is taking.

1 Complete these two sentences to sum up the start and end points of the journey your readers will take:

- As they start reading my text, readers will feel ...
- By the end of reading my text, readers will feel ...

2 Choose an appropriate planning format to help you to plan the text for the web page. Decide:

- what points you need to include in your web page help readers make the journey you want them to take
- the best order to present your paragraphs in
- how your points will be linked together.

Support

You could use a chart like this one to plan your web page.

Main points	Link words and phrases to glue text together
Introduction: Make the purpose of the page clear.	Opening sentence: *If you think parkour might be fun but are worried whether you'll end up in casualty after your first session then this page should set you right.*
Paragraph 1: Stress the importance of safety and explain how this is addressed.	***Admittedly,** to the untrained ...* ***That's why,** when you're starting out ...*

3 Working in a group of four, read the paragraphs A, B, C and D on the next page. Decide:

- which ones make a point that you would want to put in your web page
- how you can redraft these paragraphs using new or different link words so that they suit your purpose better.

A It may look easy, but to be good at parkour takes dedication, discipline and practice. Traceurs (those who practise parkour) have worked hard for a number of years to perfect their fitness and technique. But this dedication never stops, parkour is a constant work in progress. A great place to start is to watch a master in action.

B To the untrained, parkour can be dangerous. When you're starting out, it is important to have someone to train with, preferably someone who is very experienced. Most importantly NEVER BE DARED TO GO TOO FAR. Experienced traceurs have no time for newbies who just want to show off to their mates. If you're not ready to attempt a move, an experienced traceur will tell you. If you don't listen, you won't be invited to train with him, again.

C Parkour is NOT about death-defying stunts or rooftop jumps. It is about freedom of movement. Don't be misled by film and TV. Almost all stunts are performed under specific safety measures.

D The personal benefits you can enjoy are boundless. Apart from getting fit and healthy, the friendships formed can last a lifetime. Parkour is about camaraderie and even if there is no one in your immediate area to train with, you will find hundreds of parkour communities online, all with members willing to offer help and guidance.

4 a) Show where you would use any of the redrafted paragraphs in your web page by adding these to your plan.

b) What link words or phrases can you add to make each paragraph suit your persuasive purpose better? e.g. *Words and phrases such as 'Although', 'In addition' or 'In contrast' which you can use to emphasise points, trying to change readers' minds and impress them with how safe parkour is.*

5 Write your web page following your plan. Make sure you use:

- link words to guide your readers on their reading journey
- words and phrases to emphasise points or create effects that will make your text very persuasive and reassuring.

Stretch

Think about the different paragraph structures you can use in your writing to shape the reader's response. How could you:

- take into account a reader's possible concerns and answer these?
- compare parkour with other sports to emphasise its safety?
- arrange words and phrases in order of power?

Extend your skills

Whether you are writing fiction or non-fiction, every paragraph in your text should have its own purpose. It should be carrying the reader forward on the journey you planned through the text and creating the impact you want it to have. But how? Study the paragraph below which is advertising a charity fundraising event.

Whether it's Lapsang Souchong or a mug of builders' it's hard to beat a nice cup of tea. Unless it's a nice cup of tea that could help change the world. On 19th September, we're asking people across the world to get together, put the kettle on and help give poor communities the chance to work their way out of poverty.

In this paragraph the writer:

- starts by telling readers what the initial point is, i.e. that enjoying drinking tea is something people from all over the world already have in common
- ends by telling readers what the end of this paragraph's journey is, i.e. that they can share their enjoyment of tea-drinking while helping the poor
- uses the middle sentence to move readers from the beginning idea to the final one, using the word 'Unless' to emphasise the surprise the writer wants the reader to feel at the idea that there is something better still than 'a nice cup of tea'. The middle sentence leads readers to agree that 'yes, a cup of tea that could change the world would be wonderful' before the writer explains in detail what readers have to do to act upon this idea.

Skilful writers use linking words and phrases to glue their sentences together and create emphasis and effect. When you craft a paragraph, think about:

- how each sentence flows on from the last and leads on to the next
- how you can create different effects to achieve your purpose, e.g. a sense of surprise, or a sense of an argument getting stronger and stronger through emphasis.

Language

1 Plan and write a paragraph explaining how your local community could hold a fundraising Tea-Time event. Use a least three techniques from the table below to link your sentences and create particular effects.

Technique: Beginning your next sentence with …	**How to use the technique**	**Examples follow the sentence:** *You can host your Tea-Time anywhere you like.*
Repetition – this can be used to emphasise the importance of an idea	Repeat an important word from one sentence in the next sentence.	**You** could be at home, school, in the office or on top of a mountain.
A **pronoun**	Use words like pronouns that refer to a word already used in the previous sentence.	**It** can be an enormous tea-party or just you and a few friends.
A **synonym**	In your new sentence use a word that means the same as another word from your previous sentence.	**Wherever** you hold your **event** make sure you ask for a donation.
An **antonym** to surprise your reader with a fresh point	In your new sentence use a word that means the opposite to a word from your previous sentence.	**Nowhere** is too exotic for a tea-party so let your imagination run riot.
Numbering to suggest that your ideas are ordered and logical and should be agreed with	Use words that suggest the points in your paragraph are numbered.	**Firstly**, you'll need to send out invitations to everyone.
Repeated sentence structure to create emphasis of the idea that is in the repeated words	Use a similar pattern of words to echo what came before.	**You can choose** any type of tea.
A **summary** to create emphasis of the main idea that has been looked at in detail	Sum up what the previous sentence was about and build on it.	**The idea of hosting tea-parties in all kinds of locations** really fires people's imaginations.

Apply your learning

Task Teenagers are often presented negatively in the media because stories of crime and anti-social behaviour get readers' attention and sell newspapers. You don't believe that this view is fair. Plan and write a strongly argued essay that persuades readers that this is not the truth about most teenagers.

1 Plan your essay. Think about the journey you want the readers to take and how you can organise ideas to achieve your purpose. Make sure that:
   - your essay is organised effectively using link words to guide readers
   - each paragraph is organised effectively
   - you use a variety of techniques to link sentences.

2 Draft your essay using language and techniques that emphasise the strength of your points.

Assess to Progress

How confident are you now at organising a text so that the ideas flow logically? Have you shown the way you can signal the way paragraphs and sentences belong together and follow on from each other? Have you shaped the language in your paragraphs to support your purpose for writing? Look back at the ratings you gave yourself on page 181. Now rate yourself again for each of the skills.

SKILLS FOR LIFE

Your local council is putting together a programme of activities which they hope teenagers will want to take part in during the summer. They are looking for interesting suggestions from teenagers. Write a letter to the 'Summer's Cool' co-ordinator describing some activities they could include and explaining why these would be popular.

As you plan your letter, decide:

- which activities you would like and why they will be popular with teenagers
- what objections the council may have to your ideas and ways to overcome them
- the best order to organise your points so you lead the council to agree with you.

As you draft your letter, remember to use link words and vocabulary that will persuade the council to agree with you, and write using standard English so they will understand and take your ideas seriously.

Progress in ... Structuring sentences for clarity, purpose and effect

LEARNING OBJECTIVES

- Use a range of sentence structures to create deliberate effects according to your audience and purpose.
- Use different sentence structures that are appropriate to the task to enhance and emphasise meaning.
- Understand how writers adapt sentence structures and conventions to create effects and make similar adaptations in your writing.

Activate your learning

All writers vary, shape and craft their sentences to help them create the effects and meanings they want to achieve. How much can you remember about different types of sentence and how to adapt them?

1 Match each type of sentence to its correct definition. Compare your answers with a partner's.

simple sentence	does not make sense on its own and depends on the main clause for its meaning
compound sentence	a group of words with one subject and one verb which makes sense on its own
complex sentence	makes sense on its own and can form a complete sentence
main clause	a sentence with a main clause and at least one subordinate clause
subordinate clause	two simple sentences joined with a conjunction

2 Working in a pair, take turns to challenge each other to make a change to the following sentence:

She spotted the boy as he peeped through the door.

Player A: Move the subordinate clause.

Player B: Change the subordinate clause.

Player A: Make two simple sentences.

Player B: Change the main clause.

Player A: Change into a compound sentence.

Player B: Add another subordinate clause.

Language

3 With your partner, find the complex sentences in the passage below. Identify the subordinating connectives and the subordinate clauses. Join with another pair to see if you agree.

> She spotted the boy as he peeped through the door. Her anger rose, which made her even more determined. She would run away from him. She would run away from his cruel teasing that threatened to destroy her courage.

4 How many different ways can you write and punctuate the following information?
She pushed the door with all her strength. It still would not open.

Experiment with simple, compound and complex sentences and annotate the different versions to explain what you have written and the effects that each version produces.

Assess to Progress

How good do you think you are already at adapting your sentence structures to create deliberate effects? Can you make effective choices in the sentence structures you use in order to enhance and emphasise meaning? Rate yourself for each of the following skills by deciding where you would place yourself on the scale below.

1	2	3	4	5	6	7

I find this difficult. — I'm getting there. — I'm good at this.

- I can use a range of sentence structures in my writing to create deliberate effects according to who I am writing for and what I am writing.

  Self-check: Can you vary the lengths, structures and subjects of your sentences to achieve your purpose?

- I understand how writers adapt sentence structures and conventions to create different effects and can adapt the sentence structures and conventions I use to create similar effects.

  Self-check: When you read do you note powerful sentences that affect you as a reader and think about how you can use these types of sentence in your own writing?

Language

Build your skills

Skilful writers use a variety of sentence structures to create different effects in their writing, e.g. using a series of short sentences to quicken pace, or using long, flowing sentences to draw the reader in only then to stun them with the impact of a short, sharp sentence following on. Work through the skill steps to explore how to how writers use sentences effectively.

Step 1 Use a mixture of simple and complex sentences

When a writer wants to quicken the pace, they will often use simple sentences. The following extract from the novel *The White Darkness* by Geraldine McCaughrean, which describes a plane crashing in the Antarctic, is a good example of this.

> There was a huge thud. The ground moved under us. A nearby cornice of drifted snow collapsed and smashed, like a wave hitting shore. The snow all around changed colour, swallowing the glow of the explosions just then ripping through the DC-6. Within the transparent rag of red flame, the huge metal shape of the aircraft began to move, subsiding, settling, sashaying across the melting ice until the runway was too liquid to any longer support its weight. Then it keeled over onto one wingtip.
>
> Smaller explosions sent fire washing outwards in lavish swags that engulfed the piles of luggage, the bagged litter, a row of safety flags, and a skidoo. The petrol tank of the skidoo itself exploded, tossing the machine high into the air to crash back down on the kitchen tent.

1 Working in a pair, reread the text picking out examples of simple sentences. Discuss why you think the author has used them where she has.

2 Turn two of the simple sentences you noted into a compound sentence. What effect is created?

Now look at one of the complex sentences the writer included. Here she is describing several things that are happening at the same time:

The snow all around changed colour, swallowing the glow of the explosions just then ripping through the DC-6.

3 a) Change this complex sentence into three simple sentences. What different effect is created?

b) This complex sentence starts with the main clause. What different effect is created if you start it with the subordinate clause?

4 Find other complex sentences in the text and experiment by changing the position of the subordinate clauses. What effects does this create.

Language

Support

Complex sentences are often made up of a main clause and at least one subordinate clause, which usually adds detail and makes the meaning clearer. The subordinate clauses can start in several ways:

- the situation at the beginning, which is normal and everyday
- with 'who', 'which' or 'that'
- with a conjunction such as 'because', 'although', 'as'
- with an '-ing' word such as 'hoping', 'swallowing', 'sliding'.

Step 2 Use sentences to create deliberate effects

Writers are able to create a variety of effects in their writing using different types of sentence, for example, using one word as a sentence to create surprise or impact. These are called **minor** sentences and do not contain a finite verb, e.g. 'Mary!', 'Yes.', 'Perfection.'

Look at the following sentence structures that the author Terry Deary has used and explore the effects they create:

1 Here the writer adds to and builds up details. What sentence structures does he use to do this?

> *You stole fire from the gods and you gave it to those crawling creatures they call humans. You sneaked it away, hidden inside a reed – you are no better than some robber on the road.*

2 This sentence starts with the conjunction 'As'. How does this help you to understand the rest of the sentence?

> *As it climbed, the shimmering grass below gave way to grey, wind-scrubbed shrubs, and then bare rocks, too bleak for even the moss to grow.*

3 Write the next paragraph in the Geraldine McCaughrean story on page 192. Think about the effects you want to create and use the sentence structures and conventions you have explored so far.

Stretch

Rewrite the original text and your paragraph in the present tense. Adapt some of the sentences used in the original text to create different effects.

Step 3 Draw on the sentence structures used by other authors in your own writing

When you are writing in a particular genre, it can be helpful to explore the style of other writers in the genre and look at the sentence structures they use to create different effects, then draw on these in your own writing.

Working in a pair, read the following text and work through the activities below to explore how the horror writer William Peter Blatty crafts his sentences to build suspense.

The house was a rental. Brooding. Tight. A brick colonial ripped by ivy in the Georgetown section of Washington, D.C. Across the street, was a fringe of campus belonging to Georgetown University; to the rear, a sheer embankment plummeting steep to busy M Street and, beyond, the muddy Potomac. Early on the morning of April 1, the house was quiet… At approximately 12:25 A.M., Chris glanced from her script with a frown of puzzlement. She heard rapping sounds. They were odd. Muffled. Profound. Rhythmically clustered. Alien code tapped out by a dead man.

1 Discuss what effect this passage has on you as a reader. Pick out three sentences which emphasise the normality of the scene and three which contribute to the building of suspense.

2 Create your own description of an event in a way that creates suspense for your reader. Choose an idea such as going for a swim and then finding yourself out of your depth. Use the sentence structures you have explored and think about how you can vary these to create different effects.

3 Swap your writing with a partner. Compare and discuss the choices you have made and how successfully you think these have worked.

4 Look at the opening and closing sentences in your writing. Experiment with writing two more opening and two more closing sentences, changing the sentence structures you have used. Decide which is the most effective and why.

Language

Reinforce your skills

It is not only writers of fiction who craft sentences to create deliberate effects or emphasise meaning. You will see similar shaping of sentences in non-fiction texts.

The writer of the news report below is giving a recount of an event that has taken place. However, the way the writer shapes the sentences helps to engage the reader's interest in the story and emphasise the drama of the situation.

> Fire-fighters arrived at Muddleswood less than 10 minutes after the 999 call, but they'd already missed much of the drama. A plume of thick, billowing smoke greeted them. The heat from the bedroom was enough to melt one fire-fighter's helmet, but Annette Walker, who had been in the bedroom, had already been rescued. A neighbour said, 'I got out the ladder and leaned it against the roof, I went up and coaxed Annette to come over the edge...'

1 Working with a partner, list the basic facts of the incident. Then discuss how the writer uses different sentence structures to make it dramatic.

2 Experiment with changing the order of the information in the report, so it begins by describing Annette Walker's rescue. What effect does this have?

3 Write an eyewitness report of a fire that destroyed Fleetwood Pier near Blackpool using the details below. Think about how you can use a range of sentence structures to present the information in a logical and dramatic way.

- Fleetwood Pier built in 1910
- Smoke seen coming from the roof of the main building in the early hours of the morning
- 10 fire engines and 60 fire fighters sent to the blaze
- Fire crews pumped water from a nearby boating lake to try to control the fire
- Roads were closed off around the scene
- Cathy Stacey from Lancashire Fire and Rescue Service said, 'Most of the pier has been destroyed – certainly the buildings on it.'

Stretch

How would you adapt your eyewitness account if you were writing about the event in your blog? How might you adapt the sentence structures you used? Write a blog entry about this event.

Language

Extend your skills

Consciously controlling and adapting the lengths of your sentences to create deliberate effects can help you expand your ideas to add richness and detail or shape your sentences to emphasise meaning.

Read the following information:

> *He first smelled smoke when he was getting ready for bed. He choked. It was coming from the landing. He realised there was a blazing fire. He was trapped and unable to get down the stairs. He had to wait in his room until he was rescued.*

One way of adding richness and detail to a sentence is to use expanded **noun phrases**. This can be a single word that can be added to in a number of ways. Look at the sentence:

He *choked.*

One way of expanding it would be to say:

The ***boy*** *choked.*

Adjectival phrases are another way of adding interesting detail. Look at this phrase:

blazing *fire*

1 a) Discuss in pairs other ways of expanding the noun phrase 'he' to add detail that will engage a reader.

b) Write down two ways of expanding the adjectival phrase to add tension.

2 Write a first-hand account by somebody trapped in a flaming building. Think about how you can:

- emphasise the build-up of tension and fear by using a variety of simple, compound and complex sentences (Remember: Short, sharp sentences will quicken the pace and increase tension. Don't forget the possible impact of minor sentences.)
- include a combination of noun phrases and adjectival phrases to add rich detail.

3 Annotate your paragraphs to explain the techniques you have used and the effects you are trying to create.

4 Redraft your paragraphs. Think about using modal verbs and varying the position of the subordinate clauses in your sentences. Compare your work with a partner and discuss the effects the different sentence structures create.

Support

Remember that modal verbs, such as 'will', 'can', 'shall', 'may', 'could', 'should', 'would', 'might' and 'must', are used to express the future, possibilities and demands.

Apply your learning

Working on your own, use the skills you have developed through this unit to complete the following task.

Task

You have been asked to write a newspaper report about a disaster that has affected your local area. This could be a real event or an imagined one. You will need to show how you can use a range of sentence structures to report the facts of the event but also craft these in ways that engage readers and their emotions.

1 Choose an appropriate planning format to generate and organise the details you will include in the report. Think about how you can:
   - explain why the situation happened
   - describe the scene and atmosphere
   - capture the emotions of people involved
   - include snippets of interviews or eyewitness comments.

2 Draft your newspaper report. Remember to craft your writing by controlling the length and variety of sentences you use. Think about how you can use different sentence structures for deliberate effect.

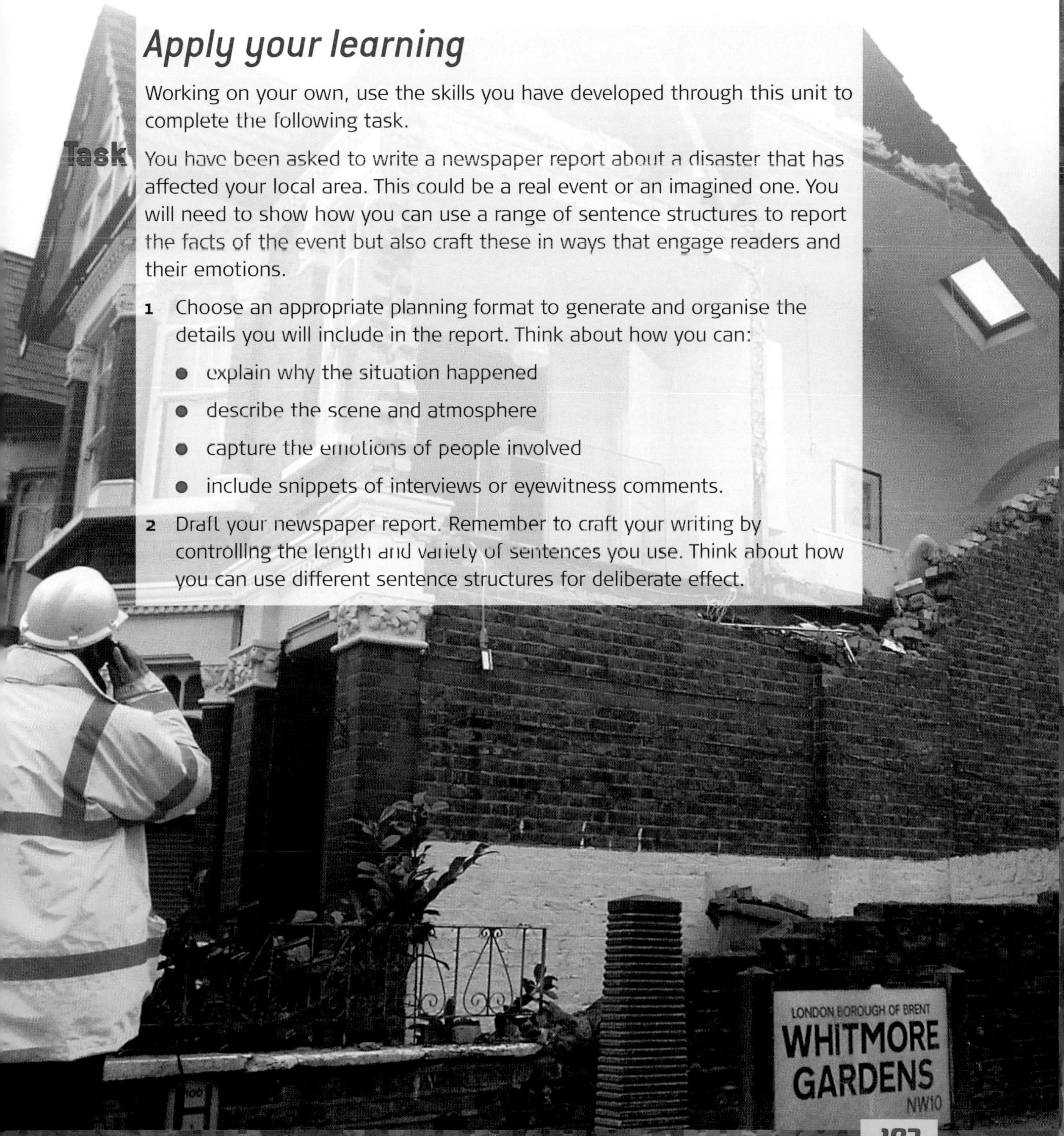

Assess to Progress

How good do you think you are now at adapting your sentence structures to create deliberate effects? Have you made effective choices in the sentence structures you have used in order to enhance and emphasise meaning? Look back at the ratings you gave yourself on page 191. Now rate yourself again for each of the skills.

SKILLS FOR LIFE

Read the following notes about what to do if you discover a fire. You have been asked to use this information to create a set of instructions that would be displayed in every classroom. Use your skills in sentence construction to make sure the important information is emphasised.

If the worst happens and a fire breaks out:

- Delay the spread of fire – close doors
- Get everyone out
- Take care
- Handles might be hot
- Stay out
- Call the fire service

If you are cut off by fire:

- Remain calm
- Close all doors
- Block any gaps
- Stop smoke spreading
- Get close to the floor – helps breathing
- Get to a window
- Attract attention
- Get someone to call fire service.

Writing AF6

Progress in ... Using a range of punctuation for clarity and effect

- Use the full range of punctuation to enhance and emphasise meaning.
- Use punctuation to create a wide range of effects.
- Evaluate the effectiveness of your writing by using your editing, proofreading and reviewing skills.

Activate your learning

You are an editor at a publishing company and you have received the following text. It is an extract from the story *The Courtship of Mr Lyon* by Angela Carter, which you are including in a book you are editing. However, the punctuation has been removed from the text as the file has corrupted.

1 Work with a partner to copy out the text and add the appropriate punctuation.

a) You may find places where you agree on what punctuation mark should be used. Mark these in one colour.

b) Where you disagree or you think more than one piece of punctuation could be used, mark these in a different colour, making a note of the different punctuation marks that could be used.

In too much need to allow himself to be intimidated he squared up to the mahogany door this door was equipped with a knocker in the shape of a lion's head with a ring through the nose as he raised his hand towards it it came to him this lion's head was not as he had thought at first made of brass but instead of gold before however he could announce his presence the door swung slightly inward on well-oiled hinges and he saw a white hall where the candles of a great chandelier cast their benign light upon so many many flowers in great free-standing jars of crystal that it seemed the whole of spring drew him into its warmth with a profound intake of perfumed breath yet there was no living person in the hall

2 Now join with another pair. Share your passages and compare the punctuation you have used.

a) Discuss where you have used the same punctuation mark. Could you have used any different punctuation?

b) Discuss where punctuation differs and where you have used punctuation when the other pair has not. Give reasons for your decision, explaining why you are correct.

Assess to Progress

How good are you at using a range of punctuation in your writing to create different effects? Do you know how to use punctuation to enhance the meaning of what you write or to emphasise certain points? Do you check and make revisions to your use of punctuation, thinking about the effect it will have on the reader? Rate yourself for each of the following skills by deciding where you would place yourself on the scale below.

1 2 3 4 5 6 7

I find this difficult. I'm getting there. I'm good at this.

- I use the full range of punctuation to enhance and emphasise meaning.

  Self-check: Do you know how to demarcate sentences accurately with full stops, exclamation marks, question marks and capital letters? Do you use commas to demarcate clauses but also to add pauses or emphasis where required? Can you punctuate direct speech accurately, use apostrophes correctly for possession or omission and semi-colons and colons accurately?

- I use punctuation to create a wide range of effects.

  Self-check: I can use a range of punctuation to insert additional information into a sentence, such as dashes, brackets and commas. I can use punctuation to slow or speed up the pace of a sentence.

- I can evaluate the effectiveness of my writing by using editing, proofreading and reviewing skills.

  Self-check: Do you know your strengths in punctuation and areas you need to develop and use these to help you review, proofread and revise my writing? Do you know which areas are your weak points and focus on these when you are checking, proofreading and reviewing.

Build your skills

When you are writing, you need to think about how you use punctuation within your sentences. The punctuation choices you make can help shape sentences and create deliberate effects. Follow the skill steps to explore how you can make appropriate punctuation choices in your own writing.

Step 1 Use punctuation to enhance meaning

Using punctuation, you can intensify and add to ideas in your writing, enhancing the effects of your words and sentences.

Read the extract below from the novel *The Call of the Wild* by Jack London, which tells the story of a dog, Buck, who is taken to Alaska at the time of the American Gold Rush. In this paragraph, Buck fights with Spitz, the leader of a pack of dogs.

> In a flash Buck knew it. The time had come. It was to the death. As they circled about, snarling, ears laid back, keenly watchful for the advantage, Buck seemed to remember it all – the white woods, and earth, and moonlight, and the thrill of the battle.

Jack London could have written the first sentence like this:

> In a flash, Buck knew it.

Adding the comma would make the reader stop slightly. It is a signal to pause and think, emphasising the phrase 'in a flash'. However, the sentence written without the comma has a faster pace, echoing how quickly Buck realised 'the time had come' to fight Spitz. The punctuation enhances the content and emphasises speed of thought.

1 Reread the sentence below. What idea do the commas enhance here? Why do you think the writer has used so many commas?

> As they circled about, snarling, ears laid back, keenly watchful for the advantage, Buck seemed to remember it all – the white woods, and earth, and moonlight, and the thrill of the battle.

2 Write five sentences in which you describe the build-up to a conflict. It should be an action scene between two main characters. Show that you can use commas to enhance the pace and meaning of the passage.

Language

Step 2 Use punctuation to emphasise meaning

Punctuation can also stress or emphasise ideas. It can draw attention to particular parts of the sentence. Look at the next part of the extract – Buck is circling Spitz, preparing to fight.

> Nothing moved, not a leaf quivered, the visible breaths of the other dogs, now drawn up in a silent, expectant circle, rose slowly and lingered in the frosty air.

Here, Jack London uses a long complex sentence to emphasise the effect of the stillness and the slow wait. But he also uses punctuation to stress particular ideas. He could have written:

> Nothing moved. Not a leaf quivered. The visible breaths of the other dogs, now drawn up in a silent, expectant circle, rose slowly and lingered in the frosty air.

Using commas makes the pauses shorter and less pronounced.

1 Reread the original version of the passage. Why else do you think Jack London uses commas rather than full stops here? Discuss your ideas with a partner.

2 Which words or phrases do the commas emphasise? What effect does emphasising these words have on the reader?

a) What other punctuation marks could the writer have used in this sentence? Rewrite this text using:

- dashes to mark clauses and adding full stops, e.g. *Nothing moved – not a leaf quivered. The visible breaths …*
- brackets, e.g. *Nothing moved (not a leaf quivered) …*

b) Discuss the effects created by using different punctuation marks.

- What effect does the use of dashes have? Does it make the writing more or less dramatic?
- How does the use of brackets change the emphasis of the information contained within them?

3 David has repunctuated the final passage from this extract. Work with a partner to compare his text the original by Jack London. Discuss the different effects the small changes in punctuation achieve.

Jack London's original text

In vain Buck strove to sink his teeth in the neck of the big white dog. But Spitz was a practised fighter. He had held his own with all manner of dogs. Bitter rage was his, but never blind rage. Wherever Buck's fangs struck for the flesh, they were countered by the fangs of Spitz. Time and time again, Buck tried for the snow-white throat, where life bubbled near to the surface, and every time Spitz slashed and got away.

David's repunctuated text

In vain, Buck strove to sink his teeth in the neck of the big white dog, but Spitz was a practised fighter: he had held his own with all manner of dogs - bitter rage was his but never blind rage. Wherever Buck's fangs struck for the flesh, they were countered by the fangs of Spitz: time and time again, Buck tried for the snow-white throat, where life bubbled near to the surface. Every time Spitz slashed and got away.

4 a) Look back at the sentences you wrote describing the build-up to a conflict. Continue writing this scene using a range of punctuation to emphasise meaning.

b) Share your writing with a partner, explaining the choices you have made.

Reinforce your skills

You are now going to practise using punctuation to enhance and emphasise meaning by writing a short description of a dramatic event. Your punctuation choices need to help create and sustain tension.

1 Make a plan for your writing. You should include a range of details, adjectives and description. Look at the plan below to help you.

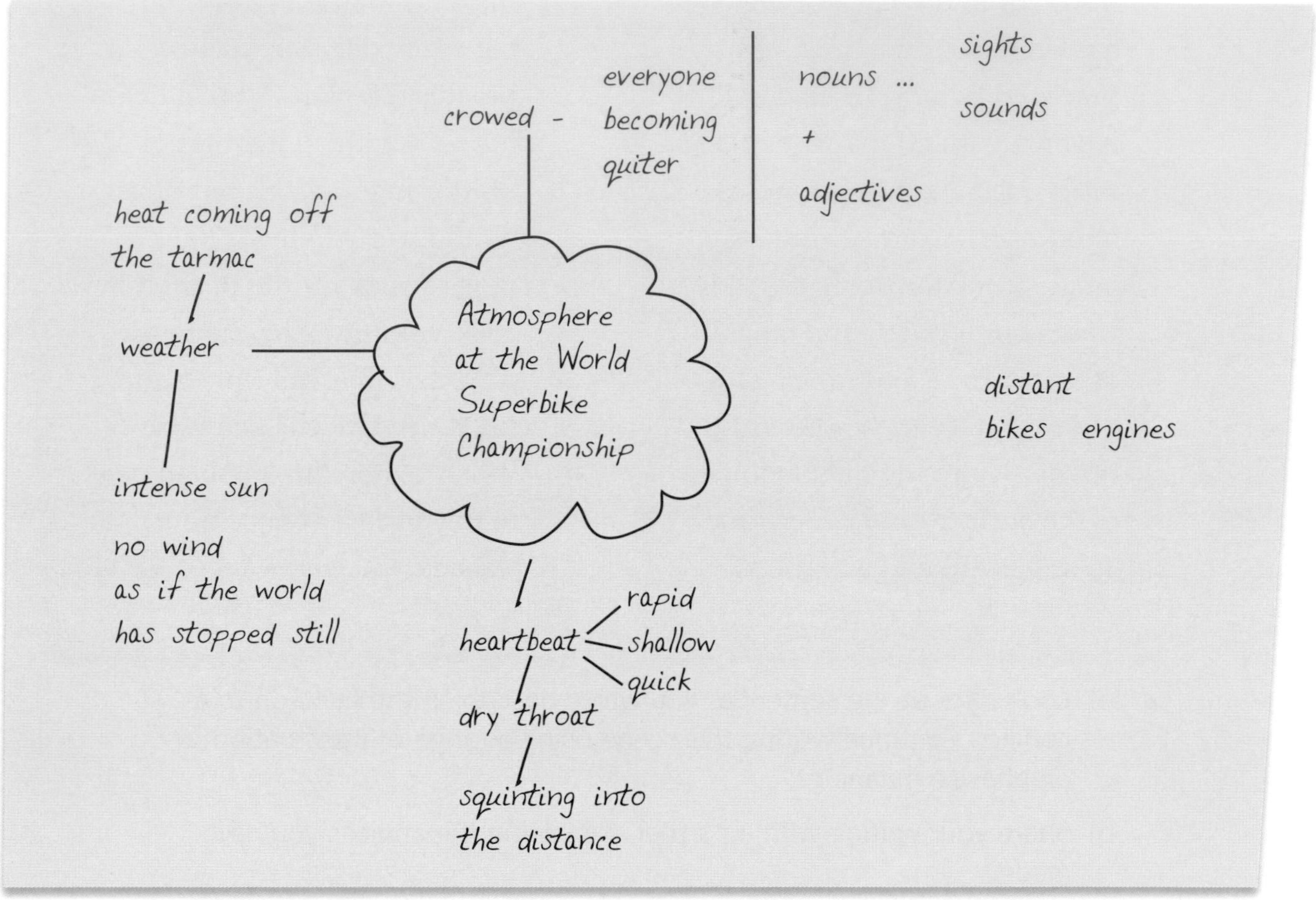

2 Decide how you can use punctuation to enhance the power of your description. Mark on your plan:

- where you want to use short, powerful sentences in combination with dramatic punctuation
- where you want to use commas and dashes to draw out the tension immediately preceding a dramatic event
- other punctuation you could use to control and shape your sentences.

3 Now write your description. Remember to use punctuation to emphasise ideas or enhance the meaning and atmosphere of your writing.

Language

Reece has written a present-tense account of a superbike race. After drafting his writing, he has reviewed it, thinking about the impact it will create for his readers. He then made additional amendments in orange and explained why he had made these adaptations.

First I put a full-stop after 'event', but I wanted the sentence to drag out as long as it could, so I put a comma and used 'and' and then another comma to really slow it down.

I used a colon after 'I daren't sit down' to explain why I daren't sit down, and then I wanted to make the explanation long like getting back up again would be.

We've been up since five this morning, listening to the hum and roar of the bikes passing our tent as the teams get ready for the big event, ***and****, for the last hour, I've been standing, waiting. My legs are beginning to ache, frozen in position, stiff from waiting. I daren't sit down: if I move, I'm sure the bikes will be gone before I've even had a chance to stand up. I'm straining to listen, but the crowd's noisy and unsettled – and I can barely hear anything above them. I want to tell them all to be quiet, but I don't. I wait,* ***turning****, frowning and tutting at the noisiest, hoping they'll get my message.*

I added some more commas after 'hour' and 'standing'. I wanted to make the reader really pause and wait, like I was waiting.

I put commas in this last sentence and made it really long as well because I'm just about to describe the bikes coming round the corner and that will be really fast with short sentences and full stops.

4 Review your own description, thinking about the impact you want your writing to have on the reader. Make any edits or amendments in a different-coloured pen and add annotations explaining your revisions.

5 Now write an additional paragraph which creates a contrasting atmosphere by using punctuation in different ways.

Extend your skills

Punctuation can also be used to clarify meaning. This can be especially important in certain types of non-fiction writing, such as instructions or explanations, where precise meanings need to be given.

1 Review the following types of punctuation and how they are used to clarify meaning.

- **Colon:** signals something will be explained in the remaining part of the sentence.
- **Semi-colon:** signals balanced or related ideas.
- **Hyphen:** links two words together to make meaning clear.

The phrase *'A **little used** car'* can mean a car that isn't used very often or a small second-hand car. To make this clear, you could use a hyphen or comma, e.g.

*'a **little-used** car'* or *'a **little**, **used** car'*

2 Work with a partner to discuss the possible meanings of the following phrases and rewrite each one using a hyphen or a comma to make the meanings clear.

- a sweet shop girl
- fifty odd people
- man eating tiger
- cross trainers

When you want to inform or explain, you can also use colons and brackets to make your writing clear. Read through the following passage, where Reece has given information about James Ellison, a bike rider.

I used brackets to explain what BSB means because I didn't think the reader would know.

James Ellison had to pull out of the Cadwell Park BSB (British Superbike) round: he had ligament damage to his right wrist. He has always made it clear what he wants: to win! He spent a two-year stint in MotoGP, then went on to race in the AMA Superbike (American Motorcyclist Association Superbike) series, before being tempted back to the new-look BSB.

I used colons to explain why he pulled out of the round after starting. I also used it to explain what he wants.

3 Now write a short information or explanation piece about a topic you are interested in. Include punctuation that makes your meaning clear.

Support

Look back over the unit, making a list of where you have used the following punctuation:

.	!	?	,	;	:	( )	-

- Colour-code each one, using red (I find it difficult), orange (I'm not always sure where to use it) and green (I know how to use this).
- Look back over your work on any punctuation you have coded red or orange. Rewrite the previous passage trying to use these punctuation marks accurately to gain extra practice.

Stretch

Semi-colons can be used to show balance or opposites in ideas. Reece wrote two sentences using semi-colons to enhance the balance or opposite idea in his introduction:

The Honda is quality and runs like velvet, sticking to the road; the Suzuki is heavier and a little lethargic, but good on twisties.
The fireblade tops out at 179.02 with a 0-60 of 3.15 seconds; the GSX-R1000 K8 has a higher top speed of 182.74, but is slower on the 0-60.

Look back over your last piece of writing. Add detail that shows a contrast or comparison between two details or between two nouns. Use semi-colons to show a balance between the two ideas, or to demonstrate a contrast.

Apply your learning

Working on your own, use the skills you have developed through this unit to complete the following task.

Task You are going to write a review of an event you have attended. This can be anything of your choice from a sports match to a music concert. Use punctuation to emphasise and enhance meaning as well as to create appropriate effects.

1 You may find it helpful to use a chronological plan to help you think about the details you could include in your writing. In this, you can work from your expectations before the event and your reasons for going, right the way through to your feelings and thoughts after the event.

2 Draft your review. Remember to accurately use a full range of punctuation. Think about when you need to use different punctuation marks.

3 When you have finished the first draft of your review, proofread it to evaluate the effectiveness of your writing. Will it create the right impact on your reader? Check that you have used:

- punctuation correctly to emphasise or enhance your meaning
- punctuation that helps your reader understand what you mean
- a range of sentences including simple and complex ones so that you can demonstrate your punctuation skills.

Make any necessary edits to your draft in a different colour and then annotate it to explain the choices you have made, so that your teacher understands.

Assess to Progress

How confident are you now at using a range of punctuation for effect and emphasis? Do you know how to use punctuation to enhance the meaning of what you write or to emphasise certain points? Do you check and make revisions to your use of punctuation, thinking about the effect it will have on the reader? Look back at the ratings you gave yourself on page 200. Now rate yourself again for each of the skills.

SKILLS FOR LIFE

You have bought a new mp3 player from an internet retailer, but when it was delivered you discovered it was faulty. Fill in the returns report on the internet retailer's website explaining what is wrong with your product and what you would like the retailer to do.

In your text, you should make sure you have:

- used punctuation to make your meaning clear
- used a wide range of punctuation marks
- punctuated your sentences accurately
- used punctuation within sentences to make your ideas clear.

Writing AF7

Progress in ... Selecting appropriate and effective vocabulary

LEARNING OBJECTIVES

- Develop awareness of the impact your word choice will have on readers and choose vocabulary to shape their responses.
- Choose vocabulary that creates precise or more subtle meanings.
- Use a wider and more unexpected vocabulary.
- Evaluate the effectiveness of your vocabulary choices and use editing and proofreading skills to make improvements.

Activate your learning

Working with a partner, write a description based on a memory that they have and vice versa. Answer the questions below to help you with the task.

1 Think back to a time when you had very strong feelings about arriving somewhere – it could be going on holiday, to the dentist's, a shocking event, moving house or another idea.

- Choose the event you are going to describe.
- Decide how you would have looked and appeared to someone meeting you as you arrived.
- Spend a few minutes picturing the event in your mind.

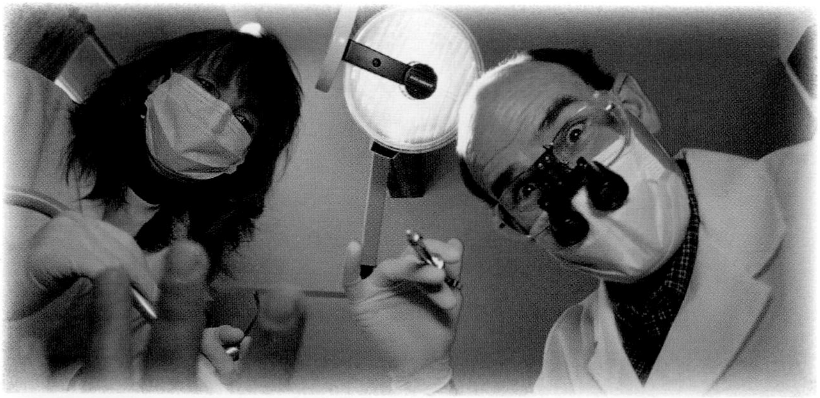

2 Working with a partner, describe your memory of this event. Then make notes as you listen to your partner's description of their memory.

- Tell each other about what happened. Include as much descriptive detail as you can.
- Ask each other questions so that you can picture clearly what happened and how your partner felt.

3 Working on your own, prepare to write about the event your partner described. Write as if your partner is the main character in a story of which this event is the opening. Use your imagination and change details to make your description really vivid and interesting.

As you write each sentence in your opening:

- pinpoint details and use words and phrases that will make your readers feel as if they are actually there watching what happened
- don't just show readers the event but hint at what kind of person this character is.

4 Reread your first draft and find ways to improve your choice of words to strengthen the effects you are trying to create. Then write the final version of your description.

Assess to Progress

How confident are you already at using a wide vocabulary in your writing and choosing words that create the precise effect on readers? When you are editing a piece of writing, do you improve the vocabulary you have already used? Rate yourself for each of the following skills by deciding where you would place yourself on the scale below.

1	2	3	4	5	6	7
I find this difficult.			I'm getting there.			I'm good at this.

- I am aware of the impact my choice of words may have on my readers.

  Self-check: How easy did you find choosing the right words to pinpoint what your experience was like when you described it to your partner? Did you use varied and interesting vocabulary when you wrote your description of your partner's experience?

- I can choose my vocabulary so that I create precise and subtle meanings.

  Self-check: When you wrote your description, which words did you choose to hint at what kind of character you were describing?

- I can use editing and proofreading skills to make my vocabulary precise.

  Self-check: How readily were you able to improve on the words you chose to create images and describe details in your redrafted text?

Build your skills

Successful writers often create fresh descriptions and intriguingly persuasive texts using well-chosen and imaginative vocabulary. Follow the skill steps to explore how a writer creates a world in which the reader can immerse themselves.

Step 1 Know your audience and your purpose

You need to make sure that every word in every sentence of your text suits your audience and helps you achieve your purpose.

Read the following text, which is taken from the novel *The Book Thief* by Marcus Zusak. Here, the writer wants readers to feel pity for Liesel, a girl living in Hitler's Germany, as she meets her foster parents for the first time. Answer the questions on the opposite page to pinpoint how the choice of words helps him achieve that purpose.

Upon her arrival you could still see the bite marks of snow on her hands and the frosty blood on her fingers. Everything about her was undernourished. Wire-like shins. Coathanger arms. She did not produce it easily, but when it came, she had a starving smile.

Her hair was a close enough brand of German-blonde, but she had dangerous eyes. Dark brown. You didn't really want brown eyes in Germany around that time. Perhaps she received them from her father, but she had no way of knowing, as she couldn't remember him. There was really only one thing she knew about her father. It was a label she did not understand.

A strange word

Kommunist.

1 What do the phrases 'bite marks of snow' and 'frosty blood' suggest about Liesel's journey? How do they provoke pity in the reader?

2 What do the words 'wire-like' and 'coat hanger' suggest about Liesel's body? Are they effective at creating feelings of pity?

3 What does 'A starving smile' suggest about Liesel's body and her emotional state? What effect achieved by leaving these words until the end of the sentence?

4 How has the writer's choice of words to describe Leisel's hair and eyes shown readers how vulnerable she is? How does the writer expand on this impression in the rest of the paragraph?

Step 2 Pick powerful words to achieve your purpose

You are now going to write two entertaining paragraphs describing the arrival of a character to stay with a family. The character and the family must be opposites of each other in some way, e.g. a free-spirited artist coming to stay with a very practical, strict family who are set in their routines. Your story will appear in a magazine aimed at mothers.

To help you craft this text try using:

- words you know in surprising ways to hint at what your character feels and thinks, as the writer of the text did when he wrote 'starving smile'.
- a thesaurus to help you find unusual words that have slightly different shades of meaning which will create a subtler impression of the characters.
- a dictionary to help you pin down the precise meaning of the words you use. Does the dictionary definition suggest any further ideas or alternative words you could use?

The following list of words could be used to suggest someone is untidily dressed:

messy	**cluttered**	**disorderly**	**jumbled**
chaotic	**unkempt**	**ragged**	**shabby**
bedraggled	**dishevelled**	**rumpled**	**scruffy**

1 a) Which of these words would you choose to support the impression that this character is poor and embarrassed?

b) Choose two words you could use to suggest that this character is happy and confident. How could you reinforce this impression?

2 Note down vocabulary you could use in your own writing to your plan. Work out how you can show readers the meanings you want to create. Make a note of words that will help you achieve the right impression.

Step 3 Use only those words that support the impression you are trying to create

Skilful writers choose words carefully to make sure that the meanings they create are the ones they want to give the reader.

In your writing you need to:

- choose words that hint at the deeper meaning that you want to give readers rather than telling them directly
- delete words that hint at meanings you don't want your text to carry
- draft and redraft as you write each sentence and paragraph – try out different words and ways of phrasing your ideas until you are happy.

Look at the vocabulary choices Josie has made and the reasons for these.

She ~~stormed~~ jostled her way on to the geometric patterned tiles and ~~left~~ deserted her rucksack at the frosty feet of my father.

I thought 'jostled' sounded like she was messy but quite confident – 'stormed' sounded too angry. I wanted the tiles to be 'geometric' to hint at just how rigid and over-neat the house and family who lived there are. I got rid of 'left' because it sounded like she'd thought about it – 'deserted' sounds more untidy and like she's not going to go back and collect it. It'll stay there.

1 Now write your opening paragraphs describing the arrival of a character to stay with a family. Use the best words that support your meaning and purpose and experiment with different vocabulary.

Reinforce your skills

You are now going to practise the skills you have developed as you write an advertisement aimed at persuading adults to buy a vehicle of your choice.

Look at the car advertisement below and think about the vocabulary choices the writer has to appeal to readers.

Touareg. Gets you to unusual places.

Able to climb 45° slopes, tow 3.5 tonnes and ford depths of half a metre, the Touareg is extraordinarily capable. The interior is equally impressive, with leather upholstery and touchscreen sat-nav as standard on the SE and Altitude models. What is more surprising, the starting price of £29,985 rrp, or where you may end up?

For more information call 0800 037 7888 or visit www.volkswagen.co.uk

Das Auto.

1 Working in a group of three, decide who the advertisement is aimed at. What impression about the car does the vocabulary create?

2 As a group, choose a vehicle to advertise, e.g. electric bike or luxury car. Discuss what impressions you want to create for your readers, e.g.

- your vehicle is fast and sporty so you want to create an impression of exhilaration and excitement
- your vehicle is going to be associated with holidays so you want to create an impression of peace and rest.

3 Find words that will support your purpose and create the right impressions. Study examples of other successful advertisements in newspapers and magazines.

Support

Think about how you could use superlative adjectives (e.g. best) to describe the vehicle or comparative adjectives (e.g. faster than) to compare it favourably with other vehicles.

Language

4 Draft your advertisement text. Keep crafting your text until you are satisfied that the way it is written achieves your purpose fully and suits your audience perfectly by creating the right impressions.

Stretch

How could you change the vocabulary used in your advertisement to make the same vehicle appeal to a different audience?

Create different banks of words that would appeal to different audiences. Then choose one of these audiences and rewrite your advertisement to appeal to them.

5 Present your advertisement text to another group. Explain why you chose the words you used and what effects you were trying to create. Discuss how successful those choices have been.

Extend your skills

While you need to work hard at writing vivid descriptions, at the same time you need to avoid over-writing.

Step 4 Ask if each description is needed to help achieve your purpose

Use the following checklist to make sure you avoid over-writing. When you evaluate your writing, check if you have:

- described too many things or gone into far too much detail
- used too many adjectives and adverbs (**Hint**: Don't feel that every noun or every verb needs describing.)
- used obvious, over-familiar words and phrases (clichés) rather than original words, names or images.

1 Working in a pair, read the text below, which is famous for having been over-written, and list any of the problems you can find.

> It was a dark and stormy night; the rain fell in torrents–except at occasional intervals, when it was checked by a violent gust of wind which swept up the streets (for it is in London that our scene lies), rattling along the housetops, and fiercely agitating the scanty flame of the lamps that struggled against the darkness.

Step 5 Cut out unnecessary detail to improve effective ideas

The writer of the text above wanted to describe a storm and build a threatening atmosphere. You might think the text could be reduced to the sentence 'It was a dark and stormy night', but this would be boring and clichéd because all nights are dark, and the use of storms to signal something bad approaching isn't fresh.

There are some interesting ideas in the text, which could be developed to better achieve the writer's purpose:

- the idea of the rain falling but being stopped by the gusts of wind
- 'the scanty flame of the lamps' (an unusual use of the word 'scanty').

1 Choose another idea or word in the text which you think is worth keeping. Explain to a partner why it is worth holding on to.

Step 6 Redraft to add more precise images

Once you have decided what to cut and what to craft spend time thinking about the effect you want to create and words that will achieve this, e.g.

> It's got to feel more threatening so what about changing the way the rain is described so it's shooting like bullets off the pavements – bits of it could be like shrapnel and the wind could be like the enemy blasting back...

1 a) Redraft the description of the storm so that it is no longer over-written and creates a more threatening atmosphere.

b) Compare your description with a partner's. Discuss the vocabulary choices you have made.

Apply your learning

Task Write a description of an important turning point in your life to be included in an anthology of real-life stories. Your vocabulary should help readers understand why it was important. You might choose a time when you:

- moved to a new home
- made a discovery
- made a big decision.

1 Plan your writing. Note down the details of event, why it was so important to you and the impressions of the experience you want to create. Make a list of words and description of details that will build the right impressions for your readers.

2 Draft your text, then evaluate the effectiveness of your writing. Review, edit and revise your text, keeping the best words and phrases and replacing those that fail to achieve your purpose.

3 Write a final version of your text.

Assess to Progress

How confident are you now at using a wide vocabulary to create precise effects? Are you able to draft and revise your writing so that you improve its effect by cutting words that don't work well and replacing them with more powerful ones? Look back at the ratings you gave yourself on page 211. Now rate yourself again for each of the skills.

SKILLS FOR LIFE

You have been offered the opportunity of a work experience placement. Write a letter of application asking for a work experience placement in the job of your dreams.

1 Plan your letter. Make a note of:

- any experience and skills you have which will suit the job
- personal qualities (e.g. punctual, polite, hard-working) that would persuade your reader to give you this chance.

2 List useful words and phrases you could use to describe yourself which will impress and persuade your reader to give you the job.

3 Draft and write your letter.

Writing AF8

Progress in … Reviewing spelling

LEARNING OBJECTIVES

- Use your knowledge of spelling rules and strategies to maintain correct spelling when writing longer and more substantial texts.
- Spell ambitious and complex words correctly.
- Use your knowledge of your own spelling challenges to guide the way you proofread, review and revise your writing.

Activate your learning

The poem below explores some of the spelling and pronunciation difficulties that people find in the English language. Working with a partner, take turns to read the poem aloud and then complete the tasks on the next page.

Hints on pronunciation for foreigners

I take it you already know
Of tough and bough and cough and dough?
Others may stumble, but not you
On hiccough, thorough, laugh and through?
Well done! And now you wish perhaps
To learn of less-familiar traps?
Beware of heard, a dreadful word
That looks like beard and sounds like bird.
And dead: it's said like bed, not bead –
For goodness sake don't call it 'deed'!
Watch out for meat and great and threat,
They rhyme with suite and straight and
debt.
A moth is not a moth in mother
Nor both in bother, broth in brother,
And here is not a match for there
Nor near and fear for bear and pear,
And then there's dose and rose and lose –
Just look them up – and goose and choose.
And cork and work and card and ward,
And font and front and word and sword,
And do and go and thwart and cart –
Come, come, I've hardly made a start!
A dreadful language? Man alive,
I'd mastered it when I was five.

1 Pick out the different letter patterns used in the poem e.g. '-ough', '-eat' and '-ear', and make a list of words that use each pattern. Use the table to help you.

Letter pattern	-ough	-oth	-eat	-ear	
Examples from the poem	tough bough cough dough				
Examples of your own	slough				

2 Look back at examples of your own writing. Have you used any of the words listed in your table? Can you spot other words where the sound doesn't match the spelling, e.g. 'rhyme'? Add these to the table.

3 Share your findings with your partner and make a collection of words that don't use sound as a guide to spelling. Discuss the strategies you use to spell these words correctly.

Assess to Progress

Complete the following questions to review your own spelling strengths.

1 How many words would you expect a confident speller to write correctly?

a) 65%? b) 75%? c) 85%? d) 95%? e) 100%?

2 How many words would you expect less confident speller to write correctly?

a) 55%? b) 65%? c) 75%? d) 85%? e) 95%?

3 How many words would you expect an average speller to write correctly?

a) 45%? b) 55%? c) 65%? d) 75%?

4 Find a page of recent writing you have completed and put a box around a section of your work that contains 100 words. Working with a partner, check your spellings in this section. Use a dictionary for any challenging words. Make a list of your spelling errors.

5 Count how many errors you made out of the 100 words and use the judgements you made in questions 1–3 to rate your spelling skills. Are you a confident speller, an average speller or a less-confident speller?

6 Discuss your spelling rating with a partner and what you think your strengths and weaknesses as a speller are.

Build your skills

It is important to think about the way that you spell not only in English lessons, but also in your writing in other subjects and outside school. This will give you a fuller picture of yourself as a speller.

1 a) Find a range of examples of your own writing. This could be work from different subjects, your diary or blog entries or any other writing. Try to find different types and lengths of writing.

b) If you can't find examples, complete the following two writing tasks:

- Describe the room you are in, focussing on the furniture, people and atmosphere.
- Write a diary entry for any day in the last week.

In order to improve your accuracy in spelling, it is important for you to identify your own strengths and weaknesses and develop your spelling strategies. Use the skill steps below to help you do this.

Step 1 Recognise what kind of speller you are

There are different categories of speller. Visual spellers, auditory (sound) spellers and intellectual spellers. You can work out what kind of speller you are by thinking about how you remember spellings.

1 Look back at a piece of your own writing and find a difficult word that has been spelt correctly. This could be a word such as 'conclusion' or 'station'. Once you have identified a word that could be tricky, ask yourself these questions.

When I'm trying to remember how to spell that difficult word, I:
1 Listen to the sound of words in my head?
2 List possible spellings and choose the one that looks right?
3 Think of a spelling rule?
4 Break a word into bits and say them aloud?
5 See the word in my mind?
6 Link the word with other similar words?
7 Say the word out loud?
8 Find that I just know it?
9 Look it up in a dictionary?

If you answered 1, 4 or 7 you are an **auditory** (sound) speller who uses **listening** strategies.

If you answered 2, 5 or 8 you are a **visual** speller who uses **looking** strategies.

If you answered 3, 6 or 9 you are an **intellectual** speller who uses **learning** strategies.

2 Working in a group of four, discuss what type of speller you are and the strategies you use to spell correctly.

Step 2 Research your personal pattern of error

1 Look at the examples of your writing that you have collected. Pick out the spelling errors you have made. Can you see any patterns?

- Do you stumble on silent letters repeatedly? ('ex**h**ibition', 'si**g**n')
- Do you find vowel combinations difficult? ('ch**ao**s', 'flav**ou**r')
- Do you struggle with double consonants? ('writting' instead of 'writing')

2 Compare your errors with a partner's. Do you make any of the same types of error?

Step 3 Reflect on the spelling strategies that suit you best

1 Work in a group of four. Discuss and decide which of the following spelling strategies you prefer to use:

- **Looking**, e.g. look/cover/write/check.
- **Listening**, e.g. saying a word in a way that reminds you of the spelling.
- **Learning**, e.g. using the structure and history of words as a guide.

Step 4 Reinforce the correct spellings of tricky words

1 Look back at the spelling errors you identified from the examples of your own writing. Use your preferred spelling strategy to practise spelling these words, e.g.

- **Looking** – put the word on a poster for you to see regularly.
- **Listening** – turn the syllables in a word into a poem or song with a catchy rhythm.
- **Learning** – use a dictionary to find out the history of the word and make links to similar words.

Step 5 Review your progress

1 Now select another writing task from page 221 (7b). Complete this new task and check your spellings for improvement.

Reinforce your skills

Good spellers use a range of different strategies to help them spell correctly.

1 Make a list of the words you often spell incorrectly. You are going to apply a range of strategies to these target spellings to see which strategy works best for you. Complete a table like the one below, using your own targets in the Word column. Then complete the other columns as you work through the activities below.

	Strategies		
Word	**Looking**	**Listening**	**Learning**
different		*I try to always say 'diff-er-ent' to remind me of the silent middle syllable.*	
remember			*I try to think about the prefix 're' joined to the word 'member' to stop me writing 'rember'.*
thoroughly			
environment			
believe			

2 a) Ask a partner to read out the first word on your list . Think about how you are trying to remember the spelling. Are you trying to picture it? Are you trying to hear the sounds? Are you trying to link the word to the spellings of other similar words or use your knowledge of how words are made up of different parts such as prefixes?

b) Fill in the appropriate strategy box to help you remember the spelling strategy you usually use and decide whether you need to try a different approach. You may need to use different strategies for each word.

3 Share and discuss your completed table with your partner. Do you have different approaches to spelling the same word? Have you changed your strategy for a particular word?

Support

Do you remember the spelling rules about double consonants, single consonants and adding '-ing'? Revise the rules and complete the activities below.

- What does a double consonant do to the vowel? *It makes it short: 'sit' becomes 'si**tt**ing' and the 'i' sound stays the same.*
  Make a list of words that follow this pattern such as 'bat' and 'spot',
- What does the single consonant do to the vowel? *It makes it long: 'hat' becomes 'hating' and the 'a' sound changes together with the meaning.*
  Make a list of words that follow this pattern such as 'rat' and 'tap'
- What happens if you add '-ing' to 'hope' and 'brake'? *You miss out the 'e' and the vowel stays long: 'hoping', 'braking'.*
  Make a list of words that follow this pattern such as 'writing'.

Stretch

Good spellers are ambitious and attempt to use unfamiliar, complex words in their writing by relying on their skills in using a range of strategies. Look at these words and decide how you would have approached the spelling of each one:

outrageous exaggerated announcing parallel

Add some challenging words of your own to the list and check your spellings in a dictionary.

Extend your skills

To avoid making spelling errors, you need to think about what could be causing the error. Common errors in spelling are often caused by:

- a mismatch between the spelling and sound of a word, e.g. 'archive'
- forgetting spelling rules, e.g. the rule for adverbs (adding '-ly' not '-ley')
- misunderstanding word roots, e.g. 'disappear', -a combination of a prefix 'dis-' and a verb 'appear'
- muddling similar words with different meanings, e.g. homophones such as 'there', 'their' and 'they're'
- forgetting when plurals require '-es' to be added, e.g. 'boxes' not 'boxs'.

1 Working in a group, compare your lists of spelling errors. Can you find any other causes? Make a list, giving examples of the mistake and the correct spelling.

Use the following checklist to help you proofread your writing:

- List the common spelling errors you make and read for each type of error.
- Try not to read for meaning as this might distract you from the spellings.
- Read each line backwards.

2 The following text has been written by a pupil in response to advice they have been given about exam revision. Working with a partner:

- try to spot the spelling error
- describe what type of error it is
- discuss what might be a helpful strategy for this pupil to use next time.

> Well at least they think revising with a friend's OK but 'be careful not to make your sessions all fun and no work' that's ridiculous, I can't be with my friends and not have fun! We're meant to go on the internet to do tests. I mean, who goes on learn.co.uk, don't they understand the concept of boring. I wonder how they'd like it if people were trying to stop them having fun, I think if I stuck to that I'd deffinitely die of boredom. We should do lots of exam questions at home ... I think I'm going to fall asleep soon! We have enough tests as it is! School Booster classes! I'd rather be popular than get totally laughed at!

3 It can be difficult to spot rare spelling errors in a piece of near-perfect writing. Proofread a longer example of your writing that you think is perfect and see if you can spot any 'rare' spelling errors. Then work out a strategy that will help you.

Apply your learning

Task Write an extended response giving your views on the ideas in the newspaper article on the next page.

1 Discuss with a partner, what you think about the ideas in the report.

2 Plan and draft a response giving your views. You could explain how spelling can be improved and how a range of strategies can be helpful for everyone. In your writing try to use ambitious vocabulary by using the spelling strategies you have developed in this unit.

3 Proofread your writing to check your spellings and review your choice of words. Make any necessary edits and revisions, marking these in a different colour.

English is too hard to read for children

The English spelling system is 'absolutely, unspeakably awful'. That is the conclusion of new research that has found that children face 800 words by the age of 11 that hinder their reading because of the way they are spelt.

Monkey, asparagus, spinach, caterpillar, dwarf, banana, handkerchief, pliers, soldiers, stomach, petal and telescope have all been included on the long list of words that baffle children because they contain letter combinations that are more commonly pronounced in a different way.

Masha Bell, the literacy researcher who carried out the work, argued that there were 200 words on the list that could be improved by simply dropping 'surplus letters' such as the 'i' in friend or the 'u' in shoulder. 'English has an absolutely, unspeakably awful spelling system,' said Bell, a former English teacher and author of the book *Understanding English Spelling*. 'It is the worst of all the alphabetical languages. It is unique in that there are not just spelling problems but reading problems. They do not exist anywhere else.'

Simplifying the system would transform literacy results, according to Bell, but she said people were resistant to change. 'People feel that they have suffered so much at the hands of English spelling that they are reluctant to look at it,' she said. Yet other countries have made changes. Last month the parliament in Portugal, where the spelling system is also thought to be complicated, voted to reform and simplify it, bringing it into line with Brazil.

Assess to Progress

How confident are you now in your spelling ability? Answer the questions from page 220 again by checking 100 words in the text you have just written. Has your success rate percentage improved?

Skills for Life

Design a leaflet to help pupils in Year 7 feel confident about improving their spelling. Remember to use:

- a simple catchy title
- a list of common errors
- straightforward explanations of how to spot errors in their own work
- clear advice about how to use the range of strategies available.

Writing

Assessing your Progress

TARGETS FOR PROGRESS

- Make arguments against another writer's point of view.
- Use connectives to create fluent writing.
- Sustain a convincing individual voice and point of view.

Working through this unit will give you the opportunity to show the progress you have made in your writing skills. You will have the chance to bring together the skills you developed in the earlier units as you prepare for a writing task that will assess how well you can argue against other viewpoints, pointing out weaknesses and offering alternative opinions.

Activate your learning

1 In this unit you will develop your skills in arguing against other points of view by developing a counter-argument. For example, what would be your argument against this statement?

> People should be allowed to download as much music as they want from the internet because CDs are overpriced.

Share your ideas with a partner and agree one counter-argument. Here is one suggestion:

> However, if people download music without paying for it in this way, then the band or singer who created the song won't receive any payment and in the end won't be able to afford to make new music.

Connective clearly indicates that an opposite viewpoint is about to be given.

The counter-argument is explained in detail to convince the reader to agree with that point of view.

Clear reference is made to the original argument

2 Working with a partner suggest the most convincing counter-argument you can think of for one of the following arguments. Organise your argument like the example on the page 227.

- Mobile phones are a waste of money since landlines are cheaper.
- There should be a law to make people recycle.
- The legal age for buying alcohol should be raised to 21 to stop teenagers behaving badly after nights out.
- Longer prison sentences for petty offenses would reduce crime.

Support

Use one of these sentence starters to help you organise your idea into a sentence:

- However, although some landlines can be cheaper, some mobile phone tariffs ...
- On the other hand, if a law was brought in to make people recycle, it ...

Progress task

Write a letter for publication in the magazine, arguing against the stance taken by the writer in the article entitled 'Teenagers should listen more!' on the next page.

1 As you read the article, think about the audience, the writers purpose and the point of view he is trying to communicate.

Assess to Progress

To be successful, you will need to:

- make arguments against another writer's point of view
- use connectives to create fluent writing and signal the structure of the writing
- sustain a convincing individual voice and point of view when addressing weaknesses in the argument and offering alternatives.

Assess how good you think you are at each of the above skills by giving yourself a rating on the scale.

1	2	3	4	5	6	7

I find this difficult. I'm getting there. I'm good at this.

Then identify the different arguments the writer makes.

Teenagers should listen more!

HEY KIDS! ARE YOU LISTENING? Yes, folks, the bad news is that the adults in your life really do know best...

You have got to admit it – teenagers do some foolish things, as they do not sense danger; girls waste time in internet chat rooms, putting themselves in danger from strangers; boys commit criminal acts for a dare in front of CCTV cameras and end up with a record that gives them the worst possible start in life. Every year large numbers of teenagers lose their lives or are seriously injured through taking drugs or drinking large amounts of alcohol. Would any of this happen if the advice of parents were taken? After all, parents are more cautious and see danger everywhere.

Main argument

Three pieces of evidence to support main argument

Connective to summarise the point

Paragraph ends with reference to listening to adults as a solution to this foolish behaviour

Seriously, adults know a lot more than you think. Just because your mum can't set the DVD or send a text message, doesn't mean she is stupid. She was your age once and survived. What's more, she can look back on her experience and see what she did right and where she went wrong. She doesn't want you to make the same mistakes that she made and still regrets. You may say that the world has changed and your parents' lives were not the same and so their fears are irrelevant or just plain old-fashioned, but the dangers don't really change, so you can learn from their experiences!

One of the biggest dangers for young people has always been that they can be led into harm's way by strangers with bad intentions. Teenagers are too trusting because they can't imagine why anybody would want to hurt them, or see how someone who seems friendly and helpful might just be putting on an act in order to trick them. However, the adults who care for you know about these people and the way they think, which is why they constantly remind you of 'stranger-danger'.

To take this argument further, some teenagers put more thought into choosing a pair of trainers than they do into selecting their option subjects as school. Making the right decisions when you are a teenager is the key to being happy in future life, but it's hard to think straight when you are 14. Firstly, your whole body is being bombarded with a massive surge of hormones which make you more likely to take huge risks on the spur of the moment rather than reflect carefully. Secondly, you are programmed to listen first and foremost to your friends who are full of the same mad hormones as you. Also, let's face it, as a teenager it's hard to think ahead; adult life is, after all, just boring. On the other hand, the adults who care about you are worth hearing out. They can think calmly about these important decisions, with the benefit of experience, and definitely will want, and will know, what is best for you. Finally, it's quite clear that mums and dads have also got far superior taste in clothes. Well, OK, I agree that's going too far, but when it comes to the important things in life, admit it, you really should listen to your elders.

Look again at the first paragraph. The main argument that the writer makes is that teenagers are foolish. Three pieces of evidence are then given to support this point of view.

2 Now read the rest of the article. What arguments does the writer make and what evidence is used to support these views? Copy and complete the table below, listing the writer's points and one piece of evidence given in the text.

Writer's points	Evidence	Your argument	Your evidence
Teenagers do some foolish things.	Girls in chat rooms		

Build your skills

Think about how you will argue against the points made in the article. You should:

- point out any weaknesses in the arguments
- offer alternative opinions.

1 For each argument the writer makes, add your own counter-argument and supporting evidence to the table, e.g.

Writer's points	Evidence	Your argument	Your evidence
Teenagers do some foolish things.	Girls in chat rooms	Adults also do foolish things.	They drink and drive, not expecting to be caught.

Check that the arguments you have made maintain your viewpoint.

When you are writing your letter, you will need to link your ideas together using connectives. These words or phrases will make your writing more fluent, create a variety of sentence structures and structure your writing.

2 Make a list of the connectives used in the magazine article. Using the headings below to organise them by purpose. One has been done for you. You won't find examples for every heading.

- Cause and effect
- Comparing
- Emphasising
- Contrasting
- Sequencing
- Summarising, e.g. After all

3 With a partner, discuss some other examples of connective words and phrases. Try to think of three for each of the above headings.

Reinforce your learning

One of the features of writing to argue is creating an individual voice. The magazine does this in different ways. Copy and complete the table, filling in the missing information about the features, examples from the text and the effect on the reader.

Feature	Example	Effect on the reader
Rhetorical questions		
	Hey kids!' 'You have got to admit it'	
Matter of fact tone		Makes writer sound honest and straightforward, which convinces the reader to agree with them.
Strong, firm expression of views		
	'Yes, folks,...'	
	'some teenagers put more thought into choosing a pair of trainers than they do into selecting their option subjects...'	
Careful choice of vocabulary		Makes the points more extreme to get the reader's attention and make the other viewpoint seem ridiculous.
Careful choice of sentence structures		To sound calm and reassuring so that ...

Extend your learning

Look at the example below of a counter-argument of the first point in the article:

Teenagers do some foolish things.	Girls in chat rooms	Adults also do foolish things.	They drink and drive, not expecting to be caught.

1 Pick out examples of the following skills used in the response below:

- Argument made against another writer's point of view
- Connectives – creating fluency and signalling the structure of the writing
- Convincing individual voice, addressing weaknesses in the argument and offering alternatives.

> *You begin your argument with a reference to teenagers doing foolish things, offering as your example girls spending time in chat rooms. Unfortunately, you choose to forget the huge numbers of both men and women who foolishly waste their time and money in pursuing football teams.*

Progress task

You are now going to write your own letter to be published in the magazine, arguing against the stance taken by the writer in the article.

Use the table of arguments and counter-arguments from page 231 as your plan. Think about the other features you should include, e.g. use connectives to make your writing fluent, an individual voice to make your argument convincing.

Feature	Example	Effect on the reader
Rhetorical questions		
	Hey kids!' 'You have got to admit it'	
Matter of fact tone		Makes writer sound honest and straightforward, which convinces the reader to agree with them.
Strong, firm expression of views		
	'Yes, folks,...'	
	'some teenagers put more thought into choosing a pair of trainers than they do into selecting their option subjects...'	
Careful choice of vocabulary		Makes the points more extreme to get the reader's attention and make the other viewpoint seem ridiculous.
Careful choice of sentence structures		To sound calm and reassuring so that ...

Assess to Progress

This unit has focused on the features of writing to argue:

- Making arguments against another writer's point of view
- Using connectives to create fluent writing
- Sustaining a convincing individual voice and point of view.

Read the extract from Victoria's letter of response to the article below and then answer the questions.

In the article, the writer describes teenagers particularly as 'too trusting' and consequently get themselves into trouble with strangers that have bad intentions. However, many teenagers nowadays are very aware of stranger danger. I would say that more than half of the teenagers in Britain today are very much aware of strangers.

Keeping on the subject of strangers, I am arguing against the writer's point that 'teenagers do some very stupid and foolish things' such as girls in chat rooms. I would like to stress that adults, above all adults in fact, also do stupid things. I would particularly like to emphasise the answer to 'who are rapists, kidnappers and STRANGERS?' Adults!

One other point mentioned by the writer was that 'Adults aren't stupid, they've survived until now'. The writer gives evidence that 'Adults know a lot more than you think' but on the contrary, a lot of kids can be cleverer than adults. Adults can at times be very stupid. Significantly when they do things such as drink and drive, not expecting to get caught!

1 What features of writing to argue has Victoria included? How do you think she could improve her response?

2 Swap your letter with a partner. Choose two or three paragraphs and look for examples of how they:

- refer to the writer's argument and then give a counter-argument
- use connectives to create fluency and signal the structure their letter
- sustain a convincing individual voice.

Assess how good you think you are now at each of the skills above by deciding where you would place yourself on the scale on page 228.

Progress in ...
Language

Progress in ... Exploring and analysing language

TARGET LEARNING

- Consider how and why the English language has developed in texts from different historical periods.
- Consider why spoken English varies in different regions and situations.
- Analyse how speakers and writers change their language in different contexts.
- Analyse the way language is used across a range of texts.

Activate your learning

Every week in *The Guardian* newspaper journalist Pascal Wise comes up with 'new' words that we never realised we needed. For example:

> **Tannoyance**: feeling cross about the endless announcements on tannoys (loudspeakers) at stations and airports about not leaving bags unattended, remembering to take all your possessions, and so on.

1 Working with a partner, think up some modern definitions of your own. **Remember**: although you are creating 'new' words, you should build these new words out of existing words and think about the meanings you want to create. If you are having difficulty, think of a word to describe:

a) being unable to decide quite which song to listen to on your mp3 player

b) knowing you've forgotten to top up your phone credit

c) someone who always boasts about their up-to-date possessions.

2 Join with another pair and discuss the way you created your new words. How did you change existing words? Did you join existing words together? Compare your approaches.

Assess to Progress

How much do you already know about how the English language is spoken in other regions of Britain? Do you understand how and why speakers and writers change the language they use in different contexts? How much do you know about how English has developed through history? Find out as you complete the tasks below.

1 Think back to the task you have just completed. How good were you at explaining how your new words were formed? With your partner talk about what you found easy and what you found difficult.

2 Now look at the statements below and decide how much you agree or disagree with them and why. Put your answers on the following scale:

1	2	3	4	5	6	7
I find this difficult.			I'm getting there.			I'm good at this.

- I recognise words that are used to describe the same thing in different parts of Britain (such as 'bap' or 'stottie' meaning bread and 'ginnel' or 'snicket' meaning alleyway) and to explain the use of dialect words.
- I understand how people can communicate better in formal and informal situations by changing the way they speak.
- I can explain some of the changes in the way that the English language has been spoken and written in different periods of history.
- I am confident in analysing a range of texts and can explain exactly how a writer has used language correctly and effieciently for their purpose.

Build your skills

The English language has changed and developed over time. One way to explore the history of the English language is by looking at the history of Britain itself.

Step 1 As you read a text search for the significant details

Read through the summary on the opposite page of the different peoples who have invaded Britain over time and the influences on the English language they brought. This is adapted from the research of a language lecturer, James Rye.

1 This is a map of part of Suffolk. Working with a partner, find ten place names which you think may have been given their names a long time ago.

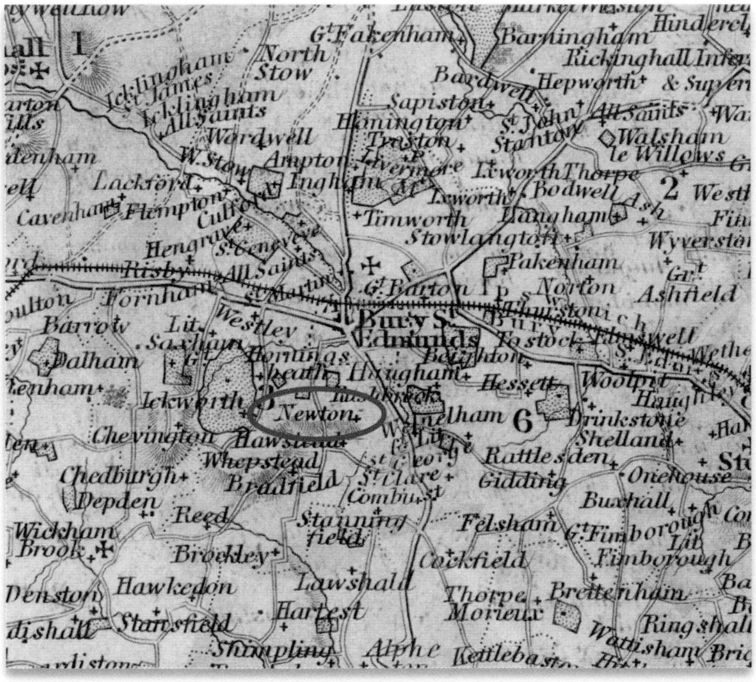

Step 2 Research details to explore the meaning of words

1 Use the information from the text on the opposite page to work out what each of the names on your list might mean.

e.g *Newton sounds like it might be an Anglo Saxon name meaning 'New farm'.*

2 With your partner, choose a different area of Britain. Make a list of as many villages and town names as you can think of. Then using the guide opposite, see if you can:

- work out which historical period some of the names might come from
- take an informed guess at what some of the names might mean.

	Invaders	Examples of place-names and their meanings
	**The Celts** The Celts were one of the many tribes living in Europe in the years before Christ. About 400 BC they began to leave Central Europe and the Celts from Northern France and the Netherlands crossed the Channel and settled in England, especially the west. They were known as the Brythons (Britons).	*aber*: mouth of a river *coombe*: a deep valley *glen*: a narrow valley *pen*: a hill tor a hill
	**The Romans** After 300 years of calling the British Isles their own, the Celts were conquered by the Romans. Between 43 AD and 410, England was the north-west corner of the vast Roman Empire. Although the Romans occupied the country for over three centuries, they only left behind approximately 300 place names. They probably used existing names instead.	*castra* (–chester, –caster): a Roman town, fort *colonia* (–coln): a settlement *porta* (–port): a gate *portus* (–port): a harbour *strata* (Strat–, –street): a Roman Road
	**The Anglo-Saxons** The Angles, Saxons, and Jutes began to invade the British Isles in 449 AD. They came from Denmark and the coast of Germany and Holland. The Anglo-Saxons named their new country Engaland (the land of the Angles) and their language was called Englisc (what modern scholars refer to as 'Anglo-Saxon' or 'Old English').	*burna* (–borne): a brook, stream *dun*: a hill *eg* (–ey) an island *halh*: a nook, corner of land *ham*: a homestead *hamm*: an enclosure, water-meadow *ingas* (–ing): the people of ... *leah* (–ley): a clearing *stede*: a place, site of a building *tun*: an enclosure, farmstead *well*: a well, spring *worth*: an enclosure, homestead
	**The Scandinavians** From 789 AD onwards, the Vikings from Denmark and Norway raided most parts of the British Isles. After much savage fighting they eventually settled down to live alongside the Anglo-Saxons. Modern Yorkshire, Derbyshire, Lincolnshire, Leicestershire, Norfolk and Suffolk became subject to Danish rule. The Scandinavian language, 'Old Norse', had the same Germanic roots as Old English so, over the years, the two languages mixed quite well.	*dalr*: a dale, valley *gathr*: a yard *gil*: a ravine *holmr* (–holm): flat ground by a river *mere*: lake *stowe*: place *lundr*: a grove *thorpe*: a secondary settlement, farm *thveit* (–thwaite): a meadow *toft*: a site of a house and outbuildings

Reinforce your skills

Below are some texts from different periods in history all of which are written in English.

Fritours: Take yolkes of egges, drawe hem thorgh a streynour, caste thereto faire floure, berme and ale; stere it togidre til hit be thik. Take pared appelles, cut hem thyn like obleies, lay hem in the batur; then put hem into a ffrying-pan and fry hem in faire grece or buttur till thei ben browne yelowe; then put hem in disshes, and strawe sugur on hem ynogh. And serve hem forthe.

Do you want me to film? She says pointing to the camera at the first security camera inside the door.

Amber is standing at the door with her eyes narrowing, scanning the inside of the supermarket. She shakes her head. She does it slowly, i.e. she is concentrating.

Go and find something for lunch, she says. Are you hungry?

Astrid nods.

He was already handling mincemeat down his throat in the most curious manner – more like a man who was putting it away somewhere in a violent hurry, than a man who was eating it – but he left off to take some liquor. He shivered all the while, so violently that it was quite as much as he could do to keep the neck of the bottle between his teeth without biting it off.

'I think you have the ague,' said I.

'I am much of your opinion,' said he.

Thus they went on till they came to about the middle of the Valley, and then Christiana said, 'Methinks I see something yonder upon the road before us, a thing of shape such as I have not seen.' Then said Joseph, ' Mother what is it?' 'An ugly thing, child; an ugly thing,' said she. 'But mother, what is it like?' said he. 'Tis like I cannot tell what,' said she. And now it was but a little way off. Then said she, 'It is nigh.'

1 Study each text and decide where you would place them on the time line below. Which clues in each text helped you make your decision?

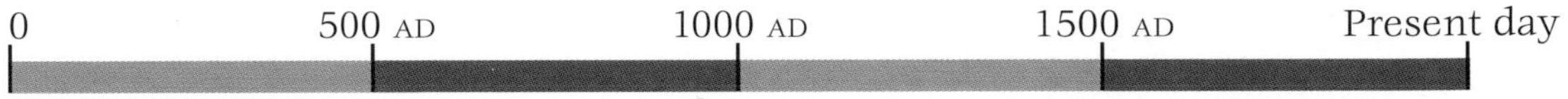

2 Working with a partner, compare the texts making notes under the following headings about the changes that have taken place in the way English language is written:

- vocabulary
- spelling
- the word order
- punctuation.

On the next page there are extracts from two versions of the epic poem 'Beowulf'. This is the oldest poem written in English and tells the story of the hero, Beowulf, killing a monster called Grendell who has been terrorising the Danish King's court. Afterwards Grendell's mother takes revenge for her son's death and kills more people. In both of the texts, a warrior is telling Beowulf where to find Grendell's mother.

3 Study both texts and decide where you would place each of them on the time line. Which clues in each text helped you make your decision?

4 Working with a partner, take it in turn to read each of the texts aloud starting with Text A and then B. As you listen to Text B try to follow it on the page. Note down any words which sound like modern words you know and jot down the words they sound like.

5 Study the glossary telling you the meaning of some of the words in Text B. Then search through the poem for words you can place in each of these four groups:

- Words which have not changed and are still used today
- Words which have kept all their sounds but changed their spelling and are still used today
- Words which have dropped a sound and changed their spelling to become a modern word
- Words which you can't recognise as being used today.

6 Try to work out which type of words are most likely to be still used today, i.e. *Is it mostly verbs, nouns, pronouns, or adjectives?* Why do you think this might be? Discuss your ideas with your partner.

7 Working in pairs, explain in one minute what you have found out so far about what has happened over the centuries to the English language and the way it is used by writers.

Text A :

They occupied the secret land,
the wolf's retreat –
windy bluffs, perilous fens,
where a waterfall
darkens under bluffs
and goes down under the ground.
It is not far from here,
by measure of miles,
that the mere stands.
Over it hangs a frost-covered
grove, woods rooted deep-
shadowing the water.
There each night
a portent may be seen:
fire on the water.
No wise one among
the sons of men
knows the bottom.
Though the heath-stalker,
the strong-horned hart,
harassed by hounds, seeks
the forest in his flight,
he will give his life
rather than protect his head
by going there

Text B

Hie dygel**lond**
warigeath, **wulf**hleoþu, **windige** næssas,
frecne**fen**-gelad, ðær fyrgen-stream
under næssa genipu niþer gewiteð,
flod under foldan. Nis **þæt** feor heonon
mil-gemearces, þæt se **mere standeð**
ofer þæm **hongiað** hrinde bearwas,
wudu wyrtum fæst **wæter** oferhelmað.
þær **mæg nihta** gehwæm nið-**wundor** seon,
fyr on flode. No þæs frod leofað
gumena **bearna** þæt þone **grund** wite

ðeah þe hæð-stapa **hundum** geswenced,
heorot hornum trum holt**wudu** sece,
feorran geflymed, ær he feorh seleð,
aldor on ofre, ær he in **wille**
hafelan (**hydan**).

GLOSSARY

bearna – bairn, child
fen – marsh
flode – flood
fyr – fire
grund – ground (bottom of a lake)
hundum – hounds
hongiað – ground (bottom of a lake)
hydan – hide
lond – land
mere – lake
mæg – may
nitha – (at) night
þæt – that
standeð – stands
wæter – water
wille – will
windige – wood
wudu – windy
wulf – wolf
wundor – wonder

Extend your skills

We all use slang, but do you know how slang has changed over the centuries? Can you explain what the difference is between slang and dialect?

Read the texts below and answer the questions on the next page to analyse how and why English is spoken differently in regions of Great Britain.

Text A

Slang words describing getting dressed in the 19th and 20th Century

To dress smartly is to get togged up, *to* get dolled up *or* to get dolled up like a barber's cat. *To dress up is to* put on dog, *from the 19th century word 'doggy' meaning stylish. Well-dressed people are in their* best bib and tucker, dap *(from the French 'dapper'),* dressed to within an inch of one's life *(19th century),* dressed to the nines *(9 was an important number in numerology),* dressed up like a dog's dinner *(20th century),* dressed like Christmas beef *(19th century),* dressed up like a sore finger and flash as a rat with a gold tooth *(20th century Australian English). You might describe well-dressed people as* dolled up *(20th century),* full fig, got up, kitted up *(all 19th century) or* kitted up *(20th century).*

Text B

Why do dialects differ?

Dialect is a regional or social variety of a language where there are differences in pronunciation, grammar, or vocabulary from the standard version

Sometimes languages break down into dialects as populations spread over larger areas. However, it is often the people who move farthest away from their 'homeland' who preserve the older patterns of speech. American English, for example, still has many words (such as 'gotten'), which were once common in England. Similarly, we still pronounce the letter 'W' in the Old English way, but in most other Germanic languages it now sounds like our 'V'. (The modern German for 'warm' is spelt the same as in English, but pronounced 'varm'.)

Also, new waves of settlers, such as the Vikings, bring in words, phrases and grammatical forms which are then adopted by the natives. This is simply so they can communicate with the newcomers.

Very often, the dialect spoken by the richest or most powerful section of the population gradually takes over and becomes the 'standard' language of a nation. This is certainly true of English, where the speech used in the triangle of land between London, Oxford and Cambridge eventually became what we now call 'Standard English'. 'Standard English' is still a dialect, but is based more on social class rather than on region.

Sometimes newcomers adopt words from older, native languages. The English spoken in the Welsh Borders is partly influenced by Welsh itself. Also, the Vikings who settled in the North West of England came via Ireland, where they had already learned some Gaelic. As a result, there have been Irish words in Lancashire speech since long before the victims of the Irish potato famine settled there in the 1840s!

1 Note down any information that you already knew and any information that you found surprising. Compare your findings with a partner's.

2 Now search through Text A and choose one expression that:

a) you have never heard before

b) you have used or heard someone in your family use

c) reminds you of an expression we might use today.

3 Read all the information on the page opposite and decide what, if any, differences and similarities there might be between slang and dialect.

4 Which slang words or dialect words do you and your friends use to describe a person's appearance. If you know where they come from add this to your notes, e.g. We call unattractive people 'Betty' after watching the American TV programme Ugly Betty (slang)

When you are analysing the language used by a writer or speaker, it is important to be able to cite and explain details that support your points.

5 In the texts on the next page, find examples where a writer:

- starts a paragraph with a short sentence about the topic
- supports the point being made with evidence (e.g. an example or a quotation) and explains what it means or shows
- avoids using 'I' and writes in an impersonal way (giving their writing authority)
- avoids joining sentences with 'and' or 'but' too much by using more interesting connectives such as 'however', 'as a result' and 'although'.

6 Use the same techniques to plan and write three paragraphs analysing:

- the way the slang used by your family has changed with time e.g. Whereas my grandparents might say.... my mother would tell her friend...
- the slang used by you and your friends today
- what makes you choose to use or avoid using dialect or slang

Apply your learning

Using all that you have learnt so far, read text A below and answer the questions.

Text A

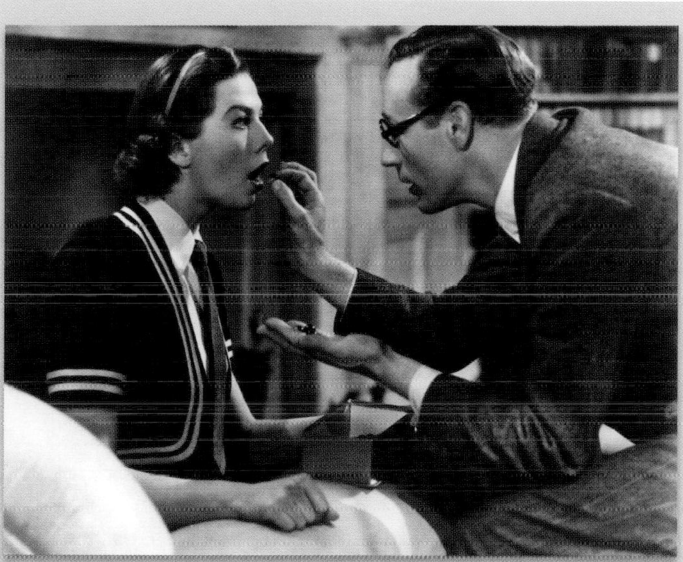

This scene is taken from the play Pygmalion by Bernard Shaw. In it, Eliza, a very poor Cockney woman is telling a rich person she has just met why she believes that her aunt's death was suspicious.

Eliza: My aunt died of influenza: so they said.

Mrs Eynsford Hill: *[clicks her tongue sympathetically]*

Eliza: *[in the same tragic tone]* But it's my belief they done the old woman in.

Mrs Eynsford Hill: *[puzzled]* Done her in?

Eliza: Y-e-e-es, Lord love you! Why should she die of influenza? She come through diphtheria right enough the year before. I saw her with my own eyes. Fairly blue with it, she was. They all thought she was dead; but my father he kept ladling gin down her throat til she came to so sudden that she bit the bowl off the spoon.

Mrs Eynsford Hill: Dear me!

Eliza: *[piling up indictment]* What call would a woman with that strength in her have to die of influenza? What become of her new straw hat that should have come to me? Somebody pinched it; and what I say is, them as pinched it done her in.

Mrs Eynsford Hill: You surely don't believe that your aunt was killed?

1 Why might Eliza be trying to speak in standard English?

2 What evidence is there in the text that Eliza is still using dialect and slang?

3 Why might these two women speak in different dialects and use different slang from one another?

4 Use clues from the text to decide where it should be placed on the time line.

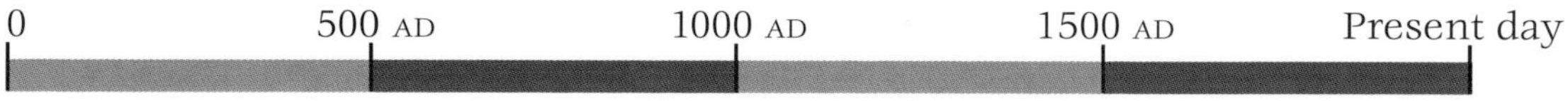

Now read texts B, C, and D.

TEXT B

In this speech a king is angry with his son and older person's behaviour

... young sir,
Whom son I dare not call; thou art too base
To be acknowledged; thou a sceptre's heir,
That thus affects a sheep-hook! Thou old traitor,
I am sorry that by hanging thee I can
But shorten thy life one week.

TEXT C

This is a description of the way a bee behaves.

The bee has thre [natures]. Ane is that scho is never ydill, and scho is noghte with them that will noghte wyrke, but castys them owte, and puttes them away. Anothire es that when scho flyes scho takes erthe in hyr fette, that scho be noghte lyghtly [raised too high] in the ayere of wynde. The thyrde es that scho kepes clene and bryghte hire wynges.

TEXT D

Antony was at the kitchen table, hunched over the telephone and a list he was drawing up with the aid of a psychedelic address book even older than the kettle. The only light was coming from the smoked glass push-up-pull-down fitting over his head.

5 Using examples from four texts in this section as well as those you have read in the rest of the unit, write three paragraphs explaining how and why the English Language has changed over time. Think about the way English is used in different situations, regions and periods of history.

Assess to Progress

Rate yourself again for each of the following skills by deciding where you would place yourself on the scale below.

1	2	3	4	5	6	7
I find this difficult.			I'm getting there.			I'm good at this.

- I can explain how and why dialect words are used in different parts of Britain.
- I can describe the way people change the way they speak in situations that are either more or less formal.
- I can comment on the way the English language has changed during different periods of history.
- I can write a detailed explanation of the way English is used in a text.

SKILLS FOR LIFE

Your local tourist information office have decided to produce a leaflet explaining to foreign tourists the way the English language is used by local people in your area. Plan and write the leaflet using the headings and ideas below. Give as many specific examples of words and phrases as you can, putting them in speech marks.

The language of this area – Think of the place names around your area. Where did some of them come from?

The language of a local family – Explain: any words you use in your family, expression an older relative uses that you don't

What makes people change the way they speak – Think about slang expressions you use when you are with your friends and how you adapt your speech for different situations.

Pearson Education
Edinburgh Gate
Harlow
Essex
CM20 2JE

Series Editor: Geoff Barton
Series Consultant: Michael Jones

ISBN: 978-1-4058-7524-0

With many thanks to Chris Edge and John Green.

We are grateful to the following for permission to reproduce copyright material

Artwork
Front cover on page 20 from *The Hogfather* (Terry Pratchett), reproduced by permission of The Random House Group Ltd; Artwork on page 20 from *The Art of Discworld* (by Terry Pratchett, artwork by Paul Kidby 2004) copyright © Paul Kidby www.paulkidby.net; Artwork on page 32 from *James Bond 007: Casino Royale* (adapted by Anthony Hern, Henry Gammidge and illustrated by John McLusky) The James Bond strip is copyright © Express Newspapers Ltd. 1987; Artwork on page 61 from "Becks: I'll coach GB Utd" front page of *The Sun*, 25 August 2008 (Clodagh Hartley), copyright © NI Syndication 2008; Artwork on page 61 from The People, *Take it Easy Magazine*, 22 November 2008 copyright © Mirrorpix 2008; Artwork on page 79 from X-Box advertorial 'A family-size box of delights' *Guardian Magazine* 15 November 2008, copyright © Guardian News and Media 2008; Artwork on page 87 from Future Visions Illustration, *The Guardian*, 16th June 2008, copyright © Guardian News & Media Ltd 2008; Artwork on page 89 from Llangollen Whitewater Active adventure park leaflet http://www.whitewateractive.co.uk; Artwork on page 98 from *"The Boater's Handbook"*, British Waterways & Environment Agency http://www.waterscape.com/media/documents/1784.pdf; Artwork on page 148 from "Welcome to Frankenfarm" and "Hydrophonics: How it works", *Daily Mail*, 12 June 2008 (David Derbyshire), copyright © Solo Syndication 2008; Artwork on page 213 from the Touareg "Gets you to unusual places" advert. Photographer Ben Stockley at Agent Orange. Reproduced with permission from Volkswagen;

Screenshots
Screenshot on page 4 adapted from www.facebook.com, granted with permission from Facebook, Inc;

Tables
Table on page 239 from *A Popular Guide to Suffolk Place-names. The Larks Press* (Rye, J. 1997), copyright © James Rye; Table on page 242 from "Learning, Changing Language - Beowulf" copyright © British Library Board. All Rights Reserved. Cotton Vitelius A. XV, f.132

Text
Extract on page 32 from The Wikipedia Foundation for details about "The Gresford Disaster"; Extract on page 34 from *Face* (Benjamin Zephaniah / Richard Conlon 2008), copyright © 2008, Benjamin Zephaniah and Richard Conlon, adapted from the book by Benjamin Zephaniah, published by Bloomsbury; Extract on page 56 from "Computer games to get cigarette-style health warnings", *The Times*, 27 March 2008 (Alexandra Frean), copyright © NI Syndication 2008; Extract on page 56 from "Playing computer games has been only a benefit to me", *The Times*, 28 March 2008 (Jack Miller), copyright © NI Syndication 2008; Extract on page 62 from "Here be monsters", *The Guardian*, 5 January 2008 (Keith Gray), copyright © Guardian News & Media Ltd 2008; Extract on page 62 from *The Stuff of Nightmares*, published by Doubleday (Malorie Blackman), Reprinted by permission of The Random House Group Ltd and The Agency (London) Ltd copyright © Oneta Malorie Blackman 2007. First published by Corgi Books an imprint of Random House. All rights reserved and enquiries to The Agency (London) Ltd, 24 Pottery Lane, London W11 4LZ fax: 0207 727 9037; Extracts on page 63 adapted from Which?, http://www.which.co.uk/reviews-ns/iphone/the-essentials/index.jsp and http://www.which.co.uk/reviews/mobile-phones/nokia-n82/review, copyright © Consumers Association; Extract on page 66 from *How I Live Now* (Meg Rosoff) Penguin Books, copyright © Meg Rosoff, 2004; Extract on page 69 from Office of Public Sector Information for extracts from Section 139 and 139A of Criminal Justice (Terrorism and Conspiracy) Act 1998, and Section 1 of the Prevention of Crime Act 1953 © Crown copyright 2002 – 2008; Quote on page 69 from The BBC for an extract from "How do the laws work?" published on www.bbc.co.uk 26 March 2008 copyright © The BBC; Extract on page 72 from "Knife teenagers may be forced to visit victims in hospital", *The Guardian*, 14 July 2008 (Michael White & Owen Bowcott), copyright © Guardian News & Media Ltd 2008; Extract on page 72 from "Youth violence: Tactics against gangs fatally flawed", *The Guardian*, 14 July 2008 (Nick Davies), copyright © Guardian News & Media Ltd 2008; Extract on page 74 from The Wikipedia Foundation for details about "George Sampson" and "Scheuermann's disease"; Extract on page 76 adapted from Clearasil advert, http://www.clearasil.co.uk/, kindly granted by The Firm; Extract on page 77 adapted from Frizz-Ease, John Frieda®, www.johnfrieda.com, kindly granted by Kao Brands Company; Extract on page 81 from *Here Lies Arthur* (Philip Reeve), Text copyright © Philip Reeve 2007. Cover image by Eamon O'Donoghue. Reproduced with the permission of Scholastic Ltd. All Rights Reserved; Extract on page 84 from "Ass of the week..." *The Telegraph*, 08 November 2007 (Charles Starmer-Smith); Quote on page 95 adapted from National Maritime Museum - Nelson's funeral Information Sheet "The state funeral of Lord Nelson, 5-9 January 1806" text and image BHC2889, copyright © National Maritime Museum, Greenwich, London; Extract on page 101 from *The Life and Times of the Thunderbolt Kid* (Bill Bryson) © 2006 The Random House Group Ltd; Extract on page 104 from *My Family and Other Animals* (Gerald Durrell), Reproduced with permission of Curtis Brown Group Ltd, London on behalf of the Estate of Gerald Durrell copyright © Gerald Durrell 1956; Extract on page 106 from "Restaurant review: Michael Winner at Park in the Mandarin Oriental hotel" *The Times*, 17 August 2008 (Michael Winner), copyright © NI Syndication 2008; Poetry on page 108 from *Read Me 2 : A Poem for every day Of The Year*, poem "Lies", Picador (Carol Ann Duffy), copyright © Carol Ann Duffy 1999 by kind permission of the author c/o Rogers, Coleridge & White Ltd., 20

Powis Mews, London W11 1JN; Extract on page 112 from *Angela's Ashes* copyright © Frank McCourt 1999, Reprinted by permission of HarperCollins Publishers Ltd; Extract on page 117 from *Daughter Of Fortune* (Isabel Allende), Reprinted by permission of HarperCollins Publishers Ltd copyright © Isabel Allende 2000; Extract on page 119 from *East of Eden*, Penguin Books (John Steinbeck 2001), copyright © 1952 John Steinbeck by permission of Penguin Books and Curtis Brown; Extract on page 128 from *The Kite Runner* (Khaled Hosseini 2004), published by Bloomsbury copyright © Khaled Hosseini; Extract on page 131 from *Paddy Clarke Ha Ha Ha* (Roddy Doyle 1994), published by Secker & Warburg. Reprinted by permission of The Random House Group Ltd and Penguin Group, Inc.; Extract on page 133 from The BBC for an extract from "Builders to rebury time capsule" published on www.bbc.co.uk 21 April 2005 copyright © The BBC; Extract on page 135 from *Toast*, HarperCollins (Nigel Slater 2004), reprinted by permission of HarperCollins Publishers Ltd and Lucas Alexander Whitley Ltd, copyright © Nigel Slater 2004; Extract on page 152 from *The Day of the Triffids* (John Wyndham 1973) With permission of David Higham Associates Limited; Extract on page 153 from *The Autobiography of Martin Luther King* (Ed Carson 2001), copyright © Little, Brown Book Group Ltd and NULL Intellectual Properties Mgmt. Copyright © 1988. By permission of Grand Central Publishing. All rights reserved; Extract on page 153 from *Anything Goes* (John Barrowman and Carole E. Barrowman 2008), by permission of the publishers Michael O'Mara Books Limited copyright © John Barrowman 2008; and the front cover jacket of *Anything Goes* by John Barrowman reproduced by permission of the publishers, Michael O'Mara Books Limited; photo: www.armandattard.com. All rights reserved; Extract on page 154 from *Being Jordan* John Black Publishing Ltd (Katie Price 2005) priced £7.99; Extract on page 154 from *A Long Walk to Freedom* (Nelson Mandela 1994) ISBN 0316-909653, copyright © Little, Brown Book Group Ltd and Hachette Group, copyright © 1994, 1995 by Nelson Rolihlahla Mandela. By permission of Little, Brown and Company. All rights reserved; Extract on page 169 from "The greatest gift of all", *TES*, 1 September 2006 (Hilary Wilce), http://www.tes.co.uk/article.aspx?storycode=2279590, copyright © Hilary Wilce; Extract on page 175 from 'Changing Sky' 1959 changed to 'A View of the World' 1986 (Norman Lewis) as published in *Faber book of Reportage* 1989 ed John Carey, Reproduced by permission of the publishers, Eland Publishing Ltd, 61 Exmouth Market, London EC1R 4QL; Extract on page 190 from *The Exorcist* (William Peter Blatty 1973), Used by permission of The Random House, Inc; Extract on page 223 from "Children find English too hard to read", *The Observer*, 8 June 2008 (Anushka Asthana), copyright © Guardian News & Media Ltd 2008; Extract on page 226 from Secondary National Strategy for "Teenagers should listen more!" from "Answering back Year 9 writing task Pupil booklet, Assessing pupils' progress in English at Key Stage 3" © Crown copyright 2006; Extract on page 236 adapted from Wyse Words: Tannoyance, *The Guardian*, 6 September 2008 (Pascal Wise), copyright © Guardian News & Media Ltd 2008; Extract on page 244 adapted from *English Varieties of the British Isles*, http://www.teachit.co.uk/armoore/lang/britishisles.htm#rhodes, copyright © Andrew Moore, Barrie Rhodes and the Yorkshire Dialect Society, 2003-2004 universalteacher@bigfoot.com.

The Reading and Writing Assessing your Progress units are adapted from the National Strategy Assessing Pupils' Progress optional tasks *Toast* and *Answering back* reproduced under the terms of the Click-Use licence.

The publisher would like to thank the following for their kind permission to reproduce their photographs:

(Key: b-bottom; c-centre; l-left; r-right; t-top)

Alamy Images: 67photo 74; Angela Hampton Picture Library 15; Bon Appetit 139; Jon Challicom 178; INTERFOTO Pressebildagentur 119; Lynne Siler Photography 9; Niall McDiarmid 137; Photofusion Picture Library 173; Chris Willson 22; **Apple Computer, Inc.:** 66cl; **BBC Photo Library:** 12-13b, 28; **Bridgeman Art Library Ltd / Look and Learn:** Saxon Raiders by Jackson, Peter (1922-2003) 239bl (Saxons); The Wonderful Story of Britain: The Coming of the Vikings by Jackson, Peter (1922-2003) 239bl (Scandinavians); Julius Caesar arrives in Britain by Embleton, Ron (1930-88) 239tl (Romans); Celtic Warriors by Peter Jackson (1922-2003) 239tl (Celts); **Corbis:** Bettmann 97br; Rolf Bruderer 233; Jim Craigmyle 226; Helen King 8; **DK Images:** 145; **Mary Evans Picture Library:** 238; Illustrated London News Ltd 95; **FLPA Images of Nature:** André Skonieczny 105; **Getty Images:** 58; AFP / Jean Claude-Chapon 26; AFP / Jose Luis Roca 177; AFP / Abdelhak Senna 48br; Bridgeman Art Library / Sir William Beechey 97tr; Andrew G Hobbs 60; Hulton Archive 124; Hulton Archive / Kurt Hutton 114; Hulton Archive / George Marks 168; Zigy Kaluzny 7; Jacopo Pandolfi 230; Zia Soleil 166; Stone / Zigy Kaluzny 7cr; WireImage 76tl; **Ronald Grant Archive:** 6, 18, 194; **iStockphoto:** 86, 116-117, 120-121, 160tr, 187 (cup), 187c (earth); **Jupiter Unlimited:** 16br, 16tr; **Moviestore Collection Ltd:** 113, 245; **Courtesy of Nokia:** 66cr; **PA Photos:** Henny Ray Abrams / AP / PA 183; Shizuo Kambayashi 205; Yui Mok 186; William B. Plowman / AP 48bl; Musadeq Sadeq / AP / PA 130; Chris Radburn 197; Dave Thompson 195; **Saxon Payne/Pearson Education:** 208; Saxon Payne/**Pearson Education Ltd:** 56 (background), 71; **Photofusion Picture Library:** Jacky Chapman 180bl; **Photolibrary.com:** age fotostock / Liane Cary 189; Corbis 111; Digital Vision 30; Fresh Food Images 140; Fresh Food Images / Rob White 107; Image Source 14; Index Stock Imagery 210; PYMCA / Oliver Grove 180br; Somos Images 179; Lars Stenman 160bl, 162; **PunchStock:** Image Source 199; Rubberball 5, 165; **Reuters:** Andres Stapff 51; **SuperStock:** age fotostock 152-153; **TopFoto:** The British Library / HIP 133; **Wellcome Images:** 76br; **Ken Wilson-Max**: 9b, 15b, 23b, 31b, 39b, 45b,65b, 77b, 88b, 99b, 110b, 122c, 136c, 157b, 169b, 179b, 189b, 198c, 209t, 218b, 226b, 247t

Cover images: *Front:* **Alamy Images:** artpartner-images

All other images © Pearson Education

Picture Research by: Harriet Mills

Illustrations provided by:

Dylan Gibson, page 2; Steve May, pages 23 and 31; Kel Dyson, pages 34, 35, 36 and 38; Teresa Murfin, pages 43 and 44; Kel Dyson, pages 68 and 70; Mark Oldroyd, page 83; Bob Doucet, page 93; Dylan Gibson, page 102; Steve May, page 108; Mark Oldroyd, page 126; Dylan Gibson, page 135; Kel Dyson, page 154; Frances Castle, page 175; Bob Doucet, page 192; Mark Oldroyd, page 202; Teresa Murfin, page 206; Kel Dyson, page 212; Mark Oldroyd, page 217; Steve May, page 219; Bob Doucet, page 242.

Printed in Malaysia, PJB CTP